PROPHECY PAST AND PRESENT

PROPHECY
PAST AND PRESENT

An Exploration of the Prophetic
Ministry in the Bible and the Church Today

Clifford Hill

Guildford, Surrey

British Library Cataloguing in Publication Data. A catalogue record for this book is available from the British Library.

Published by Eagle, an imprint of Inter Publishing Service (IPS) Ltd, St Nicholas House, 14 The Mount, Guildford, Surrey GU2 5HN.

Printed in the UK by HarperCollins Manufacturing, Glasgow

ISBN: 0 86347 170 6

CONTENTS

v

PART 2–PROPHECY IN THE EARLY CHURCH

CONTENTS

PART 3–PROPHECY TODAY

ACKNOWLEDGMENTS

I should like to express my gratitude to the late Professor F F Bruce for many helpful comments on the draft manuscript as well as his kindness in writing a Foreword to this book.

I am indebted to my colleagues David Noakes and Edmund Heddle for reading the manuscript and providing many useful suggestions.

My secretary, Jean Wolton, has given invaluable service in typing the manuscript and I am most grateful to her and to David Forbes for help in presenting the manuscript for publication.

Clifford Hill
January 1991

FOREWORD

Not long ago an English chief constable excited astonishment and controversy by a public utterance which he claimed to deliver as a prophet. The reactions were interesting and revealing. There were some, including a spokesman for his own police authority, who suggested that anyone who could claim to speak as a prophet needed to have his head examined. But such a reaction betrayed a very limited understanding of the prophet's role. A more rational response was that of the people who asked, 'Was he really speaking as a prophet, or did he only think he was?' And this is not an impossible question to answer. For hundreds, and indeed thousands, of years reliable criteria have been available for testing utterances which claim prophetic authority, and for deciding whether they are genuine or not.

Some of these criteria are laid down in the Old Testament and are further amplified in the New. They are as valid today as they were in biblical times. Today, as in biblical times, there are true prophets and false prophets, and it is important to be able to distinguish them. Dr Hill's study will give considerable help to those who are concerned to distinguish the true from the false—to 'discern the spirits', in a biblical phrase.

The great merit of this study is that it is biblically based. Dr

Hill gives a well-informed account of the rise and progress of the prophetic ministry in the Old Testament (apart from the prophets of Israel, indeed, there would be no Old Testament); he then turns to consider the role of prophets in the New Testament church. He goes on to show how the growth of institutionalism in the post-apostolic church tended to stifle prophetic spontaneity.

The institutional and charismatic ministries are both necessary for the well-being of the church. But there is an inevitable tension between the two; a tension which calls for Christian grace on both sides, neither side condemning nor despising the other, nor making exaggerated claims for itself. The institutionalists were usually in a position (where the necessary grace was absent) to suppress the charismatics. Consequently, we have to allow that there may have been a greater charismatic element in the life of the church, both before and after the Reformation, than our standard textbooks recognize.

The prophetic ministry probably receives greater recognition in today's church than it has enjoyed for a long time. And by the prophetic ministry is not meant the bizarre apocalyptic misinterpretation which has become a cult in some quarters, where the timetables of Daniel and the cryptograms of Revelation are scrutinized for the information they supposedly supply about the present day and immediate future. I remember how deeply impressed I was on the only occasion when I heard the late Martin Niemöller. I remarked to a friend that there was a genuine prophetic note in his ministry. But my friend's reaction was to ask if he took the futurist line; that was all prophetic ministry meant to him. Prophetic ministry is the declaration of the mind of God in the power of the Spirit, with a special bearing on the current situation. And it will be recognized as genuine prophetic ministry by the application of the biblical tests. Above all it must be asked: Is it in line with the authentic gospel? For, in the words of a great New Testament prophet,

FOREWORD

'the testimony of Jesus is the spirit of prophecy' (Rev 19. 10).

I am sure that many readers will be helped by Dr. Hill's study to understand the nature and purpose of prophecy—both as a means of revelation in biblical times and as a spiritual ministry today.

*F F Bruce**

*F F Bruce died in September 1990.

INTRODUCTION

The twentieth century has seen greater changes than any comparable period of history in the realms of technology, politics, economics and social structure. The incredible advancements in scientific and technological development during the century have revolutionised transport, communications and industrial production. The political map of the world has changed radically during the century. The rise and demise of the Soviet Union and its satellite Communist empire is but one example of radical political change. The growth of multi-national corporations, global financial institutions which have transformed the capitalist system from simple entrepreneurial activities to multi-national moguls, has changed the nineteenth-century concepts of the economy out of all recognition.

The twentieth century has also seen revolutionary changes in social structure in most parts of the world in both the industrialised and developing nations. These social changes have had a particularly devastating effect upon religious and moral values in the Western nations. They have also severely affected traditional concepts of family, marriage and sexual conduct which have in turn affected child-rearing and the transmission of basic moral values.

1

This in turn has produced high levels of crime and a variety of social disorders which have contributed to a strong sense of instability in society.

This social instability generates widespread feelings of uncertainty among ordinary people as well as in those who carry leadership responsibilities. People feel powerless to halt the revolutionary forces of change sweeping through society and this generates a longing for secure foundational values in life. These are just the circumstances which give rise to an openness to the unchanging word of God and create the conditions whereby those who carry the prophetic mantle can gain a ready hearing.

It was in times of crisis in ancient Israel that the great prophets arose and declared the word of God with power and authority. It is not surprising therefore that in the closing decades of the twentieth century there should be a fresh interest in the whole subject of prophecy as a re-assertion of the biblical word of God. But prophets have never been popular with those in authority. Jeremiah, for example, was constantly persecuted by both religious and political leaders.

Jesus, lamenting over the people of Jerusalem, said that they had always killed the prophets and stoned those whom God had sent to them. The third-century bishops who drove prophets out of their churches were doing just as the religious leaders of Israel had done. But it was not only the ministry of prophets that disappeared as the church became an established part of the Roman Empire and beyond, the exercise of spiritual gifts also was suppressed. Ordinary believers who were encouraged by Paul to use the gifts of the Spirit were no longer able to do so. Although there is evidence of prophetic revelation being received by individuals in different periods during the next 1,500 years, it is nevertheless true that from the fourth to the nineteenth century there was no major movement of openness to the Holy Spirit, to prophetic revelation, or to the exercise of spiritual gifts. The twentieth century has changed all that.

INTRODUCTION

Prophecy today abounds in the church throughout the world. The Pentecostal and charismatic movements have brought a new emphasis upon the Holy Spirit and a new openness to spiritual gifts. Prophecy is a subject that holds great fascination for millions of Christians today. Even among those who are sceptical of contemporary prophetic revelation there is a great interest in the study of prophecy and in the possibility of biblical prophecy being fulfilled in this present generation. But inevitably genuine prophecy is also accompanied by the counterfeit. There are the charlatans, the false prophets and the false teachers who create confusion and cause many people to want to have nothing to do with prophecy or the exercise of spiritual gifts. Jesus warned that imposters would appear among the believers, 'Watch out for false prophets. They come to you in sheep's clothing, but inwardly they are ferocious wolves' (Mt 7.15). There were at least eight books published in the USA claiming that 1988 would see the Second Coming of our Lord. Each of the authors calculated the date using various mathematical formulae based upon selective texts of Scripture. Most of them forecast that the church would be lifted out of this world in the so-called 'Rapture' at some time during 11–13 September 1988 which was the Jewish Feast of Trumpets in the fortieth year after the founding of the modern State of Israel.

As we approach the end of the second millennium of the Christian era there will, no doubt, be an increasing number of biblical speculators poring over passages from Daniel and Revelation with their calculators and computers predicting various apocalyptic events. 1988 was a record year for spurious prophecy. Two young men from Denmark announced that they were the two witnesses of Revelation 11.3 sent by God to prepare the way for Messiah. Two years earlier I had met two young Americans camping on the Mount of Olives also claiming to be the two witnesses.

The existence of false prophets and teachers, of cults and spurious prophecy, is not a valid reason for rejecting

3

divine revelation. The opposite of false prophecy is not no prophecy, but carefully weighed and tested prophecy. The western world has been in the icy grip of secular intellectualism since the days of Kant and Hegel, fathers of the eighteenth-century Enlightenment movement, and Schleiermacher, the founder of modern theology. This has dominated the thinking and preaching of all the mainline churches whose clergy and ministers have received a formal theological education. Not only have attitudes to contemporary revelation been affected by theological scepticism but so too have traditional beliefs. The very nature and existence of divine revelation has been questioned and eliminated from the theological systems of many western academics. Indeed, all the mainline churches have neglected the study of divine revelation over a long period. It has not simply been overlooked in training men for the pastoral ministry, it has been deliberately discounted.

Four years in a theological college and a doctorate in theology undermined my confidence in the presence of a personal God and invalidated the faith that originally drove me to give my life to the Lord and to spend my days preaching the gospel. Indeed, I had very little gospel left to proclaim. My experience is typical of thousands of clergy whose faith has been lost in the confused morass of critical debate and who only know the Holy Spirit in formalised credal statements or as one of the subjects of academic study in Christian doctrine.

Today millions of Christians around the world have experienced the presence and power of God through the Holy Spirit. God is doing a new thing regardless of whether or not the traditional clergy want to recognise it. God is, in fact, by-passing those churches that are resisting the Holy Spirit and are not open to fresh revelation. Hundreds of new fellowships are being planted every day with the rapid expansion of the church worldwide.

What is happening today is strongly reminiscent of the earliest days of the church when the Spirit of God was poured out upon all believers and everywhere there was evidence of the presence and power of God and the exercise of spiritual gifts. The same thing is happening in our own day. There is a new openness to divine revelation. Prophecy is again being heard in the churches. The spiritual gifts are seen among ordinary believers.

In ancient Israel God always raised up prophets in times of crisis. There can be little doubt that the fresh move of God we are seeing today is a response to the times of crisis in which we live. Today the nations of the world are being shaken by an unprecedented series of events that have shattered the complacency and self-confidence of the age. There are clear links between contemporary events and the prophecy of Haggai 2.6,7 concerning the shaking of the nations and the natural order of creation. This prophecy is interpreted in the New Testament in Hebrews 12.26–29.

We are, in fact, seeing nations shaken by natural disasters of flood, famine, plague and disease as well as by the actions of evil men through war and revolution. In a world of violence, of rapid social, economic and political change, when man's grasp of technology outstrips his wisdom in using it, there is a desperate need for divine guidance that could literally mean the difference between the annihilation of mankind and man's salvation. If the church is to be the prophet to the world, to proclaim the unchanging word of God among the nations, to meet the crisis of this age, then the greatest need today is for the church to be *hearing* from God. The church cannot proclaim the word of God with power and authority unless it is being received afresh through the ministry of the Holy Spirit.

The nature of God and the word of God are unchanging. But the prophetic task in any age is to perceive the word of God in its contemporary relevance so that it may be proclaimed with prophetic authority as the 'Now' word of God, 'Thus says the Lord to this generation . . .!' Receiving the contemporary word of the contemporary God for the contemporary world is never easy nor automatic. It was not easy for the prophets. They had to learn to listen; to stand in the presence of Almighty God. But they had one thing that is largely missing in our generation—a sense of awe. They knew the awesomeness of standing in the presence of God the Creator of the universe. They had a holy reverence and fear of God, whereas we belong to a generation that reverences nothing and fears neither God nor man; that is not afraid to blaspheme God.

The work of the Holy Spirit today is bringing new life and power into the church. But there is also a great need for reverence and awe—for learning to enter the presence of God in holy awe. The prophets of old put off their shoes to come before God. There would be less danger of the counterfeit and the spurious if we learned to approach God in holy reverence as they did. We would know his unchanging word and recognise his voice as surely as the sheep know the voice of their own shepherd. It is because of the neglect of biblical teaching on the nature of God and divine revelation that there is such fear of prophecy as well as such misuse of the precious gifts of God.

There is a great need in the churches today, both traditional and charismatic, for in-depth biblical study of prophecy and the whole area of God's self-revelation to man. The Bible provides us with the only reliable guide to the nature and purpose of revelation. It is for this reason that the major emphasis of this book is biblical. It has been written with the needs of ordinary believers in mind. I have drawn upon both critical and conservative scholarship in order to present a balanced biblical exposition of prophecy, its nature and practice. I hope the result is readable as well as informative, both for the non-theological reader, and for students.

In this second edition of *Prophecy Past and Present* I have carried out a thorough revision of the text of the original book taking note of recent scholarship. Part III on 'Prophecy Today' has been totally rewritten with three chapters replacing the original two chapters. This section brings up to date what is happening in the realm of prophecy in the churches today and takes note of recent developments particularly in the charismatic sector of the church. It is my earnest hope that this book will encourage Christians to undertake in-depth biblical study of a subject which I believe has great relevance for the contemporary world, for an understanding of great issues in society today and above all for the effective communication of the word of God among the nations and therefore the fulfilment of the Great Commission which is the prophetic task entrusted by Jesus to his church.

PART 1

PROPHECY IN ANCIENT ISRAEL

CHAPTER ONE

DEFINING PROPHECY

The right starting point of any analysis is the definition of terms. In undertaking an examination of 'prophecy' it is necessary to know how the term is used in the Bible and to note any changes in its usage in different periods of the history of Israel.

Throughout the Bible prophecy is linked with revelation and this is the key that provides the basis for a definition. This link is clearly stated in the account of the call of Samuel to the ministry of the prophet. The story in 1 Samuel 3 is too well known to recount in detail here but it is significant to note that the youthful Samuel was lying down at night, probably meditating rather than actually asleep, when he thought he heard his name called. Three times he ran to Eli thinking it was the old priest who had summoned him. Finally, Eli, realising that God was speaking to Samuel, told him to respond, 'Speak, Lord, for your servant is listening.'

This response enabled Samuel to receive a message. It is important to note that there is here no suggestion of an ecstatic experience. Samuel was not dancing, or leaping, or shouting, or singing, he was lying quietly on his bed. He responded in faith when he believed God was communicating with him; he listened attentively and he heard. This does not mean that he actually 'heard' a voice in the physical sense. We shall deal with this point more fully when we examine how the prophets received the word of God. It does mean that Samuel received a message from God. In the morning he obeyed Eli's instruction and told the priest the substance of the message he had received. The message was immediately confirmed by Eli's reaction and it subsequently received the ultimate confirmation when it was fulfilled.

The news that Samuel was hearing from God spread rapidly, 'And all Israel from Dan to Beersheba recognised that Samuel was attested as a prophet of the Lord' (1 Sam 3.20). It was no doubt the old priest's testimony that Samuel had received a true word from God that initially helped to establish Samuel's credentials as a prophet in the eyes of the nation. Eli knew that Samuel had received a genuine word from God because the things he reported, concerning the fate of Eli's family, God had already spoken to the old priest.

Revealed Truth

The link between prophecy and revelation occurs in verse 7 of the same chapter. In the middle of the account of Samuel getting up from bed and running to Eli there is an editorial note inserted into the text by the compiler: 'Now Samuel did not yet know the Lord; the word of the Lord had *not yet been revealed* to him.' Clearly this reflects the thought of a later age when the various sources which resulted in the historical books of 1 and 2 Samuel and 1 and 2 Kings were compiled. Originally these four books were one and they appear as one in the old Hebrew Bible. Even the Septuagint presents all four as a single book in four parts under the title 'The Kingdoms'. The purpose of 1 and 2 Samuel is to provide an historical account of the origins of the monarchy. The title 'Samuel' in our western Bibles is somewhat misleading since only a few chapters of 1 Samuel actually deal with the prophet's ministry and there the major concern is with Israel's request for a king and Samuel's role in inaugurating the monarchy. The editorial comment of 1 Samuel 3.7 can most likely be dated in the seventh century BC. This was when the major work on compiling the historical account of the monarchy from a variety of source material was undertaken. By that time the nature of prophecy as rooted in revelation was firmly established. The last verse of 1 Samuel 3 says, 'The Lord continued to appear at Shiloh, and there he *revealed himself* to Samuel through his word.'

Prophecy was thus regarded as the *revealed word of God*. It was not the product of intellectual attainment or rational debate. Neither was it deduced through the processes of logical deduction. Prophecy was *revealed truth* that came *directly from God*. It was the word of God delivered by God to man. Thus prophecy was 'received' rather than produced by the human mind. Yet its relationship with empirical truth, *ie* established facts in the contemporary world, gave to prophecy an immediacy and a contemporary relevance that distinguished it from contemplative meditation or speculative philosophy. Prophecy revealed facts about the present situation: it was the 'now' word of God which, in Samuel's case, was received by the simple obedience of listening attentively. No doubt as Samuel gained in experience he learned to perceive *when* God was communicating with him just as he learned to distinguish and to interpret the word of God, *ie* the *substance* of what was being communicated.

The Seer and the Nebi' im
The account of Samuel's call to ministry and his establishment as a prophet in Israel, although seen through the eyes of a later age, provides valuable evidence for an understanding of the origins of prophecy in Israel. At the time when the period of the Judges gave way to the monarchy in Israel there were two distinct types of prophet, *ie*, those who were regarded as bearers of the word of Yahweh. They were the *seer* and the *nabi* (plural *nebi'im*). The seer was the contemplative, whereas the nabi was the wilder ecstatic type of prophet. The former was a solitary figure whereas the latter went about in bands or companies and apparently lived in community.

PROPHECY PAST AND PRESENT

Our introduction to Saul, who was to become the first king of Israel, provides the setting for the contrast between the seer and the nebi'im. We meet them both in 1 Samuel 9 and 10 where some donkeys had been lost from Saul's father's farm, and Saul and a servant set out to search for them. They heard that the prophet Samuel was in the neighbourhood so they went to ask him for guidance. They took a small gift with them, not as payment for service rendered but as a mark of respect. Samuel was known as seer, according to the question Saul put to some girls they met at the local well. An editorial note, again clearly inserted into the text at a later date, states: 'Formerly in Israel, if a man went to enquire of God, he would say, "Come, let us go to the seer," because the prophet of today used to be called a seer' (1 Sam 9.9).

One might assume from this statement that there is a clear line of development from the seer in the period of the Judges through to the canonical prophets beginning with Amos in the eighth century. Such is not the case and there are a number of complicating factors that make it difficult to draw quick and easy conclusions. In the first place the terms 'nabi' and 'seer' appear interchangeable in common usage during the early period of the monarchy. Samuel, for example, was recognised as a 'prophet of the Lord' according to 1 Samuel 3:20, but he was also known as a seer. In fact this was his own witness. When Saul approached Samuel he asked, 'Would you please tell me where the seer's house is?' 'I am the seer,' Samuel replied (1 Sam 9.18,19). The same term is used of Samuel in 1 Chronicles 9.22.

Several other prophets are also referred to by both terms; for example, Gad, Iddo and Jehu, son of Hanani. In 2 Samuel 24.11 and 1 Chronicles 21.9 Gad is referred to as 'David's seer'; whereas in 1 Samuel 22.5 he is spoken of as 'the prophet Gad'. Just to add to our difficulty of interpretation 2 Samuel 24.11 speaks of 'Gad the prophet, David's seer'!

Iddo is spoken of as 'Iddo the seer' in 2 Chronicles 9.29 and 2 Chronicles 12.15; whereas in 2 Chronicles 13.22 he is referred to as 'the prophet Iddo'. Similarly Jehu, son of Hanani, is spoken of as 'a seer' in 2 Chronicles 19.2 and as 'a prophet' in 1 Kings 16.7.

This difference in the use of terms may simply be due to the use of different source material which underlies the historical books. We know that a variety of written sources, as well as oral tradition, was available to the compilers, as many of these sources are referred to in the text. For example, the chronicler, in addition to having the written records of David's reign, speaks of 'the records of Samuel the seer, the records of Nathan the prophet and the records of Gad the seer' (1 Chr 29.29).

The situation is made more complex by different styles as well as different functions of the nebi'im and the seers, both of whom are recognised as prophets and are credited with prophesying.

There are two different stories given in 1 Samuel to account for the saying 'Is Saul also among the prophets?'. No doubt these come from different sources, and because they were both current among the people they have been included by the compiler. The first is in 1 Samuel 10.5ff where, before Saul was recognised as king, he was told by Samuel to go to Gibeah, where he would meet a procession of prophets and the Spirit of the Lord would come upon him in power. This, in fact, was fulfilled exactly as Samuel had said and it led to the people asking each other 'What is this that has happened to the son of Kish? Is Saul also among the prophets?'

In the second incident, recorded in 1 Samuel 19.18ff, Saul's jealousy of David was driving him to seek his life. On hearing that David was with Samuel at Ramah Saul sent some of his men to capture him, but when they saw a group of prophets prophesying, the Spirit of God came upon them and they also prophesied. When the same thing happened to two other groups of his men Saul finally went to Ramah himself. 'But the Spirit of God came even upon him, and he walked along prophesying until he came to Naioth. He stripped off his robe and he also prophesied in Samuel's presence. He lay that way all that day and night. This is why people say, "Is Saul also among the prophets?"' (1 Sam 19.23,24).

This passage faces us squarely with the question, 'What was prophesying?' In the first of the two incidents the prophets were in a procession coming down from a high place with lyres, tambourines, flutes and harps being played before them and they were all 'prophesying'. Music clearly played a part in this kind of prophesying. This is explicitly stated in 1 Chronicles 25 where David appointed a number of musicians to work closely with those who did the prophesying. 'David . . . set apart some of the sons of Asaph, Heman and Jeduthun for the ministry of prophesying, accompanied by harps, lyres and cymbals' (1 Chr 15.1).

Prophecy in this context appears to have been an attempt to enter the presence of God both to convey worship to him and to receive guidance from him. Clearly the kind of prophesying in which the Nebi'im engaged was a very strenuous exercise, probably more akin to what some modern charismatic groups call 'praise warfare'. Certainly we may detect in their prophesying elements of praise and elements of ecstasy. But this raises the question as to whether these ecstatic activities can be regarded in any sense as genuine prophecy. (We have already defined the noun 'prophecy' as 'revealed truth'; received through the activity of God revealing divine truth to man.) We can only rightly answer this question by considering what is being described as 'prophesying' in the context of the beliefs of the day.

Any unusual behaviour in man was assigned to the in-fluence of the spirit world. It was evidence of the intrusion of the spirit world, good or bad spirits, into the everyday affairs of mankind. Thus even epilepsy or madness might be re-garded as evidence of spirit-possession. If a man wanted to enter into the presence of the gods he could sometimes do so by engendering a state of ecstasy, or trance, in which his rational thought processes were suspended and he was no longer able to co-ordinate his physical responses, at which

16

point he was believed to be possessed by the spirit of the god.

Saul was subject to fits of madness, or possession by evil spirits, which could be dispelled or overcome by David playing music and invoking the Spirit of God to calm him. The use of music was very important to create the right atmosphere for the Spirit of God to come upon the worshipper. This was no doubt what was happening in the band of prophets whom Saul joined. Their activities were highly infectious since not only Saul was affected but all of his men, who also prophesied according to the account in 2 Samuel 19, and when Saul joined them he stripped off his clothes and lay naked all day and night. Saul was evidently a highly unstable man whose moods swung dramatically from bouts of rage to ecstasy.

The difficulty for us in understanding what constituted prophecy during the period of the Judges and early monarchy is due to the strong contrast between the activities of the seers and the nebi'im. We have already noted that the seer was a lonely figure who was consulted on an individual basis by anyone seeking divine guidance. From the beginning of his ministry Samuel practised entering the presence of God by quietly listening for the inner voice of the Spirit to communicate with him. A good example of Samuel's method of seeking guidance is found in 1 Samuel 8 where Israel asked for a king. Samuel was not pleased with this as he saw it as disloyalty to Yahweh, the national God. He tried to discourage the people by telling them how a king would rule over them and exploit them but the people refused to listen. They said they wanted to be like the other nations and have a king to lead them, especially in battle.

Samuel responded by spending some time in intercession. 'When Samuel heard all that the people said, he repeated it before the Lord. The Lord answered, "Listen to them and give them a king"' (1 Sam 8.21,22). He 'repeated it', or reported it to the Lord as part of his intercession. Samuel's method of seeking guidance was very similar to that of

Hezekiah and Isaiah centuries later when the threatening letter from Sennacherib was received and the king spread it before the Lord and the two of them interceded in the Temple; *cf* 2 Kings 19.14 and 2 Chronicles 32.20.

The difference we are noting here between Samuel the seer seeking guidance from God and the ecstatic nebi'im is not as clear cut as it might appear. If we look again at the account in 1 Samuel 19.20 of Saul sending his men to arrest David, who was with Samuel at Ramah, we read 'But when they saw a group of prophets prophesying, *with Samuel standing there as their leader*, the Spirit of God came upon Saul's men . . .'. It appears that Samuel travelled the country presiding at religious feasts and festivals and when he visited a local high place he actually joined in the worship of the local group of nebi'im and assumed leadership. We are not so much concerned with what Saul did but for our purpose the pertinent question is 'Was *Samuel* also among the prophets?' It would appear that the answer was 'Yes'.

We have thus not just a confusion over the interchangeable use of terms in this period but we have a blending of roles. The answer to this apparent confusion probably lies in the gradual incursion of Canaanite worship into the religion of Israel. In the early days of the settlement under Joshua's leadership the tribes settled among the local people. It was not long before they began observing the local customs of worship at the high places which were regarded as the domain of each local god who controlled an area of land. It would have been difficult for the Israelites to ignore the harvest festivals and spring fertility rites of the local cultus.

The Israelite tribes had always been a pastoral and nomadic people apart from the period of slavery in Egypt. They were dependent upon the Canaanites to teach them agricultural skills when they settled in the land. Their lack of success and poor harvests through crop disease, drought, locusts or for any other cause provided opportunity for the Canaanites to declare that they were worshipping the wrong gods. Yahweh was believed to be a desert god who had

18

revealed himself to Moses on the mountain at Sinai but at this stage in Israel's religious development he was not seen by the ordinary people as having universal power and authority.

It was in this situation that the seers and the nebi'im arose. *They were both strong Yahwists*. The major purpose of their lives was to try to preserve the loyalty of the people to Yahweh. In the early days of the settlement, with the influence of foreign gods all around them, this was no mean task. The basic problem arose from the different conceptions of deity. At this early stage in her history Israel's idea of Yahweh was that of a tribal god who had met with them in the desert where he had entered into a solemn covenant with them; thus his relationship was to *a people*. The Canaanites' understanding of a god was *territorial*; the Baals were local gods of the land. In fact this understanding of gods who were related to territory was common throughout the Middle East and persisted long after this period. For example, when Naaman the Syrian was healed from leprosy and declared that he would worship no other God but Yahweh, he solved the problem of territorial domain by taking two muleloads of earth with him (2 Kg 5.17). This would be a piece of Yahweh's land on which he could build an altar to offer reverence to him.

We have already noted the Israelites' dependence upon the Canaanites for learning agricultural skills in the early days of the settlement. This was a period of immense sociological change from the nomadic life of the desert and the simple social order of the wandering shepherd to that of the settled farmer and trader. It meant changing from living in tents to building houses, from the concept of open land to that of private property, from constant movement in search of grazing ground to living in villages and city life, from simple tribal rules to civic law.

All these changes in the social order affected the religion of Israel and they are highly significant in terms of the rise of prophets and the development of prophecy in the national

19

life of Israel. *Prophets arise in times of crisis.* Their message is always relevant to the contemporary situation. The encounter with prophecy is always at the frontier of the social and the religious. The factors that give rise to prophecy are always both sociological and religious. They can only be fully understood in terms of a study of the sociology of religion. That is not the subject of this book and here we can do no more than make passing reference in the context of noting the antecedents of prophecy in ancient Israel. In case it should be thought that these observations relating to sociological factors rule out or diminish in any way the activity of God in prophecy, let it be clearly understood that the standpoint taken throughout this study is that prophecy is *God's direct word of response to man's situation.* In other words, the socio-political situation provides not only the backcloth for prophecy but the essential pre-conditions for the openness of man to the communication of divine revelation.

The prophets arose during the period of the settlement in Canaan to declare to the Israelites that in crossing the Jordan they had not left behind the God of their fathers, the God of Abraham, Isaac and Jacob. He had, in fact, brought them into the land and he would fulfil his covenant promise. Towards the end of his life Joshua reaffirmed the terms of the covenant and all the people declared their loyalty to Yahweh the God of Israel. This loyalty, however, was not sufficient to withstand the day-to-day influences of the local people and the impact of the major changes in the social order upon their beliefs. These were the conditions that generated the need for prophecy.

The seers were the outstanding individuals who had a wider tribal and inter-tribal role in teaching the requirements of God, reminding the people of the terms of the covenant and recounting the past deeds and faithfulness of the Lord to their forefathers.

The nebi'im were locally based communities of religious enthusiasts who were probably associated with the high places used by the Canaanites for the worship of the local territorial Baals. They probably owned no property and were supported by the people. They not only worshipped Yahweh, and were thus the guardians of religious tradition, but they also attempted to preserve the social values and ethics of the nomadic life. Their loyalty to Yahweh urged them to condemn the culture of the Canaanites.

We find such groups surviving right down to the time of Jeremiah under the name of Recabites (Jer 35). They would not drink wine because wine was the product of vineyards and vines did not grow in the desert. They did not sow seed, neither did they build houses, but they lived in tents and regarded themselves as nomads in the land (Jer 35.7). They attempted to preserve loyalty to God by trying to maintain the old social order with which the first revelation of God was associated. For the Recabites, and the tradition they represented, spiritual purity lay in resisting social change.

These then were the antecedents of prophecy in ancient Israel. Gradually the seers, as the lone figures who learned to enter the presence of God and receive divine revelation, became the outstanding religious teachers of Israel. They were neither locked in to an ethic of the past, nor fossilised into some ideal-type nomadic culture that no longer existed; nor were they imprisoned in the concept of worship that regarded ecstatic excesses as evidence of spiritual activity.

Ecstatic Prophets

The ecstatics came to be regarded as 'madmen', although they were still shown respect as religious figures and as such they were sacrosanct, being widely regarded as men who were possessed by some form of divine power. A good example is found in the account of Elisha sending a messenger to anoint Jehu king over the northern kingdom of Israel. He chose a young man who was a member of one of these groups of prophets. Jehu was sitting with some of his fellow army officers when this young man, easily identified as a member of a band of prophets, arrived. After a private consultation in which he anointed Jehu king he opened the door and ran. 'When Jehu went out to his fellow officers one of them asked him, "Is everything all right? Why did this madman come to you?"' (2 Kg 9.11). Jehu eventually told them what had happened and there was an immediate change of attitude. Far from rejecting the young man's word as the ravings of a lunatic it was accepted as the word of God and Jehu was immediately proclaimed king. This is a clear indication of the ambivalence that existed in Israel towards those who were regarded as prophets. It also underlines the different attitudes towards the messages they wanted to hear and receive and those they hated and wanted to reject.

This aura of respect that surrounded the religious man who was regarded in some way as being possessed by the Spirit of God usually resulted in the person of the prophet being sacrosanct. Despite the unpopularity of the message of many of the prophets it was very rare for a prophet to be murdered. There were many threats made against the lives of the prophets as, for example, the account of Elijah running for his life in the face of the threats of Jezebel following the carnage of her prophets that had been initiated by Elijah. There is an apocryphal tradition of Isaiah being sawn in two by Manasseh, but there are, in fact, only two recorded incidents in the whole of the Old Testament of prophets being murdered as a result of their ministry. These are found in 2 Chronicles 24.17f where Zechariah the son of Jehoida the priest declared a highly unpopular message condemning both king and people for idolatry and on the order of king Joash he was stoned to death in the courtyard of the Temple. The other incident is recorded in Jeremiah 26 where Jeremiah himself was threatened with death but a fellow prophet by the name of Uriah who proclaimed a similar message ran away to Egypt in the face of the wrath of the king. Jehoiakim, however, who had a treaty with Egypt, had him extradited and brought back to Jerusalem and executed.

The early period of the monarchy was a period of transition for prophecy and the prophets in Israel. We have already noted the major sociological changes that occurred during the period of the Judges. It was during this period that the influence of Canaanite worship put intense pressures upon the loyalty to Yahweh of the Israelites. A process of accommodation took place that continued not only into the early monarchy but right through until the exile. It resulted in the kind of idolatry that came to a head in the reigns of certain kings such as Manasseh and Ahaz in the south and Ahab in the north.

This process of accommodation is known as 'syncretism', *ie* the process by which two or more religions become fused together. From the records available to us in the historical books of the Old Testament it appears that some of the bands of prophets who were based at the high places in Canaan embraced various forms of syncretism. These became associated with Baalism and we have an example of such a group (who were regarded by the compiler of Kings as 'false prophets') in the account of Ahab and Jehoshaphat consulting the prophets before going to war against Syria at Ramoth Gilead (1 Kg 22). All the prophets said that the battle would result in victory but Jehoshaphat was not content with consulting a band of nebi'im, he wanted to know if there was a solitary prophet of Yahweh in the vicinity. Eventually Micaiah was fetched and he prophesied disaster—a true prophetic word which was ignored.

Not all the bands of prophets were, however, false prophets. In 1 Kings 18 we have the record of Obadiah taking a hundred prophets and hiding them in two caves, fifty in each, and supplying them with food and water during the famine in the reign of Ahab. This may well have been the group from which Elisha some years later selected the young man to go and anoint Jehu as king in Israel and thus to initiate a religious revolution that, in fact, resulted in enormous bloodshed in the land.

Clearly in the time of Ahab there were communities of prophets who were associated with Baalism and others who were loyal to Yahweh. There were also seers, lone figures, who were utterly loyal to the God of Israel and were outstanding for their faith and their courage; men such as Elijah, Elisha and Micaiah who all exercised prophetic ministries in the ninth century BC.

By the time we reach the eighth century the transitional period of prophecy and the prophets was drawing to a close and the picture becomes clearer. The companies of prophets were largely associated with Baalism and idolatrous practices at the high places. The true line of prophecy, in declaring the word of the Lord and maintaining absolute loyalty to Yahweh, was centred in the lone figures such as Amos and Hosea in the northern kingdom of Israel, followed closely by Micah and Isaiah in the southern kingdom of Judah. It was with these men that the written word of prophecy began, although they themselves may not have actually written down the words they declared. Prophecy, at this stage, was oral tradition.

The prophets were men of the market-place rather than the study. Indeed prophecy throughout the history of Israel was always oral. It was the *declared* word of God. The prophets were not men who composed carefully considered theological dissertations. The words that came from them were white hot. They were the word of God into the contemporary situation.

The true prophet

It is here that we need to consider the biblical definition of the prophet and the task he undertook in the life of the nation. Despite the differences we have been noting between the nebi'im and the seers the term 'prophet' is used with a consistency of meaning throughout the Bible from the time of Moses, who was the first nationally recognised prophet of Israel.

The account of Moses being called by God to confront Pharaoh and to lead Israel out of Egypt is significant for the definition it provides for the role of the prophet. In the account in Exodus 4.10–16 Moses protested:

24

'O Lord, I have never been eloquent, neither in the past nor since you have spoken to your servant. I am slow of speech and tongue.' The Lord said to him, 'Who gave man his mouth? Who makes him deaf or dumb? Who gives him sight or makes him blind? Is it not I the Lord? Now go; I will help you speak and will teach you what to say.'

At this point Moses did what all of us do when we run out of arguments. 'Oh Lord,' he said, 'please send someone else to do it.' It is small wonder that Moses experienced God's anger at his rebellious attitude which was really scorning his promise of help. Clearly Moses had not yet learned the lesson that God never calls to a task without also supplying the ability to carry it out. Moses was then told the way that help would be given through his brother Aaron.

You shall speak to him and put words in his mouth; I will help both of you speak and will teach you what to do. He will speak to the people for you, and it will be as if he were your mouth and as if you were God to him.

This arrangement was then formally identified with the term 'prophet' when God said to Moses:

See, I have made you like God to Pharaoh, and your brother Aaron will be your *prophet*. You are to say everything I command you, and your brother Aaron is to tell Pharaoh (Ex 7.1,2).

The fact that in this account the arrangement made with Moses that defined the role of the prophet was *instituted by God* gave to it a lasting significance in the history of Israel. Aaron was to be Moses' 'mouthpiece', a task which was described as being 'his prophet'. It followed, therefore, that Moses, who was the mouthpiece of God and was to speak the word he received from God to Aaron, was God's prophet. *The prophet of God was thus the mouthpiece of God.* He was God's messenger whose task was to deliver whatever God said to him. He was not simply a holy man, nor was he a man with a mission to reform the world or to accomplish any particular task of religious teaching or leadership. The prophet was simply 'a mouthpiece'.

Moses rapidly acquired an aura of respect from the people, not simply as a holy man, and certainly not because they appreciated his leadership, but as one who had the privilege of entering into the presence of the almighty God. It was said of Moses when he came down from Mount Sinai 'that his face was radiant because he had spoken with the Lord' and the people were afraid to go near him (Ex 34.29 −35). Thus the ministry of Moses established the role of the prophet as the mouthpiece of God and it also established the respect due to the office which was responsible in later years for saving the lives of the prophets when they faced ungodly rulers or proclaimed unpopular messages. It was from the time of Moses that the prophet was regarded as sacrosanct in Israel.

Antecedents of the canonical prophets

Despite the massive change in the social order brought about by the settlement in Canaan and the confusion we have noted between the seer and the nabi there is a continuous line of prophecy throughout the history of ancient Israel from the time of Moses to the close of the Old Testament canon. Most modern scholars, in tracing the antecedents of the canonical prophets, the first of whom was Amos, believe the line may be traced back to the nebi'im rather than the seers. They do this on the grounds of religious phenomena rather than historicity. Historically the weight of evidence is in favour of the seer as the true antecedent of the lonely figures of the prophets of the eighth century onwards while the nebi'im became increasingly associated with Baalism or, at best, with syncretism and false prophecy.

The reason why many modern scholars regard the nebi'im as the antecedents of the canonical prophets is due to a misunderstanding of the nature of true revelation. Most Old Testament scholars today emphasise the ecstatic characteristics of the prophets. For example, Ezekiel is almost universally regarded as an 'ecstatic' because of the numerous visions he received which were the basis of his

26

ministry of declaring the word of God. Typical of the views of modern scholars is that expressed by John Wevers in his introduction to the New Century Bible Commentary on Ezekiel. He outlines the four main sections of visions in the book of Ezekiel and then says:

> These visions are all ecstatic visions. Each is introduced by the technical phrase 'The hand of Yahweh was upon me', describing entrance into the trance state, whereas the technical term of ecstasy as such is 'visions of God'. Unlike Isaiah's vision in Isaiah 21, which records the nightmarish reaction of the prophet (cf also Habakkuk 3.16), there is no hint of any personal response on the part of Ezekiel (but see 11.13). (John W. Wevers, *The New Century Bible Commentary, Ezekiel*; Marshall Morgan and Scott).

It is a mistake to think that all visionary experiences are necessarily ecstatic and that the prophets were always 'in a trance' when they received revelation through prophetic pictures. Ezekiel was not one who went away alone and worked himself into a trance or had around him a band of musicians like the nebi'im of old and danced and leapt and shouted until he was in a frenzy of activity that put his rational mind in limbo and he entered into a state of trance. That is certainly not the impression Ezekiel gives us when he describes how he received some of his visions. For example, he says, 'While I was sitting in my house and the elders of Judah were sitting before me, the hand of the Sovereign Lord came upon me there. I looked, and I saw the figure like that of a man . . .' (Eze 8.1).

That certainly does not sound like a man in a trance. It sounds more like a man sitting with a group of responsible leaders considering the situation in which they found themselves as exiles in Babylon, separated from Jerusalem and the Temple, and given the task of religious leadership among a people who had largely regarded God in territorial terms. It certainly does not sound like an ecstatic orgy.

His vision described in Ezekiel 8 was of events taking place in Jerusalem. They were events that Ezekiel had probably seen with his own eyes before the captivity and certainly he would have discussed many times with other leaders. They were vividly fixed in his mind and during a time of prayer they came back to him. Ezekiel himself describes this as being transported from Babylonia to Jerusalem. But this still does not imply a trance, although today it would be classed as a 'paranormal experience'. As these scenes ran through his mind he received a strong word from God concerning them.

That is the nature of revelation. God uses the everyday events and scenes of human activity, recalled by his Spirit to our minds when we enter into his presence, to communicate a message to us. There is nothing psychosomatic about this as many modern scholars believe. When the prophets speak of the 'hand of the Lord' coming upon them or of the 'Spirit of God' coming upon them they simply mean that at that time they were able to shut out from their minds the things of the world to the extent that they were able to be wholly attentive to, and to respond to, the presence of God through the ministry of the Holy Spirit. At such times God would either bring into their mind a picture or words. It is these phenomena that we shall be examining in the next chapter. The point we are emphasising here is that revelation is not something that needs the tools of abnormal psychology for analysis. The prophet who received a true vision was not in a trance and the one who declared the true word of the Lord had not entered into an ecstatic state in order to receive that word.

Revelation through pictures or words is the normal experience of millions of Christians today in their quiet times of prayer or in group prayer meetings. This is something that seems to be outside the experience of most modern biblical scholars who live in a world of form criticism and literary analysis from which they rarely emerge to enter into any personal spiritual experience of the presence of the living God. Hence revelation is regarded by many scholars as strange and unfamiliar phenomena from a past age that can only be understood in terms of psychoanalysis and is outside the realm of personal experience.

In the following pages we shall be attempting to understand the ministry and the message of the prophets of ancient Israel, in the context of a contemporary understanding of revelation as the direct encounter of God with man through the ministry of the Holy Spirit.

CHAPTER TWO

RECEIVING THE WORD

We have already defined prophecy as 'the revealed word of God' and we have noted that the prophet was one who declared that word. The content of prophecy will be discussed in chapter nine but it is relevant here to note that the content of the truth conveyed by God to the prophets (apart from the Law given through Moses) concerned the divine nature; the divine purposes; God's word on contemporary issues, and God's word on the course of future events.

The task of the prophets was to know the will of God so that they could convey it to the nation. Their ministry consisted in handling revelation, *ie* the knowledge that God revealed to them. We have already noted that receiving revelation was not an intellectual process but a spiritual activity. We must now ask the questions: How did this spiritual activity occur? How was prophecy received?

From earliest times prophecy was conceived as being the activity of God rather than the activity of man. This is true not only for the receiving of prophecy but also for its delivery. When the prophet actually conveyed the word of the Lord to the people he was deemed to be under the power of God. The hand of the Lord was upon him, empowering and directing the delivery of the word. Even the prophet's manner changed when the Spirit of God came upon him and he was energised

31

by a force outside himself. This force not only produced great boldness and fearlessness in proclaiming the word of God regardless of personal danger, but it also sometimes produced extraordinary physical energy. A good example is the way Elijah ran ahead of Ahab's chariot all the way from the top of Mount Carmel down to Jezreel. Anyone familiar with the rocky terrain of Carmel will realise that this was no mean feat, but would tax the strength of an Olympic long-distance runner. But Elijah actually reached the city ahead of Ahab who was no doubt driving his chariot at full speed! Elijah's superhuman energy soon evaporated under Jezebel's malevolent threat to his life which illustrates the prophet's frail humanity during the ordinary course of his life when the Spirit of God was not upon him.

Divine Invasion

The coming of the Spirit of God upon a man from earliest times in the history of Israel was regarded as a divine invasion. The Hebrew term 'ruach' is used for the power of God. Literally it means 'wind'. The Spirit of God came upon man like the rushing of a mighty wind which was the way Luke described the events at Pentecost that occurred more than a thousand years after the period with which we are presently dealing.

From beginning to end the Bible is a record of the activity of the Spirit of God. The first page of Genesis presents a picture of darkness and chaos with the Spirit of God moving across the watery deep. The last page of the book of Revelation presents the Spirit of God joined with the church in making the great evangelising appeal to mankind, 'The Spirit and the Bride say, Come.'

The 'ruach' of God was seen as divine power. In the time of Moses and the period of the early settlement in Canaan the term 'ruach' was used of invasive energy to account for any abnormal behaviour that was believed to be connected with the presence of God. Thus when Samson was attacked by a young lion 'the ruach of Yahweh came upon him in power' and 'he tore the lion apart with his bare hands' (Jd 14.6). But the term could be used for ordinary human physical energy, as when Samson was tired and thirsty after killing a thousand men, he had a drink of water and 'his ruach returned and he revived' (Jd 15.19). In this context it means that Samson's life energy returned.

Where 'ruach' is used in connection with prophetic revelation it really means that the divine life energy was transmitted from God to man. Probably the best example in the whole of the Old Testament of the transformation brought about by the invasive ruach of God is to be found in Ezekiel's vision of the valley strewn with bones where thousands of young men met their death. As he watched, the bones came together, joined by sinews and covered by flesh until the whole valley was filled with bodies, but they were still lifeless forms until he pronounced the word of the Lord and a blast of wind swept through the valley filling the bodies of dead men with new life. The ruach of God turned death into life. The valley of slaughter became a place of resurrection and they stood up on their feet, an exceeding mighty army. The divine energy was released into the valley as the divine intention, revealed to the prophet, was spoken aloud (Eze 37).

The 'ruach' of God was closely connected with the word of God. David referred to this at the end of his life when he acknowledged how God had directed him: 'The Spirit of the Lord spoke through me; his word was on my tongue' (2 Sam 23.2). It was when the ruach of God came upon the prophets that they received the revelation of divine truth as well as the power to deliver the word. We have already referred to the ecstatic behaviour of the nebi'im and we have seen how seers such as Samuel on occasions exhibited ecstatic behaviour. When the wind or power of God rushed upon a man his behaviour became abnormal. A vivid description of this is found in Numbers 24.2–4 where the ruach of God came upon Balaam.

> The oracle of Balaam, son of Beor, the oracle of one whose eye sees clearly, the oracle of one who hears the words of God, who

sees a vision from the Almighty, who falls prostrate, and whose eyes are opened.

In this description Balaam was behaving perfectly normally when the Spirit of God came upon him. He continued to see clearly and was actually receiving the word of God when suddenly he began to see a vision at which point he was struck down by the Spirit and lay prostrate. This is not too dissimilar to the experience of Ezekiel, although Ezekiel usually saw the vision first which led to his hearing from God and to the Spirit lifting him up on his feet or telling him to stand up *cf* 1.28–2.3; 3.22–24.

Even Jeremiah refers to some kind of physical experience of the coming of the Spirit of God upon him that caused his whole body to tremble and sway.

> My heart is broken within me; all my bones tremble. I am like a drunken man, like a man overcome by wine, because of the Lord and his holy words (Jer 23.9).

Hosea refers to the prophet being 'considered a fool, the inspired man a maniac' (Hos 9.7) which appears to indicate some kind of abnormal behaviour associated with those who proclaimed the word of the living God.

Thus even with the major prophets from the eighth century onwards there were certain physical signs of the presence of the ruach of God coming upon them. It may well be that this divine invasion was associated in the later prophets with their call into the ministry of the prophet and their appointment by God rather than with the continuing activity of the Spirit in their lives.

The initial appointment of a prophet had to be purely the activity of God approaching man and not man seeking God, for it was God who appointed those who were to proclaim his word. It was not an office to be sought by men. Indeed one of the marks of the genuine call of the prophet appears to have been his reluctance to accept the appointment. It would also appear that a test of the genuineness of an experience of the presence of God was the *persistence of God*. If God truly was making an approach to a human being he would not let go. The mark of the call of God upon the individual was that despite his reluctance due to his personal sense of inadequacy, he could do no other than yield. Examples of this are to be seen in the call to ministry of Moses (Ex 4.10f); Isaiah (Is 6.1f); and Jeremiah (Jer 1.4f).

Once the prophet had the anointing of the ruach of God upon him he never knew when the Spirit of God would speak to him. On those occasions when he had to take the initiative in seeking divine guidance he then had to find a way of entering the presence of God so that the Spirit of God could communicate with him. Moses used to get away from the crowd and make the lonely climb up Mount Sinai to seek the presence of God. This underlines the strong sense of the holiness of God that was shared by all the prophets and drove them to seek the presence of God outside the company of people and separated from the ordinary secular pursuits of daily life. Jeremiah tells us that he often sat alone when the hand of God was upon him. He shunned 'the company of revellers' and 'never made merry with them' (Jer 15.17).

Hearing and Seeing

The ministry of the prophet required spending time in the presence of God. Jeremiah calls this standing 'in the council of the Lord to see or to hear his word' (Jer 23.18).

This statement of Jeremiah neatly sums up the way in which all the prophets received divine guidance. They learned to listen to God, to meditate upon his word, to allow their thoughts to be directed by the Spirit of God and sometimes to receive pictures through which he communicated a message to them. The prophet learned to allow the divine invasion to take place from the time when God had first made his unsought invasion into the life of the one who was to serve him by revealing his word to the nation.

The mind of the prophet was never passive as it would be if he were in a trance. The mind was active in co-operation with God so that the ruach could blow upon him. This was

35

the willing joining of the spirit of man with the Spirit of God made possible by God breathing into man and pervading his spirit that had been created by God in his own image. It was the active response of the spirit within man to the Spirit of the living God.

The excesses of ecstasy are nowhere to be seen in Moses. But were introduced into the religion of Israel through the influence of Canaanite religion and gradually disappeared from Hebrew prophecy as the ministry of the true prophet emerged from the syncretism of the period of the Judges and the early monarchy into the more refined and purer revelation of the eighth-century prophets.

The true prophet was always in control of his mind, even when receiving a vision. He was conscious of the presence of God and willingly reaching out to him to enable the transference of revelation to take place. This is what Paul later described as the spirit of the prophet being under the control of the prophet (1 Cor 14.32). Each of the mainline prophets of ancient Israel could have similarly testified.

The prophets learned to recognise the symptoms of the ruach of God coming upon them and at such times they were attentive, ready to listen to words brought into the conscious mind, or to receive a picture formed on the retina of the mind and discerned through the Spirit.

Thus we see that revelation was communicated to the prophets through the Spirit of God using the ordinary human attributes of sight and hearing. Most of the prophets received the word of God through words and pictures, although with the canonical prophets the emphasis is usually upon one or the other as their principal means of receiving the word of the Lord.

Visions and words
A glance at the beginning of each of the canonical prophets illustrates the two principal ways of receiving the word of God. Isaiah was a 'seeing' prophet; 'the vision concerning Judah and Jerusalem that Isaiah son of Amoz saw during

the reigns of Uzziah, Jotham, Ahaz and Hezekiah, kings of Judah' (Is 1.1).

This, however, does not mean that Isaiah only saw visions. Sight and sound were always mingled in the ministry of the prophets. Jeremiah was primarily a 'hearing' prophet, but he also received the word of God through pictures.

Jeremiah's own account of his call by God emphasises that he was a hearing prophet.

> The word of the Lord came to me saying, 'Before I formed you in the womb I knew you, before you were born I set you apart; I appointed you as a prophet to the nations.' 'Ah, Sovereign Lord,' I said, 'I do not know how to speak; I am only a child.' But the Lord said to me, 'Do not say, "I am only a child." You must go to everyone I send you to and say whatever I command you.' . . . Then the Lord reached out his hand and touched my mouth and said to me, 'Now, I have put my words in your mouth' (Jer 1.4–9).

It is clear from Jeremiah's personal testimony that God spoke directly to the prophet. The phrase used at the beginning of verse 4 gives an indication of the manner in which he heard from God. The Hebrew verb translated here 'came' literally means 'came into being' or 'was created'. Thus Jeremiah's personal account of receiving the word of God is that it was formed within him or conceived within him. God actually spoke directly into his spirit; he moulded the thoughts of his mind, so using his normal human thought capacity to enable him to think the thoughts of God and to express them in human words. Thus the word of the living God was communicated into his mind.

Jeremiah did not hear a booming voice in the sky; or, indeed, any kind of physical sound. Neither was he in a trance. His mind was very much alert so that he was able to respond actively and rationally to what he was hearing and to test its veracity. He protested against his commissioning as a prophet on two grounds: he was not a good orator, and also he was very young. God's response was to ignore both of these human limitations and to remind him, as he had

37

reminded Moses, that he would be with him. 'Do not be afraid of them, for I am with you and will rescue you' (Jer 1.8). At the beginning of his ministry Jeremiah had learned the lesson that if God calls to a task he never leaves his appointed one alone. His presence guarantees the power to fulfil the task.

Ezekiel was a *seeing* prophet. He remembered the exact day when the Spirit of God first came upon him. 'In the thirtieth year and in the fourth month and the fifth day, while I was among the exiles by the Kebar river, the heavens were opened and *I saw* visions of God' (Eze 1.1).

Hosea was primarily a *hearing* prophet. 'The word of the Lord that came to Hosea son of Beeri during the reigns of Uzziah, Jotham, Ahaz and Hezekiah, kings of Judah' (Hos 1.1). Amos, on the other hand, was said to be a *seeing* prophet. 'The words of Amos, one of the shepherds of Tekoa—what he saw concerning Israel two years before the earthquake, when Uzziah was king of Judah and Jeroboam son of Jehoash was king of Israel' (Am 1.1).

This does not mean that any of the prophets of Israel were confined to a single mode of communication in receiving the word of God. Although Ezekiel was principally a 'seeing prophet' he also heard from God. So too did Amos. Although there were many times when the prophets received a picture through which God conveyed a message to them they also heard words brought directly into their minds.

Ezekiel was one who saw many visions, such as the glory of God departing from the Temple before the destruction of Jerusalem and then returning at the end of the exile. 'Now the glory of the God of Israel went up from above the cherubim where it had been and moved to the threshold of the temple' (Eze 9.3). 'The glory of the Lord went up from within the city and stopped above the mountain east of it' (Eze 11.23). 'I saw the glory of the God of Israel coming from the east. . . . the land was radiant with his glory. The vision I saw was like the vision I had seen when he came to destroy the city' (Eze 43.2,3).

Ezekiel is really the outstanding prophet of visions and their interpretation such as the valley of the 'dry bones' in chapter 37 and the vision of the 'new Temple' that was to be built in Jerusalem followed by the vision of the 'river of life' in chapter 47 that would bring cleansing and healing to the whole land. But Ezekiel also heard the word of God as he spoke directly to him on many occasions. Sight and sound often appear to merge for this prophet. He says, 'This was the appearance of the likeness of the glory of the Lord. When I *saw* it, I fell face down, and I *heard* the voice of one speaking.' Ezekiel records the words that he heard formed in his mind. 'He said to me, "Son of man, stand up on your feet and I will speak to you." As he spoke, the Spirit came into me and raised me to my feet, and I heard him speaking to me' (Eze 1.28–2.2).

Hearing and seeing were therefore the major characteristics of the manner in which the prophets received the word of God that they were to declare to the people. All of them testified that it was the presence of God that enabled them to receive from him. It was the coming of the Spirit of God upon them that enabled them to receive the word of God. Thus it was the Spirit of God that was the means by which God communicated with the prophets. As we have seen, he did so by using the ordinary senses that are part of our humanity so that either words or pictures were formed in the prophet's mind. The Spirit of God then enabled spiritual perception to take place so that the word of God came into being within the mind of the prophet thus enabling him to know what he was to declare. We shall see later the manner in which the same Spirit gave power to declare the word publicly.

The thing we are emphasising here is that there was nothing magical or occultic in the way the prophets received from God. God used the ordinary attributes common to all humanity that he himself had formed when creating men and women in his own image. The prophets, moreover, were not superhuman beings—a race set apart. Neither were they superhuman in the sense that they had special attributes not available to ordinary men and women.

Certainly they were different in their absolute commitment to God and in their commissioning by him to the task of prophecy, and in the heightening of their spiritual faculties that enabled them to receive the word of God, to perceive his purposes and to declare the word of God publicly. But the prophets were men like us. That is the witness of Scripture. All of them were born in the same manner as the rest of humanity by the normal means of human procreation and were raised as ordinary children by their human parents. Certainly, they were set aside for their special task by the commissioning of God whose call was received directly. And certainly the coming of the Spirit of God upon them changed their lives. But in terms of the substance of their humanity the prophets were in no way different from us. James declares this explicitly, 'Elijah was a man just like us. He prayed earnestly that it would not rain, and it did not rain on the land for three and a half years. Again he prayed, and the heavens gave rain, and the earth produced its crops' (Jas 5.17,18).

The prophets, moreover, despite their devotion to God were not always walking in the power of the Spirit. We read of Elijah running away after the tremendous victory over the prophets of Baal at Mount Carmel. He was clearly utterly depressed and going through a period of black despair feeling far from the presence of God. But through the experience of the great storm on the mountainside God was finally able to get through to him again as he listened to the still small voice within him and the word of the Lord returned to him.

The prophets were not always hearing from God every day. Many times we read of the word of the Lord coming to the prophet, or the Spirit of God taking hold of the prophet. Sometimes it was a struggle of concentration to receive the word and to discern clearly what God was saying. It required careful meditation, quiet listening, intercession and prolonged concentration to discern an important message, as, for example, the occasion when it took Jeremiah ten days to receive the word of the Lord (Jer 42.7). We shall examine this more fully when we look at the method of the prophet.

The prophets therefore were men or women who had been chosen by God and endued with the characteristics that were essential for receiving revelation. They possessed the ability to seek the face of God, to enter into his presence and thus to receive his word which was the essential prerequisite for the proclamation of the word of God to the nation.

CHAPTER THREE

THE CHARACTERISTICS OF
THE PROPHET

The individualism of the prophets of ancient Israel is unde-
niable, yet there are certain characteristics that are common
to all the genuine prophets. These characteristics distinguish
them from others, notably the false prophets, and thus form
an important body of evidence as to the true nature of
prophecy and the exercise of the ministry of the prophet. In
this chapter we will outline eight characteristics of the
prophet that can be discerned through the biblical accounts
of their ministries and their recorded words.

Messengers of God

The first major characteristic that all the prophets have in
common is that they were sent by God. They were messengers rather than orators. They did not make up their own
speeches; they simply relayed the words that they had been
given.

Each of the prophets was able to point to a personal
experience of 'being called' by God into the ministry of the
prophet. We do not have a recorded account of each
prophet's experience but the marks of having been called by
God and set aside for this ministry are clearly to be seen.

Among those whose experience of 'a call' to ministry have

been recorded in the Bible there is none more vivid and powerful than that of Isaiah. His experience of God in the Temple is classic, coming as it did soon after the death of the leper king Uzziah whose sickness had cast a shadow over the entire nation and whose death signalled the beginning of a new era of hope. Isaiah's experience of the holiness of God and the awesomeness of being in his presence provided the foundational knowledge from which the prophet undertook his ministry. In the presence of the holy and almighty God whose glory filled the whole earth Isaiah experienced his own humanity and uncleanness. There was nothing he could do about this except to cry out to the Lord Almighty who immediately responded by cleansing him and removing the guilt of his sin. It was after this experience of atonement that he received the call to ministry and was able to respond 'Here am I. Send me!'

The experience of being called by God into ministry came to Amos while he was out in the southern hills of Judah, where he lived the simple life of a shepherd and also did some tree cultivation. The details of his call to ministry are unknown to us but the effect left an indelible mark upon his life. It was a conviction that enabled him to withstand a face-to-face confrontation with Jeroboam, king of Israel, and to be undaunted by the rage of Amaziah the priest who ordered him to leave the king's sanctuary at Bethel and to go back to Judah. Amos calmly referred to the call of God upon his life and continued to speak the words he had been sent to deliver. Even the combined religious and secular power of the state could not silence the prophet who had been sent by God to deliver a message (Am 7.10ff).

Jeremiah also refers briefly to his experience of being called by God into ministry as a young man. He traces the call of God upon his life back to his birth saying that God had actually formed him in the womb and set him apart for the special task of 'a prophet to the nations' (Jer 1.5).

Jeremiah's experience of God actually touching his mouth was similar to that of Isaiah. It was followed by the specific injunction, 'Now, I have put my words in your mouth'. It was this experience of being sent by God with a message that was common to all the prophets. They were not in the service of man but in the service of God. In this sense, they were not finally responsible for the message they bore, it was God's responsibility. The words were his, not theirs. If the message was rejected it was not the words of men that were being spurned, but the word of the living God.

Under Authority

It was the experience of being sent by God that gave each of the prophets his authority. They were not giving voice to their own ideas, they were under the direction of the Spirit of God. It was the living God who gave them authority not simply to distinguish between good and evil, as ethical reformers, but actually to speak in his name. It was the use of the first person singular in respect to the Almighty God that distinguished the prophets from all other religious functionaries.

The priests had authority to perform ritual, the scribes had authority to copy the law and even to interpret it, but only the prophets had the authority to speak in the name of God. 'Thus saith the Lord' became one of the marks of the true prophet. Their task was recognised by the whole nation both in Israel and Judah, among high and low, rulers and people. They were expected to declare what God was saying to the nation in the circumstances of the day.

Very often the message was hated or rejected because it was unpalatable or ran contrary to the political policies of the ruling party. Jeremiah nearly lost his life for prophesying an unpopular message at the time of the fall of the Assyrian empire. There was a strong pro-Egypt party among the politicians of Jerusalem who advised the young king Jehoiakim, son of Josiah. Josiah had been killed at Megiddo while trying to prevent the Egyptians from going to the aid of the Assyrians. Nineveh had fallen in 612 BC, and in 609 the final stronghold of the Assyrian army, Haran, had been crushed by the rising power of Babylon. Despite the exultant declaration of the prophet Nahum—'Everyone who hears the news about you claps his hands at your fall, for who has not felt your endless cruelty?' (Nah 3.19)—Jeremiah perceived the real danger. He warned sternly against putting trust in Pharaoh Necho and duly provoked the wrath of the pro-Egypt party.

Jeremiah even went so far as to proclaim Nebuchadnezzar king of Babylon as the servant of the Lord (Jer 25.9). He perceived that Nebuchadnezzar was a mere pawn in the hands of the Almighty God who would use him to punish Judah for their apostasy, 'Do not follow other gods to serve and worship them; do not provoke me to anger with what your hands have made. Then I will not harm you' (25.6). When God had finished using the Babylonians he would cast their empire down, 'But when the seventy years are fulfilled, I will punish the king of Babylon and his nation' (25.12). This prophecy was fulfilled exactly. From the defeat of the Assyrian army in 609 to the fall of Babylon to Cyrus the Persian in 539 BC was exactly seventy years.

Jeremiah was seized by 'the priests, the prophets and all the people', who said that he must die: 'Why do you prophesy in the Lord's name that this house will be like Shiloh and this city will be desolate and deserted?' (26.9). His defence was to declare that he was not responsible for the words he had spoken. 'The Lord sent me to prophesy against this house and this city all the things you have heard' (26.12). He followed this with a further plea to the leaders of the nation to put their trust in God. He perceived with incredible accuracy, as Isaiah had done before him, that the Egyptians were like a broken reed which, if a man leaned on it, would pierce his hand.

The Egyptian power was indeed short-lived and in 605 BC Nebuchadnezzar dealt them a crushing defeat at Carchemish. From there he swept south to deal with Judah and, just as Jeremiah had said, there was no Egyptian army to save Jerusalem from the onslaught of the enemy.

Jeremiah's personal disclaimer of responsibility for the declaration that the Temple and the city of Jerusalem would be destroyed was not simply a response to the unanimous threat of death pronounced by the priests, prophets, politicians and all the people, it was a mark of his absolute conviction that he had been given that word by God. He was a man under authority and could do no other than utter the word he had been given.

An outstanding example of the way the God-given authority possessed by the prophet over-rode all other considerations including that of the personal safety of the prophet is seen in the account in 2 Chronicles 18 of Micaiah being summoned to counsel Ahab and Jehoshaphat. The messenger who went to summon Micaiah informed him that all the other prophets were advising the two kings to go into battle against the Syrians and that they would be successful in recovering Ramoth Gilead. 'Look, as one man the other prophets are predicting success for the king. Let your word agree with theirs, and speak favourably.' To this Micaiah responded, 'As surely as the Lord lives, I can tell him only what my God says' (2 Chr 18.12,13).

The prophet could not change the message to suit the convenience of men, however powerful. He was a man under authority. He was under obligation to speak the word of God. He could do no other.

Absolute Obedience

The prophet, being a man sent by God and under his authority, was required to show absolute obedience. When God spoke to him he had to be able to discern what was being said so that he knew what was required of him. Once he was sure of the mission and the message he was under the obligation of absolute obedience to do exactly as he was told.

Ezekiel had to learn this lesson when some of the elders of Israel came to him and sought his counsel. The account in Ezekiel 14 indicates that while the prophet was pondering the matter brought to him by the elders the word of the Lord came to him instructing him to give them no answer to the matter upon which they were seeking guidance. 'These men have set up idols in their hearts and put wicked stumbling-blocks before their faces. Should I let them enquire of me at all?' The prophet was then instructed to tell them the consequences of idolatry. The only message to be given to the house of Israel was a call to repentance. 'This is what the Sovereign Lord says: Repent! Turn from your idols and renounce all your detestable practices!' (Eze 14.6).

Ezekiel was instructed to tell the elders of Israel that they were not to be commended for coming to the prophet to seek guidance while they were involved in idolatrous practices which put a spiritual stumbling-block in their hearts. In fact this was simply evidence of their gross hypocrisy and God would answer this by bringing disaster upon them. There is considerable threat in the statement 'I the Lord will answer him myself'. It is followed by the statement 'I will set my face against that man and make him an example and a byword' (14.7,8). God's direct answer would be not with words, which would normally be delivered through a prophet, but directly, which means by deed or action that would bring swift retribution upon the sinner. God's action would result in his being cut off from the rest of the people. He would be made an example that would be highly public and everyone would be talking about it.

Ezekiel himself also learned a lesson through this incident. He was told that if the prophet was persuaded to utter a prophecy when God had refused to answer, the prophet himself would be as guilty as the ones who consulted him.

Ezekiel probably remembered the fate of the unnamed prophet in 1 Kings 13 who was sent from Judah to Bethel where Jeroboam was standing beside the altar making an offering. The prophet cried out against the altar in the words God had given him, saying that it would one day be desecrated with the bones of the priests who served there. The implication was that the king and all who performed religious rituals at Bethel were involved in idolatry and practices that were detestable to God.

King Jeroboam ordered the seizure of the man but as he did so his arm became paralysed and the altar itself split apart. The king turned from aggression to entreaty and when the prophet responded by praying and the king's hand was restored he could not do enough for the prophet.

It was at this point that the prophet showed his obedience to God. He refused food and gifts saying, 'I was commanded by the word of the Lord; you must not eat bread or drink water or return by the way you came.' Thereupon he left Bethel immediately by a different route.

All was well until he met a man who claimed also to be a prophet and to be bearing a word from God for him. It countermanded the word that he had been given from God and led to disaster in which he lost his life. He had fearlessly confronted the king, faithfully proclaimed the word of the Lord, refused gifts, food and even a drink of water in order to be absolutely obedient to the word of God. Now, through an elderly prophet whom he believed, he brought disaster upon himself by his disobedience.

The ministry of the prophet was never easy. He had to learn to obey God rather than men. He was not his own; he had been set apart by God for his service. The fear of the Lord never left the prophet. Once he was called into ministry he was under the obligation of absolute obedience to the one who had set him apart for this ministry.

No doubt the events of Bethel and the fate of the disobedient prophet were known to Amos, who similarly was sent from Judah to Bethel during the reign of Jeroboam to speak against the northern kingdom of Israel. All the subsequent prophets from Hosea to Ezekiel and beyond to the post-exilic prophets such as Haggai—all would be aware that the Lord required from his prophets absolute obedience.

Total Commitment

The message of the prophets was never popular. They called

for loyalty to God and adherence to a strict ethical code that ran contrary to the desires of the people and to the selfish ambition and self-indulgence of the rulers. All the prophets encountered opposition but one of the marks of the true prophet was the fortitude with which he met the opposition and the tenacity with which he continued to proclaim the message. Each of the prophets displayed the quality of total commitment to the ministry to which he was called. There was no turning back or weakening. Once the prophet had embarked upon his public ministry he was marked out as a man of God. His loyalty was to God alone whatever the consequences.

Each of the prophets was driven by a kind of inner compulsion to fulfil whatever task was given regardless of the danger or personal suffering that may result.

Jeremiah is probably the best example of the prophet who could not be silenced or induced to vary the message despite threats, abuse, physical violence and the menace of imminent death.

Throughout his life Jeremiah faced opposition. He was no stranger to threats and physical violence but even he was brought to the extremity of pleading with the king not to have him sent back to prison during the lull in fighting prior to the final Babylonian assault on Jerusalem. The prophet had been put into prison for declaring that the lifting of the Babylonian siege of Jerusalem was only a temporary respite. Jeremiah declared that they would be back and that Jerusalem would fall because God himself was against the city for its idolatry and rebellion against him. He declared, 'Even if you were to defeat the entire Babylonian army that is attacking you and only wounded men were left in their tents, they would come out and burn the city down' (Jer 37.10).

Zedekiah gave orders for Jeremiah to be brought secretly from his dungeon cell into the palace where he asked him privately 'Is there any word from the Lord?' 'Yes,' Jeremiah replied, 'You will be handed over to the king of Babylon' (37.17).

50

On another occasion Jeremiah was flung down a well and left to die in the mud. It was on the king's orders that men were despatched to lower ropes to him and pull the prophet out of the cistern (38.1–13).

It was only the prophet's total commitment to his mission and utter conviction that he was rightly hearing from God that enabled him to maintain an unswerving witness in the face of severe suffering. His suffering was not always physical. Chapter 20 reveals some of the personal cost of the ministry he exercised. In a moment of black despair he actually cursed the day he was born and wished he had died in the womb. 'Why did I ever come out of the womb to see trouble and sorrow and to end my days in shame?' (20.18). His cry to God not only revealed the pain and suffering he endured through his ministry but it shows the extent of his commitment to the ministry. Despite all the opposition of men and the suffering it brought to him he simply could not keep quiet, he had to proclaim the word that God had put into his heart.

> I am ridiculed all day long; everyone mocks me. Whenever I speak, I cry out proclaiming violence and destruction. So the word of the Lord has brought me insult and reproach all day long. But if I say, 'I will not mention him or speak any more in his name,' his word is in my heart like a burning fire, shut up in my bones. I am weary of holding it in; indeed, I cannot (Jer 20.7–9).

Compassion
There is a deep compassion running right through the ministry of the prophets that reveals their understanding of God as merciful, compassionate and overflowing with loving-kindness.

Hosea speaks with great tenderness of God's love for the nation Israel, 'When Israel was a child, I loved him,' he reports God as saying. He clearly sees God as a loving Father tenderly caring for his children. 'It was I who taught Ephraim to walk, taking them by the arms; but they did not

51

realise it was I who healed them. I led them with cords of human kindness, with ties of love; I lifted the yoke from their neck and bent down to feed them' (Hos 11.1–4).

It was because of God's great love for his people that the prophets were able to declare that he hated injustice and oppression. Hence, on those occasions when the prophets speak very sternly to the rulers or to the rich and powerful, it is because they perceive that God loves all his people equally and does not favour a small powerful élite. It is thus out of a great compassion for the oppressed that Amos thundered, 'Hear this, you who trample the needy and do away with the poor of the land.' He accused the merchants of greed and corruption, 'skimping the measure, boosting the price and cheating with dishonest scales,' and he saw the rich 'buying the poor with silver and the needy for a pair of sandals' (Am 8.4–6).

Amos knew that God is always on the side of the poor and the oppressed when the rich and powerful misuse their positions of privilege in the nation and are driven by greed and self-interest. Even the harshest words of the prophets are not spoken out of a motive of vindictiveness or a desire to bring judgment, wrath and disaster upon the people, but rather to turn them from the path of self-destruction. They foresaw the consequences of man's rebellion against God and they knew God's great love for his people, so they trusted his purposes were for good and not for ill, that, as Jeremiah declared, God had good plans for his people—plans to give a future and a hope (Jer 29.11).

The prophets were so aware of the loving and good purpose of God that they saw even his harsh words as words of warning for the good of the people and not for their destruction. It was because of God's compassion for the people that he spoke to them so urgently when they were heading for disaster. Their idolatry, false religion or the sins of the flesh had made them blind and deaf to God's word so that he was unable to guide them. The prophets so identified with their message that they actually experienced the compassion of God as a deeply felt emotion. Even when they had a harsh word to bring it was pronounced as *judgment upon evil actions and faithlessness rather than judgmentalism against individuals*.

The deep compassion of the prophet who internalised the message from God is seen very clearly in Jeremiah, who sometimes openly wept at the message he had to bring: 'Let my eyes overflow with tears night and day without ceasing' (Jer 14.17). And sometimes he sat and wept in private, 'I sat alone because your hand was on me and you had filled me with indignation. Why is my pain unending and my wound grievous and incurable?' (15.17,18).

Jeremiah's greatest anguish came as a result of seeing vividly the disaster that was to come upon the nation. Yet however clearly he described this and however urgently he warned the people, they were dull and unresponsive. Jeremiah occasionally gives us a glimpse of the great personal suffering this brought to him:

> Your own conduct and actions have brought this upon you. This is your punishment. How bitter it is! How it pierces to the heart! Oh, my anguish, my anguish! I writhe in pain. Oh, the agony of my heart! My heart pounds within me, I cannot keep silent. For I have heard the sound of the trumpet; I have heard the battle cry. Disaster follows disaster; the whole land lies in ruins (Jer 4.18–20).

It was because he felt the pain and compassion of God that Jeremiah was able to speak in such terms. And it was because he knew that God was longing to save his people not to condemn them that he continued to proclaim the message in the hope that it would be received and heeded despite the personal suffering and physical abuse it brought him.

Patriotism
All the prophets were great patriots. In fact compassion and patriotism were very much linked in their ministry. It was

53

because God loved the people and had good purposes for them that the prophets were driven to communicate the message they were given. The link between compassion and patriotism is seen in the word we have just quoted from Jeremiah 14.17 where the prophet was told to speak these words to the nation, 'Let my eyes overflow with tears night and day without ceasing; for my virgin daughter—my people—has suffered a grievous wound, a crushing blow.' The grievous wound is vividly described by Jeremiah in the next sentence: 'If I go into the country, I see those slain by the sword; if I go into the city, I see the ravages of famine.'

The prophet was expressing through his own sorrow the grief that was in God's heart over the terrible calamity that had occurred to the nation that had been ravaged by enemy invasion. The context places this prophecy in the year 598 BC when the young king Jehoiachin, who had just succeeded his father, was carried captive to Babylon in Nebuchadnezzar's first invasion of Judah (2 Kg 24).

The patriotism of the prophets was never a blind loyalty to the nation, right or wrong. It was always seen primarily as loyalty to God to whom the land belonged. God had given the land to Israel and had established a covenant relationship between himself and the people; therefore the people and the land were holy to God. They were the place and the people through whom he was working out his purposes among the nations. Isaiah spoke of God as using Israel to be a light to the Gentiles through whom he would reveal himself, the one and only true God, creator of the universe. 'I will also make you a light for the Gentiles that you may bring my salvation to the ends of the earth' (Is 49.6). Although that word, and a similar one in 42.6, was part of the prophecies to the 'Servant of the Lord' and are therefore within a Messianic context that we know to be fulfilled in the person and work of the Messiah, Jesus, nevertheless, in their original context the Servant was seen as a personification of the nation Israel through whom God was longing to convey his salvation to all the nations of the world. It is part of the tragedy of Israel's history that it was not through the whole nation but only through his 'only begotten Son' that God's purposes could be worked out.

The patriotism of the prophets is beautifully illustrated in the song of the vineyard in Isaiah 5, where God's relationship to the land and the people is expressed through the simile of a gardener who loved his vineyard situated on a fertile hillside. He planted the choicest vines and did everything he could to care for them and ensure they produced a good crop. When he came to reap the harvest he found only bad fruit. The interpretation given in verse 7 is that 'the vineyard of the Lord Almighty is the house of Israel and the men of Judah are the garden of his delight. He looked for justice, but saw bloodshed; for righteousness, but heard cries of distress'.

This passage neatly summarises God's possession of the land, his love and care for it and his purpose in planting the nation Israel in the land. It illustrates God's deep disappointment at the frustration of his good purposes by the rebelliousness of his people.

Nevertheless, all the prophets believed in the sovereignty of God. Isaiah saw that he was even able to summon a pagan king, Cyrus, to do his bidding (Is 45). God was in absolute control of the nations and while his purposes could be frustrated in any generation through the foolishness and rebellion of his people he would nevertheless find a way of working out his purposes. Even though his purposes may be delayed, as Habakkuk declared (2.3), the revelation of his truth would not prove false, it would certainly come to pass.

In the face of the continued rebellion of the people of Israel and Judah the prophets saw that God could work his purposes out through a faithful remnant. Isaiah is the first to speak of a remnant who would survive from the house of Israel and would return to the land after God had allowed destruction to come upon it (Is 10.20–23).

More than a century later Jeremiah took up the same theme when the destruction and exile originally foreseen by

Isaiah had actually taken place. The disaster had been averted during Isaiah's lifetime through the repentance of Hezekiah who heeded Isaiah's warning and experienced revival that spread throughout the nation (2 Chr 30).

Jeremiah was totally convinced that God would bring the survivors of the exile back to the land. 'I will bring Judah and Israel back from captivity and will rebuild them as they were before. I will cleanse them from all the sin they have committed against me and will forgive all their sins of rebellion against me' (Jer 33.7,8). This was the word he was hearing from God even in the midst of the turmoil and tragedy that struck the nation during his ministry. He was convinced that God would never break his promise to carry out his purpose through the land and the people. He said, 'This is what the Lord says, "If I have not established my covenant with day and night and the fixed laws of heaven and earth, then I will reject the descendants of Jacob and David"' (Jer 33.25).

So great was Jeremiah's confidence in God's love of the land and the people that he actually bought a field in Anathoth, his home village, at the time of Nebuchadnezzar's invasion. It was a time when no one was buying land because it was already in enemy-occupied territory. But Jeremiah saw his cousin Hanamel's coming to offer him a field, recorded in chapter 32, as an opportunity to demonstrate God's commitment to the land and the prophet's own conviction that God would never abandon his people.

How it must have hurt Jeremiah to be accused of being a traitor! He hotly denied the charge of deserting to the Babylonians. 'That is not true!' Jeremiah said. 'I am not deserting to the Babylonians' (37.14). It was his total loyalty to God that caused him to advise people to stand against the policies of their faithless rulers and made him say such apparently unpatriotic things as, 'Whoever stays in this city will die by the sword, famine or plague. But whoever goes out and surrenders to the Babylonians who are besieging you will live; he will escape with his life' (21.9). He would not have seen these words as unpatriotic because his first loyalty was to God who would not be able to bless the land and the people whom he loved unless they were faithful to him.

Fearlessness

The absolute loyalty to God of the prophets led them to display a fearlessness in public that probably none of them felt in private. We have already noted James' observation that the prophets were men like us. They experienced the same emotions and they shrank from pain and suffering in the same way as any normal human being, but their consciousness of being messengers of God and their total commitment to carrying out their divine instructions produced a fearlessness in the face of even brutal opposition, naked force or overwhelming numbers such as those faced by Elijah on Mount Carmel. He was confronted with the belligerent opposition of 850 false prophets and a despotic king and his army, together with a vast crowd of ordinary people from the nation who formed a sullen and silent audience determined only to be on the side of whoever won the contest. Rarely can one man have stood alone against such a powerful array of opposing force.

The account of Elijah's victory on Mount Carmel is too well known to recount in detail. (1 Kings 18) King Ahab already held him responsible for the severe drought that was afflicting the land and there is no doubt that in initiating this confrontation Elijah actually put his own life on the line. He would have been mercilessly hacked to death if the prophets of Baal had prevailed. It was his own utter confidence in God that produced the fearlessness with which the lone prophet faced the multitude.

Elijah rebuilt the altar of the Lord that was in ruins, not with ten stones symbolising the ten tribes over which Ahab ruled, but with *twelve* stones. He thus emphasised that in God's eyes there was still an essential spiritual unity in the nation with whom he had entered into a covenant. It took a special kind of confidence in God to make such a witness in the presence of a capricious despot like Ahab.

There are numerous examples of the prophets displaying great courage in the face of naked secular power. One of the earliest is the account of Nathan facing David after his adultery with Bathsheba. His accusation, 'You are the man!' (2 Sam 12.7) is in complete disregard of the fact that David had only to clap his hands to have the prophet executed.

Many times the prophets faced actual danger to their lives. Amos knew this when he confronted Jeroboam at Bethel and was ordered to leave by Amaziah the priest (Am 7.12). Elisha took his life in his hands on numerous occasions, not only in Israel when dealing with such madmen as Jehu but also in Syria, which was constantly at war with Israel. He actually went to Damascus on one occasion and prophesied that Hazael would succeed Ben Hadad.

The fearlessness of the true prophet is seen not only in the major figures but also in unnamed prophets such as the man in 1 Kings 20.35f who faced Ahab with the fact of his unfaithfulness. The king was proudly returning from a victorious battle when the prophet accused him of not fully carrying out the will of God in that he had made a treaty with the king of Syria.

It was not only kings the prophets faced but priests, merchants, and political rulers—any who were misleading the people and misusing their positions of responsibility in the life of the nation. Isaiah on one occasion sent a devastating message to a political leader, Shebna, the steward in charge of the king's palace, challenging his actions and his misuse of his authority. He ended the message by saying that God would depose him from his office and oust him from his position (Is 22.15–19).

According to Hebrew tradition, Isaiah's fearless opposition to corruption and evil wherever it was found eventually cost him his own life. Despite the great deliverance of the nation, for which in many ways he was responsible during the reign of Hezekiah, Isaiah suffered the ultimate penalty of his faithfulness to God during the reign of Manasseh, who is reported to have sawn the prophet in two. (The apocryphal book *The Ascension of Isaiah*)

Faith

It was the prophets' faith in God that gave them the confidence to carry out their ministries in the life of the nation. All the characteristics we have been noting in this chapter are linked; and the link is faith. Throughout their ministries the prophets staked their lives upon their understanding of God, their experience of his presence and power and their confidence that if they rightly heard from him and undertook a task in his name he would take responsibility for the consequences. For their part, the prophets simply had to put their trust totally in God and do whatever he told them—the key to their trust was faith.

This faith in God stemmed from the knowledge which the prophets had of God; of his nature, of his purpose, and of his faithfulness. The prophets were not primarily miracle workers. Indeed, there is no record of any of the writing prophets ever having performed a miracle such as those recorded of Elijah and Elisha.

From the eighth century onwards, beginning with the ministries of Amos and Hosea in the north, and Micah and Isaiah in the south, the prophets took their place in the nation as men who declared the word of God for their times. They were far from being magicians or wonder-workers. They were men who carried the mark of the authority of God upon their lives, who feared God rather than men, and whose power lay in the declaration of the word of God by both word and deed.

The prophets were not leaders of men. They carried no responsibility for the Temple, for worship, for the institutional side of religion. They had no political power, no party following, no organisation, no priestly or pastoral function. They were not involved in the commercial life of the nation, neither were they rulers of men. They were simply servants of the living God whose task was to declare what he was saying to the people.

We shall see in the next chapter the method by which the prophets carried out their ministry in the nation. Our task in this chapter has been to look at the basic characteristics that were common to all the prophets and to note finally that it was their faith in God which gave them the confidence to carry out their ministries. That faith in God came not from textbooks or theoretical propositions, or even from intellectually perceived knowledge. The faith of the prophets was rooted and grounded in personal experience—the knowledge that they were called by God to be his messengers, that he had given them authority and that he was a faithful God. Provided they were totally obedient to him, he would never leave them alone and would be faithful to perform his word through the lives of his servants.

CHAPTER FOUR

THE METHOD OF THE PROPHET

Personal Experience

The prophets were not hermits. They were not men who lived in caves, separated from the life of ordinary men and women. They were actively involved in the life of the nation both at a local community level and in wider national affairs. Far from living the contemplative life of a recluse, the prophets were normally to be found mixing with the crowd and moving among the people. They often spoke to large crowds when they publicly declared the word of God. The things they said indicate an intimate knowledge of contemporary social life.

Despite their active social involvement the prophets each had a strong personal experience of God which was the starting point of the prophetic ministry. As we have already seen, it was the consciousness of being called by God to be his messenger to the nation that was the essential dynamic underlying the ministry of the prophet.

Students of History

The prophets were students of history. Alongside their personal experience of God was placed the heritage of Israel. Until the time of David and the establishment of the court in Jerusalem this had largely been passed on by word of mouth from generation to generation. By the time of the great writing prophets, beginning in the eighth century with the ministries of Amos, Hosea, Micah and Isaiah, there was a considerable collection of writing available that recorded the history of the nation, its religious heritage and the law. The prophets were each aware of the history of the nation and saw it in terms of the 'deeds of the Lord'.

The central historical event in the life of the nation was the escape from Egypt led by Moses. It was also a milestone in the spiritual heritage of the nation. The spiritual significance of the events surrounding the crossing of the Red Sea lay not in Moses' inspired leadership or the people's reluctant obedience but in what God had done for the nation.

The prophets saw in the release from slavery in Egypt a pure act of salvation by God that revealed both his nature and purposes. The Exodus was the archetypal 'enacted parable' that conveyed a deep spiritual message in a physical act. The prophets regularly used this kind of spiritual visual-aid to convey the message they were given to declare to the nation. It was God himself who first taught them to do this. He had revealed his own nature as a God of salvation through his great saving act of responding to the cries of his people in slavery and miraculously releasing them. Through this act of salvation he had demonstrated his commitment to the people of Israel; they were his people, adopted by him and later drawn into a covenant relationship that established mutual rights and obligations. God's action in saving his people from Egypt also demonstrated, not only to Israel, but in the eyes of all the nations, his power to carry out his declared intentions. God demonstrated his divine om-nipotence. His actions showed that he held the nations in the hollow of his hand. None of the nations or their gods could stand against him.

The history of Israel, which the prophets saw as the record of God's dealings with his people, provided both the foundation and the framework for the message of the prophets. They saw the whole of the nation's history as the record of

THE METHOD OF THE PROPHET

God's dealings with his people and the criteria of judgment and blessing lay in the faithfulness of the people, their adherence to the terms of the covenant and their obedience to the law and commandments, particularly in relation to the recognition of one God and abhorrence of idols and all forms of idolatry.

The way in which the prophets used the historical record in their teaching and as the basis of their message is well illustrated in Samuel's farewell speech to the nation recorded in 1 Samuel 12. After speaking of some personal matters he began to recount God's dealings with his people.

> It is the Lord who appointed Moses and Aaron and brought your forefathers up out of Egypt. Now then, stand here, because I am going to confront you with the evidence before the Lord as to all the righteous acts performed by the Lord for you and for your fathers.

Samuel then recounted briefly the history of the nation from which he drew the teaching:

> If you fear the Lord and serve and obey him and do not rebel against his commands, and if both you and the king who reigns over you follow the Lord your God—good! But if you do not obey the Lord, and if you rebel against his commands, his hand will be against you, as it was against your fathers.

The lesson Samuel drew from history was that when the nation was faithful to God and obedient to his commands all went well with them and they experienced his blessing, but that when they did evil in his sight it led to disaster. This teaching is a basic factor in the message of all the prophets. It is a common element in all their teaching. A good example is found in Hosea.

> I am the Lord your God, who brought you out of Egypt. You shall acknowledge no God but me, no Saviour except me. I cared for you in the desert, in the land of burning heat. When I fed them, they were satisfied; when they were satisfied, they became proud; then they forgot me. So I will come upon them

like a lion ... I will destroy you, O Israel, because you are against me, against your helper (Hos 13.4–9).

There are many instances of the prophets referring to the Exodus as God's great saving act in the history of the nation. The following are a few examples: Isaiah 11.16, 43.16; Jeremiah 2.6, 7.22, 11.4, 16.14, 23.7, 32.20, 34.13; Hosea 2.15, 11.1, 12.9, 13.4; Amos 2.10, 3.1, 4.10, 9.7; Micah 6.4 and Haggai 2.5.

In addition the prophets sometimes dwelt at length upon the history of God's dealings with his people along similar lines to that which we have already noted in Samuel's ministry. A good example is found in Ezekiel 20, where he dwells at length upon the idolatry and rebellion of the nation seen throughout her history from the time of Egypt onwards.

> This is what the sovereign Lord says: on the day I chose Israel, I swore with uplifted hand to the descendants of the house of Jacob and revealed myself to them in Egypt. With uplifted hand I said to them, 'I am the Lord your God.' On that day I swore to them that I would bring them out of Egypt ... and I said to them, 'Each of you, get rid of the vile images you have set your eyes on and do not defile yourselves with the gods of Egypt. I am the Lord your God.' But they rebelled against me and would not listen ... (Eze 20.5–8).

Ezekiel's purpose in using the historical record was to show that over the centuries the nation had continually rebelled against God through idolatry and that God had been merciful and spared them time after time. 'I withheld my hand, and for the sake of my name I did what would keep it from being profaned in the eyes of the nations in whose sight I had brought them out' (Eze 20.22).

Ezekiel's message was that now God had allowed judgment to come upon them as a consequence of their continued apostasy, but the day would come when God would release them from exile in Babylon and bring them back from the nations where they had been scattered and take them into the desert. There, face to face, he would execute judgment just as he had done after the Exodus from Egypt and he would re-establish 'the bond of the covenant' (Eze 20.34–38).

The prophetic method of teaching was to use the historical record of good times and bad in the fortunes of the nation as illustrative of God's dealings with his people, the basic criterion being their faithfulness to him. From the historical record the prophets learned to understand the requirements of God and this, together with their personal experience of God's holiness, his mercy, his forgiveness of sin and his requirement of absolute obedience, determined their understanding of the nature and purposes of God. Out of this sprang their ministry and message to the nation. There are, of course, individual differences in the message of each prophet, determined in part by the different circumstances of the day; hence *Amos* stresses the *justice of God* and therefore his requirement of justice in the lives of his people, while *Hosea* emphasises the *loving-kindness and mercy of God*, and *Isaiah* lays stress upon the *moral righteousness of God* and his ethical rather than ritualistic requirements of his people. Yet these are differences in emphasis rather than in the basic conception of the nature and purposes of God.

In a later chapter, when we examine the message of the prophets, we shall look in greater detail at their understanding of the nature of God but it is essential to note here the broad agreement between them. Unlike the gods of the nations surrounding them, who were but idols of wood and stone, the God of Israel was the one and only true God. He was the God of history who directed the affairs of the nation and gave rewards and punishment according to the faithfulness of his people. He was sovereign Lord of all the nations and nothing happened without his permission. Even a foreign tyrant could have success over Israel only if God allowed it and when he did so it was to chastise his people. The victorious enemy was in fact the sword of the Lord.

Perhaps most important of all, the prophets understood the nature of God in terms of his faithfulness; he was a God of

65

law. He was not a capricious God like the gods of the other nations whose whim might change from hour to hour. He had declared to his servant Moses the standards of behaviour that he required of his people and he did not change from one generation to the next. What was once declared sin would always be sin and what was once declared right would never be declared wrong.

The closing verses of Micah are an excellent illustration of the prophet's combination of personal experience of God with his understanding of the deeds of the Lord in history and how this was applied to the contemporary situation to produce a powerful message:

> Who is a God like you, who pardons sin and forgives the transgression of the remnant of his inheritance? You do not stay angry for ever but delight to show mercy. You will again have compassion on us; you will tread our sins under foot and hurl all our iniquities into the depths of the sea. You will be true to Jacob and show mercy to Abraham, as you pledged on oath to our fathers in days long ago (Mic 7.18–20).

Students of contemporary events

We have already noted that the prophets were not hermits living in isolated caves, but were active in the life of the community. They were keen students of contemporary affairs in social life, in the economy, in political affairs and in the religious life of the nation. The prophets, however, did not confine themselves to taking an interest in local or national affairs, they took an equally keen interest in what was happening on the international scene.

The prophets often referred to international events and in particular to the threat of foreign invasion. They saw a major part of their task as warning the nation of danger or the threat of impending disaster, hence they keenly followed the movement of foreign armies and the political intrigues of neighbouring states.

Jeremiah, in particular, spoke many times of the threat of foreign invasion. His urgent warnings in chapter four 'sound the trumpet throughout the land! . . . flee for safety without delay! For I am bringing disaster from the north, even terrible destruction' (4.5,6), followed by his graphic description of the disaster in verses 23 to 26, have led some scholars to conclude that he was actually describing a devastation of the land that had already taken place and that he had seen with his own eyes, possibly the Scythian invasion. His vivid description of desolation and destruction is followed in verse 27f by the warning that the whole land will be ruined unless there is repentance and turning from rebellion and backsliding.

Throughout Jeremiah's ministry it is clear that he followed events on the international front with great care so that he was aware of the intrigues of the pro-Egyptian party within Israel, the movements of the Egyptian army, the weakness of the Assyrian army and the growing power of Babylon. Jeremiah undoubtedly accepted it as part of his prophetic calling and responsibility to the nation before God to follow the news of the shifts in international power so that he could rightly bring the word of God to the nation.

All the prophets were active in following international events. Isaiah, soon after his call into ministry, must have been aware of the Assyrian onslaught first upon Syria then upon Israel and the devastating destruction and slaughter of her people that ensued. His ministry began with the advent of the new king Jotham, but it was not until the succession of Hezekiah that he found a ruler with whom he could converse and speak the same spiritual language. The early part of Isaiah's ministry is marked by the clearest warnings that the consequences of the evil practices in the life of the nation would be that God would use the Assyrians as the instrument of his judgment. Because the people had rejected God he could say, 'Therefore the Lord is about to bring against them the mighty flood-waters of the river—the king of Assyria with all his pomp' (Is 8.7).

Amos reveals the depth of understanding and breadth of knowledge that the prophets possessed in regard to international affairs. In chapters 1 and 2 he gives a brief word-picture of what was happening in each of the neighbouring nations surrounding Israel. He began with Syria, then turned to Gaza, then to Tyre. He followed this with Edom, then Ammon, then Moab, and finally Judah before bringing the subject home to what was happening in the nation of Israel itself. It is here that Amos turned from international affairs to an examination of many aspects of national life. He described the injustice of the rulers, their misuse of power and the oppression they exercised over the powerless. 'They trample on the heads of the poor as upon the dust of the ground and deny justice to the oppressed' (2.7). Slavery was rife in the land. 'They sell the righteous for silver, and the needy for a pair of sandals' (2.6). It was not only the men but also the rich women who oppressed the poor. 'Hear this word, you cows of Bashan on Mount Samaria, you women who oppress the poor and crush the needy' (4.1).

The great gap between rich and poor was emphasised by the extravagant luxury with which the rich surrounded themselves. 'You lie on beds inlaid with ivory and lounge on your couches. You dine on choice lambs and fattened calves. . . . You drink wine by the bowlful and use the finest lotions, but you do not grieve over the ruin of Joseph' (6.4–6). The above passage clearly indicates the uncaring attitude of the rich. There was complacency among the rulers. 'Woe to you who are complacent in Zion, and to you who feel secure on Mount Samaria, you notable men of the foremost nation, to whom the people of Israel come!' (6.1). This complacency the prophet was determined to shatter. 'Woe to you who long for the day of the Lord! Why do you long for the day of the Lord? That day will be darkness not light' (5.18).

There was dishonesty and cheating among the merchants. Each one cared only for himself and was driven by the desire to get rich at the expense of others. Amos had observed them in the market 'skimping the measure, boosting the price and cheating with dishonest scales, buying the poor with silver and the needy for a pair of sandals, selling even the sweepings with the wheat' (8.5,6).

The spiritual life of the nation was a hollow sham. Amos was instructed to declare, 'I hate, I despise your religious feasts; I cannot stand your assemblies . . . Away with the noise of your songs! I will not listen to the music of your harps' (5.21,23). The hypocrisy underlying religious observance was exposed by the obsession with wealth. Religious festivals were a tiresome interruption of the real business of acquiring wealth which would be consumed in complacent self-indulgence. Amos had heard the traders saying, 'When will the new moon be over that we may sell grain, and the sabbath be ended that we may market wheat?' (8.5).

Amos' references to the contemporary situation in Israel reveal an intimate knowledge of the social, economic, political and religious situation. But Amos was not alone in such an awareness of national affairs. Indeed it was an essential part of the ministry of the prophets that they understood the contemporary national situation. Isaiah gives a graphic picture of the moral and spiritual apostasy of Jerusalem in his day: 'See how the faithful city has become a harlot! She once was full of justice; righteousness used to dwell in her—but now murderers! . . . Your rulers are rebels, companions of thieves; they all love bribes and chase after gifts. They do not defend the cause of the fatherless; the widow's case does not come before them' (1.21–23).

Jeremiah, in one purple passage of a few sentences, describes the situation in Jerusalem in his day. He puts his finger upon six major sins that are abhorrent to God and were common practice among rulers and people. The six are: false religion; injustice; oppression; murder; idolatry, and immorality. They are all to be found in Jer 7.4–11. He describes how the people were trusting in false religion saying, 'This is the temple of the Lord, the temple of the Lord, the temple of the Lord!' and then briefly referring to injustice, oppression, the shedding of innocent blood and following other gods, he almost exploded with the force of the

word God had instructed him to say to the people at the
entrance of the Temple:

> Will you steal and murder, commit adultery and perjury, burn
> incense to Baal and follow other gods you have not known, and
> then come and stand before me in this house, which bears my
> Name, and say, 'We are safe'—safe to do all these detestable
> things? Has this house, which bears my name, become a den of
> robbers to you? But I have been watching! declares the Lord.

There are many other examples that could be given of the
intimate knowledge the prophets possessed of the contemporary situation in the life of the nation to which they were
ministering, but the above words of Jeremiah are among the
most powerful of any uttered by the prophets. Their force
still has revelance today since the six sins which God declared to be abhorrent in his sight must still be abhorrent
to God today if we accept the basic teaching of the prophets
and the entire witness of Scripture in both the Old and
the New Testaments concerning the unchanging nature of
God.

Jeremiah used the vivid word picture of the sins of the
people in Jerusalem to pronounce a fierce and urgent warning of the danger that confronted the nation saying that God
would thrust them from his presence as he had done the
northern kingdom of Israel unless there was repentance and
turning from their evil ways (7.12–15).

Standing in the Council of God

The reason why the prophets were avid students of contemporary affairs on both the international and the national
fronts was so that they would be in full possession of the facts
in order to bring the word of God to the nation. This was not
motivated simply by a desire for relevance but by the deeper
spiritual objective of being faithful messengers of God. It was
only as they were able to come with understanding of the
contemporary world situation into the presence of God that
they were able rightly to discern what he was saying and

therefore able faithfully to declare the word of the living God to the people.

We have already noted that one of the characteristics of the prophets was the authority with which they proclaimed the word of God. This authority derived not simply from an intimate knowledge of God gained through personal experience and a knowledge of the history of the nation but through their constant seeking of the presence of God.

A good example of the way the prophets received the word of God is to be seen in the ministry of Isaiah at one of the most critical crisis points in the life of the nation. It happened during the reign of Hezekiah when the Assyrians, fresh from their victorious conquest of the northern kingdom of Israel, launched their assault upon Judah and prepared for the siege of Jerusalem. Sennacherib, who was laying siege to Lachish, sent a letter to Hezekiah saying that as the gods of the other nations had not been able to deliver their land from his hand so the God of Judah would equally be powerless to resist his assault. Hezekiah promptly sent a message to Isaiah and went into the Temple to spread the letter before the Lord. Isaiah also went before the Lord and then joined Hezekiah in the Temple for intercession (2 Chr 32.20). Isaiah 37, 2 Kings 19 and 2 Chronicles 32 give a clear picture of king and prophet coming before God and laying the situation before him as Hezekiah spread the letter out before the Lord in the Temple.

This action in laying the matter before God is what Jeremiah refers to as 'standing in the council of the Lord'. In chapter 23 Jeremiah speaks bitterly of the deception and wickedness of the false prophets. He says that just as the false prophets of the northern kingdom of Israel prophesied by Baal and led the people astray so, among the prophets of Jerusalem, he had seen something horrible. 'They commit adultery and live a lie. They strengthen the hands of evildoers, so that no-one turns from his wickedness' (v14).

Jeremiah then spelt out the consequences of the religious leadership exercised by these false prophets. They not only

71

strengthened the hands of evildoers but 'from the prophets of Jerusalem ungodliness has spread throughout the land' (v15). Their false preaching and teaching actually encouraged rebellion against God and evildoing.

The nub of the problem was that these false prophets were speaking out visions 'from their own minds, not from the mouth of the Lord' (v16).

Jeremiah then puts his finger upon the root of the problem. The reason why these false prophets give their own opinions and speak about revelations that have been generated in their own minds is because none of them has 'stood in the council of the Lord to see or to hear his words'. He asks the question, 'Who has listened and heard his word?' (v18). He then declares that God was saying, 'If they had stood in my council, they would have proclaimed my words to my people and would have turned them from their evil ways and from their evil deeds' (v22).

In this important passage Jeremiah lays down the principal fundamental to receiving revealed truth from God; that alone gave the prophet the right to say 'thus says the Lord' and to speak as the mouthpiece of the living God. It was only those who entered the throne-room of God, who came humbly into his presence and listened attentively to his word, who had the right to proclaim the word of God to the nation.

Proclaiming the Word
When the prophets were sure of the message they had to deliver they proclaimed it unequivocally. We have already noted this as being one of the characteristics of the prophet. They were uncompromising with the truth, even when speaking to powerful rulers. There is nothing hesitant about the way Isaiah, for example, spoke to the leaders of Judah in Jerusalem,

> Hear the word of the Lord, you rulers of Sodom; listen to the law of our God, you people of Gomorrah! The multitude of your sacrifices—what are they to me? says the Lord (Is 1.10,11).

72

THE METHOD OF THE PROPHET

We have already given many examples of the directness and the authority with which the prophets spoke the word of God publicly. The spoken word was the most usual means of communication although on some occasions the prophet wrote down the message, possibly to reinforce a spoken word and to ensure that it was conveyed accurately. Jeremiah did this, using his servant Baruch as the messenger.

Jeremiah did not write the message simply because he thought it would be a good idea but because he was directed by the Spirit of God to do so. It was to be a summary of the words he had been publicly declaring in Jerusalem; words that had been ignored by Jehoiakim and his court officials, who cared nothing for the word of God and who in the prophet's eyes were leading the nation headlong to disaster. Jeremiah wrote down a summary of the warnings he had been giving and spelt out explicitly the consequences of continued rebellion against God. He instructed Baruch, 'Read them to all the people of Judah who come in from their towns. Perhaps they will bring their petition before the Lord, and each will turn from his wicked ways, for the anger and wrath pronounced against this people by the Lord are great' (Jer 36.7).

The scroll was read not only to the people but also to the king who cut it up and burned it following which Jeremiah re-wrote the message with some additional words. This is one of the few occasions that we know of where the prophet actually wrote down the message. Ezekiel was shown a scroll with words of revelation written on it but there is no indication that he actually wrote the words himself.

In addition to the spoken and the written word many of the prophets also used what may best be described as 'enacted parables'. These were prophetic visual aids which the prophets often used to accompany the spoken word and sometimes used alone without verbal interpretation. They were always a powerful means of communication.

It should be emphasised that the prophets did not use enacted parables simply as visual aids that they themselves had thought up to illustrate and give dramatic effect to their spoken word. The enacted parable was essentially a prophetic act which the prophet undertook not because he wanted to, but because he was told what to do. Hence Jeremiah was instructed by the Lord to go and buy a clay jar from the potter and then to take some of the elders of the people and of the priests and to go out to the valley of Ben Hinnom near the entrance of the potsherd gate. He was told that when he reached there the Spirit of God would come upon him and he would be given a word to proclaim. That word was:

> This is what the Lord Almighty the God of Israel says: Listen! I am going to bring disaster upon this place that will make the ears of everyone who hears of it tingle. For they have forsaken me and made this a place of foreign gods; they have burned sacrifices in it to gods that neither they nor their fathers nor the kings of Judah ever knew, and they have filled this place with the blood of the innocent. They have built the high places of Baal to burn their sons in the fire as offerings to Baal (Jer 19.3–5).

The prophet was unable to express in mere words God's utter abhorrence of these abominable deeds of child sacrifice that had become part of the idolatrous practices that were carried out within sight of the Temple at Jerusalem. He declared that the whole area would one day be called the valley of slaughter because God would bring about the ruin of Judah and Jerusalem. He would 'make them fall by the sword before their enemies, at the hands of those who seek their lives'. Their carcasses would be given as food for the birds of the air and the beasts of the earth. 'I will devastate this city and make it an object of scorn; all who pass by will be appalled and will scoff because of all its wounds' (Jer 19.7,8).

Even these terrible words were not sufficient to describe the revulsion that God felt when the precious gift of life that he alone could give was so despised that they murdered innocent little children. Something further had to be done to reinforce the spoken word and to convey the utter devastation that God would bring upon the nation unless there

74

was immediate repentance before him. The prophet was instructed:

> Then break the jar while those who go with you are watching, and say to them, 'This is what the Lord Almighty says: I will smash this nation and this city just as this potter's jar is smashed and cannot be repaired' (Jer 19.10,11).

There are many other examples of the prophets using enacted parables to reinforce the word such as when Micah went about barefoot and naked howling like a jackal and moaning like an owl and actually rolled in the dust in the streets of Jerusalem to demonstrate dramatically the humiliation and degradation that would come upon the people if God finally gave them over to their enemies (Mic 1.8–12). On a happier note Jeremiah purchased a field in his home town of Anathoth despite the fact that it was in enemy occupied territory. He did this to demonstrate his confidence in the fact that God would never finally abandon his people and that the day of restoration would come and 'houses, fields and vineyards will again be bought in this land' (Jer 32.15).

Ezekiel on one occasion was told to act like a refugee. He had to pack his belongings for exile and go out through a hole in the wall that he had dug with his own hands. He was not to say anything until the people actually asked him what he was doing. Then he was to explain to them, 'I am a sign to you. As I have done, so it will be done to them. They will go into exile as captives' (Eze 12.11).

The enacted parable was not always used to reinforce the message but rather as a prophetic demonstration of the message. On one occasion Jeremiah was told to undertake a certain action and he was not given the reason for it. He was told to go and buy a linen belt and put it around his waist but not to let it get wet. He did this as directed and then he received the second part of the instruction which was to take the belt to a place called Perath which we understand to symbolise the river Euphrates. There he was told to hide the

75

belt in a crevice in the rocks. Some time later he was told to go and retrieve the belt and when he did so he found it was ruined.

The prophet still did not know the reason why he had been told to bury the belt and then find it again. It was only after all the actions had been completed that the interpretation came to him, 'This is what the Lord says: "In the same way I will ruin the pride of Judah and the great pride of Jerusalem . . . For as a belt is bound round the man's waist, so I bound the whole house of Israel and the whole house of Judah to me," declares the Lord, "to be my people for my renown and praise and honour. But they have not listened" ' (Jer 13.1–11).

In addition to the enacted parables the prophets sometimes used a 'word parable' to convey the message they were given. The classic example of this is the story told by the prophet Nathan to king David after he had arranged the death of Uriah so that he could marry the man's wife. In the parable a rich man took a lamb belonging to a poor man to feed his guest. The prophet presented the story in such a way that David immediately pronounced sentence upon the rich man. Nathan then gave the interpretation with the unforgettable words, 'You are the man!' (2 Sam 12.1–10).

Another example of a word parable is found in Ezekiel 17 where the prophet is instructed to 'set forth an allegory and tell the house of Israel a parable'. The parable concerned two eagles and a vine. The interpretation was then given by the prophet in reference to the rebellion of Zedekiah when the breaking of his oath and treaty he had made with Babylon led to disaster coming upon Jerusalem. The historical events would undoubtedly have been well known among the exiles in Babylon to whom Ezekiel was addressing his words, but in this case the teaching would probably be better remembered in the form of the story in the parable.

The prophets thus used many methods of proclaiming the word of God: in writing, through spoken parables, through public proclamation of the word and through enacted parables or prophetic actions. Their task was to convey the message they had been given in the manner that God directed, even if it meant discomfort or brought humiliation and ridicule. It was God's word and the prophets were his messengers, responsible to him alone.

Summary

We may summarise the prophetic method as involving first a personal relationship between the prophet and God. There was no substitute for this. Secondly, the prophets were students of history, which they saw as illustrating the deeds of the Lord. This led them to an understanding of the nature of God and his purposes for the nation. Thirdly, the prophets were students of contemporary events. They studied both international affairs and every aspect of life in the nation. Fourthly, the prophets took all this into the presence of the living God and sought for understanding of what he was saying through them to the nation in the context of the contemporary situation. Finally, when they received the word of God as they stood in his council they were enabled to proclaim the word publicly in word and deed, through the spoken and the written word and by undertaking prophetic actions.

CHAPTER FIVE

INTERPRETING THE SIGNS

A major part of the ministry of the prophets was the interpreting of signs. A sign in biblical language is an event, either
natural or of human origin, that has spiritual significance. It
is allied to the parable, but whereas the parable focuses upon
a fictional story followed by a spiritual interpretation, the
sign is an actual empirical event with a spiritual interpretation. The contrast lies in the fact that the story both embo-
dies and conveys the message, which is usually fairly plain
for the hearers to understand. The sign, on the other hand, is
an event that the whole community may know about, may be
sharing from one to another and discussing, but its significance is not perceived until someone with prophetic insight
interprets its meaning and proclaims its message.

This is how the prophets used signs. They would refer to
an event that everybody knew had happened and was the
topic of general conversation. They did so not simply to be
topical or to gain a hearing but to convey a message. The
prophets were men with a mission. Their lives were God-
centred. Thus, although they lived among the people and
were not recluses, withdrawn from society, they also spent
much time in the presence of God. Their task was to span
both dimensions—the human and the divine. They lived in
the world and observed carefully all that was taking place

around them in the economy, in family life, in the market-
place, in politics, in international affairs, in religious observance, in moral behaviour, in social and tribal affairs. At the
same time they could not exercise the prophetic ministry
without spending time quietly alone with God and meditating upon the things they observed and experienced in the life
of the nation.

It was as they stood in the presence of the Almighty that
they perceived the significance of everyday events and were
able to determine the genuine signs. It was then simply a
matter of timing to find the right opportunity to declare the
interpretation and message that God was conveying through
the sign.

Relationship with God

It was only by revelation from the Spirit of God that the
prophets were able to recognise the significance of ordinary
everyday events. The prophets were men like us (Jas 5.17).
They received the insight that enabled them to interpret
everyday events in precisely the same way as revelation is
received today. God does not change. He has always spoken
to his servants through his Spirit. The faithfulness of the
prophets in listening to God and their confidence in discerning what God was saying to them stemmed from their close
relationship with God. This was bound up with, and inseparably linked to, the call of God upon their lives. The life
and ministry of each of the prophets can only be understood
in the context of their personal relationship with God that
was rooted in his call and anointing upon their lives.

Isaiah describes in some detail the experience that
brought him into the ministry of the prophet. He was
probably at prayer in the Temple, looking up at the carved
figures of the seraphim, when he received the experience
of the presence of God that brought with it his own commission. Through the vision he found himself in the very
throne-room of God. It was here in the presence of the living
God, in his 'council chamber', that every prophet had to

learn to enter with quiet attentiveness and reverential awe to receive the word of the Lord. Isaiah's immediate reaction is characteristic of the man; his overwhelming sense of the holiness of God immediately reminded him of his own sinfulness and the sinfulness of the people among whom he lived.

The prophets identified with the people of their generation. Although they were set apart for the special ministry of the prophet they were not separated from responsibility for the sinfulness of their generation. Hence Isaiah's cry, 'I am ruined! For I am a man of unclean lips, and I live among a people of unclean lips, and my eyes have seen the King, the Lord Almighty' (6.5). The remainder of Isaiah's vision is the classic experience of redemption. Through the action of God he was cleansed and forgiven. Then the call came, 'Whom shall I send? And who will go for us?' Isaiah's response was immediate, 'Here am I. Send me!' which was followed by the commission, 'Go and tell this people.'

Amos was a poor country shepherd when he received the call of God. He was not a prosperous sheep farmer but just a simple shepherd who also did some part-time fruit tree cultivation to ensure an adequate livelihood. But it was while he was tending the flock alone out in the countryside that he had an experience of the presence of the living God that brought him into the ministry of the prophet. His commission came, as did all the prophets', in the vast loneliness of personal experience, the encounter of a frail created mortal with the infinite eternal creator God.

Jeremiah's experience of the presence of God coming into his life brought the immediate reaction of a sense of his own inadequacy. His response was similar to that of Moses, 'Ah sovereign Lord,' he protested, 'I do not know how to speak; I am only a child.' Like Isaiah he experienced the cleansing touch of the Lord upon his lips. 'Then the Lord reached out his hand and touched my mouth.' This was followed by the commission, 'See, today I appoint you' (Jer 1.4–10).

There was no substitute for this personal encounter with

God from which each of the prophets derived his commission, his authority and his confidence in the message he
bore. This confidence grew as the prophets saw their words
confirmed and fulfilled. We have already noted the call of
Samuel and how God revealed to him that a disaster was
going to overtake Israel, but the immediate confirmation of
the words he was hearing came through the personal
message he received for Eli.

Signs and Symbols

The interpretation of signs was a major part of the ministry
of the prophets. They found God speaking to them through
the ordinary everyday things that they were seeing around
them. Suddenly a physical object would take on a new
significance and through it a message would be formed in
their minds that would convey the word of God.

Ezekiel had an experience that began by seeing banks
of thick cloud rolling across the sky followed by a fierce
thunderstorm with brilliant lightning flashing across the
heavens. The storm clouds gradually took on the appearance
of a fire and the physical storm gave way to a vision that
brought an intense spiritual experience conveying a powerful message. The vision lasted throughout the storm and
came to its climax as the storm clouds gave place to a
beautiful rainbow. Its radiance symbolised the glory of the
Lord and caused the prophet to fall face downwards in the
presence of the living God. It was then that the words came
to him, 'Stand up on your feet and I will speak to you. As he
spoke, the Spirit came into me and raised me to my feet, and
I heard him speaking to me' (Eze 1.4–2.2).

For Ezekiel the physical experience led to a vision which in
turn enabled him to receive a word from God. This contrasts
with Jeremiah who received the word directly from the
physical experience. For him the physical symbol became
the sign without the intermediary of a vision. Nowhere do we
find Jeremiah saying that he saw a vision. His phrase is 'the
word of the Lord came to me'. Jeremiah was out walking in

the early spring when he saw an almond tree. Immediately he felt God drawing his attention to it and saying, 'What do you see, Jeremiah?' As he responded, 'I see the branch of an almond tree' the pun struck him, as 'almond' and 'watching' sound the same in Hebrew. The message formed in his mind, 'You have seen correctly for I am watching to see that my word is fulfilled.'

The nearest Jeremiah got to visions were nightmare experiences in which he perceived clearly the disaster that was coming upon the land and the people unless they turned to God in humility and penitence and reformed their ways. 'How long must I see the battle standard and hear the sound of the trumpet?' he cried, and then described graphically the fearful picture of the devastation he foresaw.

> I looked at the earth, and it was formless and empty; and at the heavens, and their light was gone. I looked at the mountains, and they were quaking; all the hills were swaying. I looked, and there were no people; every bird in the sky had flown away. I looked, and the fruitful land was a desert; all its towns lay in ruins before the Lord, before his fierce anger (Jer 4.21–26).

This was an unusual experience for Jeremiah, who more usually saw something in front of him and straight away received a message, as for example when he looked at some fruit traders in front of the Temple. There were two baskets full of figs. One was full of good fruit and the other contained figs that were so bad that they could not be eaten. Immediately he saw the interpretation of this and God conveyed a message contrasting the people who had gone away into exile with those who had remained behind and were still pursuing their faithless ways that were an offence to God (Jer 24).

On another occasion Jeremiah was actually told to go down the street to the potter's house and watch him at work, through which God would give him a message. He found the potter shaping a pot from a lump of clay on his wheel and no doubt talked to the man while he was working. The potter probably explained that sometimes you get a piece of clay that simply won't run in your hands. In his mind he could see the beautiful vase he was attempting to create but the stubborn obstinacy of the clay resisted the touch of his skilled hands. Eventually he abandoned the task crushing the clay in his hands and removing it from the wheel.

Jeremiah immediately saw the significance—the obstinacy of the nation refusing to be directed by the hand of God; their stubbornness would lead to them being crushed and removed from his presence.

Was this to be the end of the nation? Would God cast them away for ever? Suddenly, his attention was rivetted upon the potter once again. Here was the completion of the sign. He had expected to see the man hurl that unyielding piece of clay across the floor of his yard into the dust of oblivion, but instead, the potter patiently kneaded the lump of clay into a ball and placed it back on the wheel. His skilled hands again set about the task of shaping a pot. He would not be able to create the thing of beauty he had originally intended, but he would nevertheless fashion a useful pot that would bless the kitchen of a housewife somewhere in the land of Judah.

The realisation of God's love and mercy overwhelmed the prophet. God would not cast away his people. Although they were faithless he would remain faithful. It was his nature to forgive and to love mercy. Even though a man's sinful stubbornness may spoil God's best intention for him, yet if he is willing, God will patiently remake his life. Even through breaking, or the experience of being crushed, God can and will refashion his life to make him useful in his service.

The word of the Lord came, ' "O house of Israel, can I not do with you as this potter does?" declares the Lord.' Then followed the promise of God, which holds good for any nation at any time, that even if they are heading for disaster and are about to be destroyed, 'If that nation I warned repents of its evil, then I will relent and not inflict on it the disaster I had planned' (Jer 18.1–10).

Interpreting Events

A major part of the prophet's task was to interpret current
events. All the prophets refer to events in their own day and
use them as a means to bring the word of the Lord. The use of
signs is quite distinct from reference to the social, moral or
spiritual state of the people. It is the use of specific events
through which the prophet was able to declare the word of
the Lord. These were either natural events such as drought,
famine, volcanoes, earthquakes, plagues of locusts or
disease; or man-made events such as economic problems,
military defeats, international affairs, social or political
situations.

Natural Events

Natural events were usually ascribed to the direct action of
God, as when Haggai boldly declared that God was responsible for the current famine that was afflicting the people,
'I called for a drought on the fields and the mountains, on the
grain, the new wine, the oil and whatever the ground produces, on men and cattle, and on the labour of your hands'
(Hag 1.11).

Elisha told the Shunammite woman that the Lord had
decreed a famine in the land that would last seven years.
Elijah had actually pronounced a drought in the name of the
Lord.

Jeremiah referred to the drought that had come upon the
land with the failure of the spring rains, and interpreted it as
the direct act of God as a consequence of his outrage in
the face of the idolatry and spiritual prostitution that had
polluted the land. 'You have defiled the land with your
prostitution and wickedness. Therefore the showers have
been withheld and no spring rains have fallen' (Jer 3.2,3).

On another occasion Jeremiah referred to the failure of
harvest due to the lack of autumn and spring rains and he
said, 'Your wrong-doings have kept these away; your sins
have deprived you of good' (Jer 5.24,25).

There are numerous instances in scripture of the prophetic

use of natural events where God either allowed them to happen or directly sent them. The classic example of the latter is in Amos 4 where the prophet probably spoke at Bethel in the presence of the king and a large gathering of the people of Israel. He reeled off a catalogue of recent events, following each terse description with the punch-line, '*Yet you have not returned to me, declares the Lord*'. He spoke of famine and hunger; then he referred to drought and people staggering from town to town searching for water. He recalled how crop disease and mildew had struck gardens and vineyards. He described the plagues of locusts that had devoured everything in the fields including the fig and olive trees. He referred to plagues that had come among the people and a catastrophe similar to that which destroyed Sodom and Gomorrah. The dramatic effect of his constant repetition of the phrase 'Yet you have not returned to me, declares the Lord', must have mounted as he reeled off the events one after the other—events that everybody knew about but had steadfastedly ignored or explained away as 'one of those things that just happen'.

The prophet left the people with no uncertainties concerning the interpretation of these natural events. They were specifically stated to be the result of God's direct action. Through them he was communicating a message to his people. It was a clear message of warning that worse would befall them if they did not heed the warning signs he was sending. Hence Amos declared, 'This is what I will do to you, Israel, and because I will do this to you, prepare to meet your God, O Israel' (Am 4.6–12). The threat implied in this visitation of God spelt judgment upon the whole house of Israel which would undoubtedly be carried out if the nation continued to ignore God's warning signs.

Man-made Events
Amos' list of recent events included a military defeat which he also directly ascribed to the action of God. 'I killed your young men with the sword, along with your captured horses.

86

I filled your nostrils with the stench of your camps, yet you have not returned to me, declares the Lord' (4.10).

Despite Amos' stern warnings that God would bring disaster, the severest form of judgment upon the nation if they did not turn to him, it is a plain fact of history that these warnings were ignored and the consequences were indeed terrible. The terse record in 2 Kings 17.5 masks the fearful suffering of the three-year siege in Samaria and the subsequent atrocities when the city finally fell to the Assyrian invaders in 722 BC. The remnant were deported and scattered across the Assyrian empire while foreigners were brought in to repopulate the land of Israel, to prevent the nation ever again being reformed and rebelling against their overlords.

The historian records 'All this took place because the Israelites had sinned against the Lord their God . . . so the Lord was very angry with Israel and removed them from his presence . . . therefore the Lord rejected all the descendants of Israel; he afflicted them and gave them into the hands of plunderers, until he thrust them from his presence' (2 Kg 17.7–20).

More than a century later a similar fate befell the southern kingdom of Judah, which also refused to heed the word of the Lord through the prophets. No-one could have brought clearer warnings than did Jeremiah but they fell on deaf ears and God allowed military defeat to crush the nation as Jeremiah had foretold. The fall of Jerusalem recorded in 2 Kings 25 and repeated in Jeremiah 52 still makes fearful reading despite its brevity. Lamentations 4.13 pronounces the reason why God allowed the slaughter of his people and the destruction of the city that bore his name. 'It happened because of the sins of her prophets and the iniquities of her priests, who shed within her the blood of the righteous.' The disaster that befell the nation is here directly ascribed to the sins of the religious leaders. This illustrates the basic biblical principle that runs right through the mission and message of the prophets that when disaster strikes a nation God holds the religious leaders accountable to him if they have not faithfully declared the word of God to the people.

It was this commission to declare the word of God that drove all the prophets to speak publicly even the most unpopular interpretation of an event. Haggai told the people in straight unvarnished terms that the reason they were experiencing economic hardship was because they were living for themselves and paying no heed to the Lord.

> You eat, but you never have enough. You drink, but you never have your fill. You put on clothes, but you are not warm. You earn wages, only to put them into a purse with holes in it (Hag 1.6).

Jeremiah constantly referred to the developing international crisis and said that God would not protect the nation from powerful neighbours unless they put their trust completely in him.

> I am bringing a distant nation against you—an ancient and enduring nation, a people whose language you do not know, whose speech you do not understand. . . . They will devour your harvests and food, devour your sons and daughters . . . with the sword they will destroy the fortified cities in which you trust (Jer 5.15–17).

He warned urgently, 'Look, an army is coming from the land of the north; a great nation is being stirred up from the ends of the earth. They are armed with bow and spear; they are cruel and show no mercy' (Jer 6.22,23).

Despite all his appeals and vivid references to the reports of advancing enemy armies and the interpretation of these international events, the warnings still went unheeded. Such was the measure of Judah's stubborn rebellion that eventually brought disaster and exile.

Thus the interpretation of signs was an important part of the ministry of the prophets. They had to be constantly alert to what was happening around them so that they did not miss something that God was wishing to convey to the nation. But they also had to be men or women of prayer, who constantly sought the presence of God so that they could understand the significance of current events whether they were the deeds of men or of God. The prophets learned that once the call of God was upon their lives they could never be 'off duty'. Theirs was a ministry in which they were constantly called, by day and night, to 'watch and pray'.

CHAPTER SIX

FORETELLING THE FUTURE

The evidence we have examined so far of the ministry of the canonical prophets in ancient Israel amply supports the view we are taking in this book that the prophets were not primarily known as foretellers of the future. They were undoubtedly regarded as those who possessed supernatural knowledge not readily accessible to ordinary men and women. But their knowledge was seen primarily in the context of the contemporary situation. It was as servants of God in the present tense that they were perceived by people in their own day. The chief task of the prophets was to bring the word of God to their own generation, rather than to forecast events one thousand or two thousand years hence.

Clearly, however, the prophets did also speak about future days, so it is necessary for us to examine both the context and the motives underlying their reference to future events. There are three levels of prophecy to be discerned in the writings of the eighth-century prophets and their successors. These may be defined in simple chronological terms as contemporary prophecies; prophecies concerning the near future, and prophecies concerning the distant future.

Contemporary Prophecy
We have been largely preoccupied with contemporary

prophecy in the earlier chapters since this was the basic ministry of the prophets. We cannot over-emphasise the fact that the prophets were men of their own day and that they were students of the contemporary world, taking note of both the deeds of the Lord and the works of men.

If we are to make a right approach to prophecies concerning the future and to a right understanding of their purpose leading to a clear method of interpretation, then the starting point lies in the contemporary ministry of the prophets. Contemporary prophecy as the proclamation of the word of God for their own generation was the bedrock of the ministry of the prophets. We say this despite the danger of falling into repetition through over-emphasis because there has been so much misunderstanding and misinterpretation of the words of the prophets that have a bearing upon future events. If we are to be faithful in rightly handling the word of God we must understand the context in which it was given and the purpose for which it was given. It is a gross mishandling of Scripture simply to take isolated references to the future and to try to apply them to events in our own day or to events that we imagine may happen soon.

Prophecies concerning the near future were always related to the contemporary scene and usually grew out of the words the prophets were speaking into the contemporary situation. It was the prophets' intimate knowledge of what was happening around them that enabled them to describe vividly the situation in the nation and thus to pinpoint the word of God to actual situations with telling accuracy.

From the description that Amos gives of life in the market-place of Samaria it is clear that he had actually seen the merchants cheating with dishonest scales and the traders selling even the sweepings with the wheat. He had actually listened to their conversations and knew what was happening among rich and poor, among the political rulers and among those who were supposed to dispense justice.

As we have seen, it was the practice of the prophets to stand in the council of God and to bring before him all the information they had gleaned about the international scene and of what was happening in the nation, Israel or Judah. The prophets learned to analyse the social, political and economic forces at work in their day. They did this not, as happens in our own day, through using the tools of analysis in the disciplines of sociology, political science, or economics. Their analysis was carried out in the presence of the living God. They learned to spread the facts before God, to meditate upon them in his presence and to have listening, receptive minds so that they could hear from the very throne room of God the word he wanted conveyed to the nation.

The Near Future

A good example of the relationship between the contemporary and the near future is to be seen in Amos 2 where he flows easily from the present tense to the future. From verse 6 he begins a description of contemporary life in Israel.

> They sell the righteous for silver, and the needy for a pair of sandals. They trample on the heads of the poor as upon the dust of the ground and deny justice to the oppressed. Father and son use the same girl and so profane my holy name. They lie down beside every altar on garments taken in pledge. In the house of their God they drink wine taken as fines.

Amos then reminded them of their history, of how God had brought them up out of Egypt and had sent prophets among them but they had commanded the prophets not to prophesy. Then in verse 13 he moves smoothly into the future:

> 'Now then, I will crush you as a cart crushes when loaded with grain. The swift will not escape, the strong will not muster their strength, and the warrior will not save his life . . . Even the bravest warriors will flee naked on that day,' declares the Lord.

Prophecy, for Amos, was a mixture of contemporary analysis and of recorded history which showed both the deeds of God which were good and faithful, and the actions of men which were wicked and faithless, and from this he flowed easily and naturally into the future tense. For Amos the future was governed by the past and the present; not in the sense of predetermination according to a plan of God arbitrarily imposed upon men, but governed by the actions of men themselves. If men deliberately chose to ignore the word of the living God and to shut their eyes and ears to what was happening in their own generation, they brought upon themselves the inevitable consequences of their own actions.

It was because men did not want to know what God had done in the past that they failed to understand the nature of God and his purpose for the nation. They were therefore unresponsive to his messengers, the prophets, who warned them against the consequences of their own actions. Amos declared that 'the Sovereign Lord does nothing without revealing his plan to his servants the prophets' (3.7) but his message went unheeded. In fact, as Hosea said to the same generation of Israel, 'The prophet is considered a fool, the inspired man a maniac' (9.7). Hosea went on to say, 'The prophet, along with my God, is the watchman over Ephraim.' This is a very significant phrase. The prophets often speak of God 'watching over Israel' or 'watching over his word to perform it'. All the prophets taught that God was active in keeping watch over his people. The task of the watchman was to be always alert and to observe what was happening so that he could give forewarning of what was going to happen. While the city slept at night or went about its business during daytime the watchman would be up in his tower scanning the horizon for a coming messenger or the approach of a foreign army so that the city could be alerted and its defences fully mobilised.

Hosea's statement was that the prophet shared this responsibility with God as the watchman over the nation despite the opposition he encountered from secular men and the hostility of religious leaders. He said, 'Snares await him on all his paths, and hostility in the house of his God' (9.8).

Ezekiel, in the same way, saw his prophetic ministry as that of a watchman. His testimony was that the word of the

Lord came to him saying, 'Son of man I have made you a watchman for the house of Israel; so hear the word I speak and give them warning from me' (3.17).

Through Jeremiah God said, 'I appointed watchmen over you and said, "Listen to the sound of the trumpet!" But you said, "We will not listen." Therefore hear, O nations; observe, O witnesses, what will happen to them. Hear, O earth; I am bringing disaster upon this people, the fruit of their schemes, because they have not listened to my words and have rejected my law' (Jer 6.17–19).

There are two points here of major significance in understanding the ministry and message of the prophets. The first is Jeremiah's declaration that God was blowing the trumpet in the nation which was the traditional warning of approaching danger and call to arms, to mobilise the defences so that the attack of the enemy could be resisted. The second point was that the people refused to listen and therefore God called upon all the nations of the world to witness what would happen to them, that he would bring disaster on his own people. But the disaster that would come upon the people would not be the direct action of God pouring out his wrath upon his own people but his action in withdrawing his protection from them and allowing them to be exposed to the violence of their enemies. Thus in the same passage quoted above Jeremiah went on to say

> This is what the Lord says: 'Look, an army is coming from the land of the north; a great nation is being stirred up from the ends of the earth. They are armed with bow and spear; they are cruel and show no mercy. They sound like the roaring sea as they ride on their horses; they come like men in battle formation to attack you, O daughter of Zion' (6.22,23).

This clear warning of impending disaster was accompanied by yet another appeal from the prophet; 'O my people, put on sackcloth and roll in ashes; mourn with bitter wailing as for an only son, for suddenly the destroyer will come upon us' (6.26). This is a perfect example of the prophet acting as watchman to the nation. He had stood in the council of the Lord and seen what was coming. He recognised the danger of the approaching army that as yet could not be seen by the physical eyes of the watchman high up in the watchtower, but could clearly be perceived by the prophet whose inner sight and perception had been heightened by the presence of the Lord. As a faithful watchman his task was to describe clearly what he saw and to call for immediate action to avert the danger. Hence the call to repentance, to turn to God so that his strong shield of protection would be put around the nation; this was the only hope of salvation.

Most of the prophecies concerning the near future are of this nature in keeping with the watchman role of the prophet. They describe the danger the prophet perceived, sometimes giving specific details of the direction from which the attack would come, as in the passage just quoted from Jeremiah. The early chapters of Isaiah have many similar passages warning of oncoming danger. These usually begin with a description of the contemporary scene and then move smoothly into the future by warning of what will happen as a consequence of the present evil ways of the nation.

> See how the faithful city has become a harlot! She once was full of justice; righteousness used to dwell in her—but now murderers! . . . Your rulers are rebels, companions of thieves; they all love bribes and chase after gifts. They do not defend the cause of the fatherless. . . . Therefore the Lord . . . declares: '. . . I will turn my hand against you; I will thoroughly purge away your dross and remove your impurities . . .' Rebels and sinners will both be broken together, and those who forsake the Lord will perish (Is 1.21–28).

The prophecies concerning the near future are not always of a threatening nature. There are those that look forward beyond the devastation, or after the disaster has already taken place, to a time of restoration. Usually there is the recognition among the prophets that not all the nation will be destroyed. Certainly from the time of the fall of the northern kingdom of Israel there developed the belief that a remnant would survive, that God would not allow the whole nation to be destroyed. Isaiah gave voice to this belief,

> In that day the remnant of Israel, the survivors of the house of Jacob, will no longer rely on him who struck them down but will truly rely on the Lord, the holy one of Israel. A remnant will return, a remnant of Jacob will return to the mighty God (Is 10.20,21).

A similar prophecy was given for Judah that after the exile in Babylon a remnant would return. They would be those who had been purified by the terrible experience of exile and slavery. They would come back along a highway provided by God.

> But only the redeemed will walk there, and the ransomed of the Lord will return. They will enter Zion with singing; everlasting joy will crown their heads (Is 35.8–10).

Jeremiah wrote a letter to the exiles who had been taken to Babylon in the first wave of captivity following the surrender of Jerusalem ten years before its destruction in 586 BC. His letter recorded in chapter 29 is a beautiful message of hope and encouragement. It begins with a warning against the false expectation of immediate release. The prophet perceived that the purpose of God in allowing his people to go through the devastating experience of exile was for the cleansing and purifying of the nation. The purposes of God could not be hurried so he warned them to prepare for a number of years in exile. They were not to let the false prophets and diviners among them encourage them to false hope. He nevertheless declared his confidence that God had not, and never would, forsake his people and that after seventy years, from the time of her ascendancy through the crushing of Assyria, Babylon would fall. That would be the signal for God to fulfil his gracious promise to bring the people back to the land of Judah.

97

'For I know the plans I have for you,' declares the Lord, 'plans to prosper you and not to harm you, plans to give you hope and a future. . . . You will seek me and find me when you seek me with all your heart. I will be found by you,' declares the Lord, '. . . and I will bring you back to the place from which I carried you into exile' (Jer 29.4–14).

Thus not all the words of the prophets concerning the near future were declarations of doom and disaster. They also perceived the good purposes of God that would be worked out despite the tragedies that men brought upon themselves by their faithless behaviour and by their deliberate rebellion against God despite the clear warnings he sent them through his watchmen, the prophets.

God's intention always was for the good of his people, but even his good plans could be thwarted by the deliberate refusal of those who were in a covenant relationship with him and who owed him their very existence to heed his warnings or to obey his word. This was the tragedy of their history; God was watching over his people for their good but they were determined to go their own way and therefore suffered the inevitable consequences of disobedience and folly.

The Far-Distant Future
The task of the prophet as watchman over Israel and Judah, as we have already stated, was to gather information regarding the contemporary world scene and especially to observe carefully what was happening in every aspect of the life of the nation. Armed with that information they sought the presence of the Lord and in his presence they received clear direction so that they were able to proclaim his word with power and authority. It was this experience of coming into the presence of God while considering what was happening in the nation that enabled the prophets to discern the 'signs of the times' and to receive revelation of what would happen in the near future if the nation did not turn from its present course.

This experience of coming into the presence of the almighty God on behalf of the nation enabled them to perceive the purposes of God. In this divine encounter between the prophet and God the great mysteries of time were sometimes unveiled. The good purposes of God were perceived by the prophet on a wider scale than the mere near-future events surrounding the nations of Israel and Judah.

As the prophet entered the very throne-room of God so occasionally a glimpse of supreme reality and the ultimate purposes of God was revealed. The prophet stood in awe at the majesty of God and then tried to describe, through the frailty of human language and the limitations of the encounter of the finite with the Infinite, the ultimate truths that he had glimpsed.

The far-distant prophecies given by the prophet are always sketched in outline rather than in detail. Looking at the message of the prophets is rather like looking at a beautiful landscape picture where the foreground is in clear detail, the middle ground may be seen in unmistakable relief but the distant scene is only in hazy outline.

The prophets spoke vividly and in clear detail of the contemporary scene of which they were eye-witnesses. They also gave an unmistakable picture of things that would happen in the near future. Dealing with the far distant scene, they perceived the purposes of God being worked out for the nations of the world, but the detail is missing: the hazy outline requires the eye of faith to discern and to interpret.

There are numerous passages among the prophets which speak of the distant future, often referring to what they saw as 'the Day of the Lord'. This is just one of the elements in the teaching of the prophets concerning future events that over a period of several hundred years developed into what we now know as Hebrew eschatology, *ie* a study of the last days. It is not possible within the scope of a single chapter even to summarise the eschatology of the Old Testament. Our task in this chapter is to do no more than note the different elements in the teaching of the prophets and the development of their concepts in regard to the future as they sprang out of their contemporary experience.

There are five major elements in the teaching of the prophets in regard to the future. They are:

(1) The Day of the Lord
(2) The Ingathering of the Exiles
(3) The Messianic Age
(4) The Conversion of the Gentiles
(5) Eschatological and Apocalyptic Concepts.

The Day of the Lord

The idea of a Day of the Lord when God would deal with the sinfulness of mankind runs right through the ministry and message of the prophets of ancient Israel. It grew out of the prophetic understanding of the nature of God, that he is a God of justice, faithfulness and holiness. This meant that he required faithfulness and holiness of his people. Israel and Judah were a people in a covenant relationship with their God and therefore they should not allow the spiritual life of the nation to be contaminated by divination, idolatry or occultic influences coming in from the idolatrous practices of the surrounding nations or the people of the land among whom the Israelites settled in Canaan.

Gradually the teaching of the prophets acquired an ethical as well as a purely spiritual dimension. It was not enough simply to observe the Sabbath or to fulfil the sacrificial requirements of the law. Indeed, God was not primarily interested in sacrifice, the blood of bulls and goats, he was interested in right behaviour. 'Stop bringing meaningless offerings! . . . Learn to do right!' was the message they thundered (see Is 1.10–17).

It was because Israel and Judah were in a covenant relationship with God that he could demand from them right behaviour which included both moral and spiritual right-eousness. When the nation failed to live up to the standards required by God it broke the terms of the covenant, disturb-ing the covenant relationship between God and his people,

100

and inevitable consequences followed. God who was holy and just could not simply turn a blind eye to the promises made by the nation at Sinai and reaffirmed at the time of the settlement in the Promised Land under Joshua. At that time they solemnly renewed the covenant and Joshua made sure they understood what they were doing.

> 'If you forsake the Lord and serve foreign gods, he will turn and bring disaster on you and make an end of you, after he has been good to you.' But the people said to Joshua, 'No! We will serve the Lord.' Then Joshua said, 'You are witnesses against yourselves that you have chosen to serve the Lord.' 'Yes, we are witnesses,' they replied. . . . 'We will serve the Lord our God and obey him' (Jos 24.20–24).

Hence the ministry of the prophet in each generation was to remind Israel of the solemn terms of the covenant and the dire consequences of breaking it. Isaiah declared that, 'The Lord Almighty has a day in store for all the proud and lofty . . . The arrogance of man will be brought low and the pride of men humbled; the Lord alone will be exalted in that day and the idols will totally disappear.' He said that men would flee to the caves in the rocks and hide in holes in the ground 'from dread of the Lord when he rises to shake the earth' (Is 2.12–19). But although Isaiah speaks of the day of the Lord being an earth-shattering experience, it is within the context of God bringing judgment upon his *own people* who were 'full of superstitions from the East'; who practised divination like the Philistines; who made deals with pagans; whose chief object in life was the acquisition of wealth so that their land was 'full of silver and gold'; who did not put their trust in God but who put their trust in building up a mighty army so that there was 'no end to the chariots', and who were utterly unfaithful to God so that their land was 'full of idols'.

God could not tolerate such behaviour from a people bearing his name. They had broken the covenant relationship and were guilty of dishonouring his name among the nations. He looked to them as representatives of the truth and of the very nature of the God whom they claimed to serve and whose action in times past in bringing them out of Egypt and establishing them in the land of Canaan was known to all the surrounding nations.

Therefore, Isaiah declared, in order to maintain his own standards of holiness God had to bring about a day on which he would judge the nation. It would be a day of disaster for Judah and the people of Jerusalem because God would actually banish them into exile. It would happen because of their 'lack of understanding' of the true nature and requirements of God (Is 5.13).

The disaster that God would bring upon his own people would actually be a vindication of the nature of God, of his good name, of his holiness and justice. This is a concept of the utmost importance for understanding the message of the prophets. It is expressed most clearly by Isaiah who describes graphically the disaster about to come upon the people in which the grave would 'enlarge its appetite and open its mouth without limit' to engulf the slaughter of the people. But in allowing this terrible thing to happen to his own people Isaiah said that, 'The Lord Almighty will be exalted by his justice, and the holy God will show himself holy by his righteousness' (Is 5.14–16).

Amos was the first of the eighth-century prophets to declare that the day of the Lord would not be a pleasant experience for the covenant people. He shattered the popular expectation of a day of the Lord in which God would intervene and destroy all the enemies of Israel and leave them rejoicing in a time of peace and prosperity. He saw clearly that God could not do this and remain faithful to his own holiness, so he shattered the composure of those who were perfectly satisfied with the injustice, immorality, and idolatry of the age because they themselves were enjoying life. 'Woe to you who are complacent in Zion; and to you who feel secure on Mount Samaria.' They were enjoying a life of self-indulgent luxury but, he declared, 'You do not grieve over the ruin of Joseph' (Am 6.1–7).

It must have been a salutary experience for the people to hear Amos declare, 'Woe to you who long for the day of the Lord! Why do you long for the day of the Lord? That day will be darkness, not light' (5.18).

Hosea, writing in the same period as Amos, declared much the same message, that the day of the Lord would be one of judgment for Israel. 'In that day I will break Israel's bow in the valley of Jezreel' (Hos 1.5). But Hosea perceived that it is the purpose of God to chastise those whom he loves. He saw the purpose of the chastisement as being that of cleansing the nation. 'I will remove the names of the Baals from her lips; no longer will their names be invoked' (2.17). Hosea began to feel his way towards a time of reconciliation beyond the period of judgment: God would have achieved his purpose in allowing destruction to come upon his people and he would be able to re-establish his covenant of right relationships with his own people. He said:

> Bow and sword and battle I will abolish from the land, so that all may lie down in safety. I will betroth you to me for ever; I will betroth you in righteousness and justice, in love and compassion. I will betroth you in faithfulness and you will acknowledge the Lord. In that day I will respond, declares the Lord . . . I will show my love to the one I called 'Not my loved one'. I will say to those called 'Not my people', 'You are my people'; and they will say, 'You are my God'. (Hos 2.18–23).

The Ingathering of the Exiles

The theme of restoration is found in a more developed form in the teaching of Jeremiah more than a century later. Jeremiah had been preaching for thirty years in Jerusalem when 'Jehoiachin son of Jehoiakim, king of Judah, and the officials, the craftsmen and the artisans of Judah were carried into exile from Jerusalem to Babylon' (Jer 24.1). He had warned them in the straightest possible terms that God would not protect Jerusalem unless they turned from following other gods and put their trust in the Lord. But once the disaster had happened and the exile had begun he immediately began to see beyond it to the way God would eventually work out his purposes for the good of his people. Hence his encouraging letter to the exiles in chapter 29, to which reference has already been made. For those who remained in Jerusalem he continued to prophesy a message of judgment, 'This is what the Lord Almighty says, I will send the sword, famine and plague against them . . . for they have not listened to my words, declares the Lord, words that I sent to them again and again by my servants the prophets' (29.17–19).

In chapter 30 Jeremiah begins to look forward to the days of restoration when the exiles will return. 'The days are coming, declares the Lord, when I will bring my people Israel and Judah back from captivity and restore them to the land I gave to their forefathers to possess' (v3). He looks forward to a time of peace and security for the nation and declares his confidence that God would not completely destroy his covenant people. 'I will not completely destroy you. I will discipline you but only with justice' (30.11).

God would not turn back from his fierce anger until he had fully accomplished the purposes of his heart (30.24) but the day would come when he would restore the remnant of Israel (31.8) and there would be great rejoicing. 'Then maidens will dance and be glad, young men and old as well. I will turn their mourning into gladness' (31.13). 'So there is hope for your future, declares the Lord, your children will return to their own land' (31.17). 'Just as I watched over them to uproot and tear down, and to demolish, overthrow and bring disaster, so I will watch over them to build and to plant, declares the Lord' (31.28).

God would actually renew his covenant. 'The time is coming, declares the Lord, when I will make a new covenant with the house of Israel and with the house of Judah' (31.31).

As a sign of his complete confidence in this prophecy of the future restoration of the people to the land, Jeremiah bought a field in his home community at Anathoth in the belief that the time would come when 'houses, fields and vineyards will

104

again be bought in this land' (32.15). He believed that the new covenant relationship that God would establish would be of a lasting spiritual nature, written in the minds and hearts of the people (31.33).

> I will surely gather them from all the lands where I banish them in my furious anger and great wrath; I will bring them back to this place and let them live in safety. They will be my people and I will be their God. . . . I will make an everlasting covenant with them; I will never stop doing good to them (32.37–40).

Jeremiah's confidence in this declaration of the restoration of Israel and Judah into a right relationship with God was based upon his knowledge of the faithfulness of God and that once God had spoken nothing could break his word. His promise was from everlasting to everlasting. 'This is what the Lord says, If you can break my covenant with the day and my covenant with the night . . . then my covenant with David my servant . . . can be broken' (33.20,21). Such was the certainty of the word of God, it was as sure as the fact that the sun would rise and set each day.

Isaiah, who was a contemporary of Hosea, more than a century before the ministry of Jeremiah, did not live to see the exile of Judah but he did witness the fall of the northern kingdom and the exiles from Samaria being scattered across the Assyrian empire. Isaiah knew that they would not all return. He saw the survivors as a remnant whom God would one day bring back to the land. 'A remnant will return, a remnant of Jacob will return to the Mighty God. Though your people, O Israel, be like the sand by the sea, only a remnant will return' (Is 10.20–22). He believed that God would establish 'a highway for the remnant of his people that is left from Assyria, as there was for Israel when they came up from Egypt' (11.16).

It was, however, only after the destruction of Jerusalem and the Babylonian exile that the expectation arose that both Israel and Judah would be returned to the land as a reunited nation. (It is for this reason that many scholars assign Isaiah

105

PROPHECY PAST AND PRESENT

11 to the post-exile period.) Ezekiel received a word for the *whole* house of Israel. 'I am concerned for you and will look upon you with favour . . . even the whole house of Israel. The towns will be inhabited and the ruins rebuilt' (Eze 36.9–10). Ezekiel's teaching is exactly in line with that of Isaiah two centuries earlier when he had declared that God would allow disaster to come upon Judah and Jerusalem as an act of his own justice and holiness. Ezekiel saw that God had allowed the enemies of Israel and Judah to prevail 'because they had shed blood in the land and because they had defiled it with their idols' (Eze 36.18). But now the exile had achieved its purpose in ridding the land of an idolatrous generation and the day was near when God would fulfil his promise of restoration. In fact the exile could not continue much longer because it was now becoming a cause of profaning the holy name of God because the nations among whom his people were scattered were saying, 'These are the Lord's people, and yet they have had to leave his land' (36.20). The implication was that God did not have the power to protect his own people so for his own name's sake he had to act.

> This is what the Sovereign Lord says: It is not for your sake, O house of Israel, that I am going to do these things, but for the sake of my holy name, which you have profaned among the nations where you have gone. I will show the holiness of my great name . . . I will gather you from all the countries and bring you back into your own land (36.22–24).

Ezekiel then elaborates the cleansing purpose of the exile and says that God would now use it to break down the division between the tribes and to re-establish *one new nation*, a holy people under his sovereign rule.

> I will sprinkle clean water on you, and you will be clean; I will cleanse you from all your impurities and from all your idols. I will give you a new heart and put a new spirit in you; I will remove from you your heart of stone and give you a heart of flesh. I will

put my Spirit in you . . . You will be my people and I will be your God. . . . Then the nations around you that remain will know that I the Lord have rebuilt what was destroyed and have replanted what was desolate . . . I will make them one nation in the land . . . They will never again be two nations or be divided into two kingdoms . . . I will make a covenant of peace with them; it will be an everlasting covenant . . . Then the nations will know that I the Lord make Israel holy, when my sanctuary is among them for ever (36.25–28,36; 37.22,23,26,28).

The same thought runs through the beautiful prophecies of Isaiah 48–54. It was unthinkable that God could forget his own people.

Can a mother forget the baby at her breast and have no compassion on the child she has borne? Though she may forget, I will not forget you! See, I have engraved you on the palms of my hands; your walls are ever before me (Is 49.15,16).

The reference there was to the walls of Jerusalem that had been smashed down and destroyed by the enemy. But God was still in charge of the destinies of the nations whom he held like a drop in a bucket (Is 40:15) and the day would soon come when he would use these same foreign nations to bring his people back:

See, I will beckon to the Gentiles, I will lift up my banner to the peoples; they will bring your sons in their arms and carry your daughters on their shoulders (49.22).

They would return with great rejoicing. The prophet could already 'see' the scenes of great celebration in Jerusalem as the returning exiles entered the city.

The ransomed of the Lord will return. They will enter Zion with singing; everlasting joy will crown their heads. Gladness and joy will overtake them, and sorrow and sighing will flee away (51.11).

It would be as though even the desecrated ruins of the shattered city that the enemy had left behind would rise up and sing praises to God.

Burst into songs of joy together, you ruins of Jerusalem, for the Lord has comforted his people, he has redeemed Jerusalem (52.9).

Messianic Age

The passages we have just been quoting from Isaiah 49–54 are all set within a messianic context. The hope for a Messiah grew out of the bitter experience of exile, the failure of the monarchy and the humiliation of the nation. Ezekiel had foreseen the reuniting of the tribes after the exile under one king: 'There will be one king over all of them and they will never again be two nations or be divided into two king-doms,' he had said. He foresaw an idealised kingship after the pattern of David. 'My servant David will be king over them and they will all have one shepherd ... And David my servant will be their prince for ever' (Eze 37.22,24,25).

The pattern of an idealised kingship which the prophet foresaw was not divine; the king was still in his understand-ing simply a human being related to the household of David. In the immediate post-exilic period the expectations of a Messiah were still connected with a human figure. Haggai and Zechariah who returned with the first wave of released exiles and prophesied in Jerusalem about the year 520 BC (before the rebuilding of the Temple in 516 BC) both speak in messianic terms of Zerubbabel the governor of Judah. Hag-gai addressed his plea for the rebuilding of the Temple to Zerubbabel and Zechariah called him 'the Branch'. Refer-ring to Joshua and Zerubbabel, Zechariah said, 'These are the two who are anointed to serve the Lord of all the earth' (Zec 4.14).

It is in the Servant passages of Isaiah in chapters 49 to 54 that we find the truly sublime concept of Messiahship. The Servant of the Lord would be one who would act wisely and who would be exalted above all the kings of the earth (52.13–15). His mission was the cleansing of the sins of the people to prepare for a new nation who would be taught by

108

the Lord and a new city whose walls would be built of precious stones (54.12,13).

It is not clear, however, whether in the original prophecy the Servant of the Lord was the personification of Israel, cleansed and redeemed through the sufferings of the exile and banishment from Judah and now miraculously restored to the land by the Lord her Redeemer, or whether the Servant was an individual raised up by God to complete the work begun in the exile and to prepare the nation for her new world-wide mission.

The Conversion of the Gentiles

The world-wide mission of the newly restored nation was to be 'a light for the Gentiles', in order to bring God's 'salvation to the ends of the earth' (49.6).

The middle chapters of Isaiah, chapters 40 to 55, are vibrant with the faith, confidence and joy of those who have been rescued from slavery; brought through the terrifying experience of suffering to the joy of once again living in their own land in freedom and peace. But of far greater significance is the transforming experience of having been apparently separated from God as a consequence of their own sinfulness in much the same way as there had been physical separation from the land of Israel and Judah (see 48.17–21). Now, having been set free from the captivity of Babylon, they were realising that God had, in fact, never left them; he was actually with them, even in Babylon. For a brief moment he had abandoned them to their enemies but with deep compassion he was bringing them back (54.7). Now, the nation would not only know God's blessing, forgetting the shame of her youth and remembering no more the reproach of widowhood (54.4), but should prepare for growth because God was going to bless in a mighty way.

> Enlarge the place of your tent, stretch your tent curtains wide, do not hold back; lengthen your cords, strengthen your stakes. For you will spread out to the right and to the left (54.2,3).

109

It was not only the descendants of Abraham by the flesh who would be included in the Lord's blessing but he would include all the Gentiles who truly sought the Lord. 'Let no foreigner who has joined himself to the Lord say, "The Lord will surely exclude me from his people"' (56.3). God's intention was through the newly restored Israel to reach out to the Gentile nations and bless them with the knowledge of his salvation.

> Foreigners who bind themselves to the Lord to serve him, to love the name of the Lord, and to worship him, all who keep the Sabbath without desecrating it and who hold fast to my covenant—these I will bring to my holy mountain and give them joy in my house of prayer . . . for my house will be called a house of prayer for all nations. The Sovereign Lord declares—he who gathers the exiles of Israel: I will gather still others to them besides those already gathered (Is 56.6–8).

Gone is the old particularism and narrow nationalism that characterised both the religion and the national outlook of Israel and Judah in pre-exilic times. Now, God's purpose in re-establishing his people was that they should be a servant to the Gentile nations. The sovereignty of God and his power over all the nations of the earth which the pre-exilic prophets of the eighth and seventh centuries had boldy declared would now be seen to be worked out through a nation purged of idolatry, immorality and faithlessness. 'I, the Lord, have called you in righteousness; I will take hold of your hand. I will keep you and will make you to be a covenant for the people and a light for the Gentiles' (42.6).

God's purposes would be worked out on a world-wide scale. He now addressed himself not simply to one nation but to all people on earth. There were to be no geographical boundaries to the message of salvation.

> Turn to me and be saved, all you ends of the earth, for I am God and there is no other. By myself I have sworn, my mouth has uttered in all integrity a word that will not be revoked; before me every knee will bow; by me every tongue will swear. They will

say of me, 'In the Lord alone are righteousness and strength.' All who have raged against him will come to him and be put to shame (45.22–24).

Eschatological and Apocalyptic Concepts

A number of new elements arose in the teaching of the prophets of Israel in post-exilic times which we may broadly regard as apocalyptic concepts. Of these the chief elements that need to be noted are (a) resurrection; (b) judgment of the nations; (c) cosmic destruction, and (d) the reign of God.

Resurrection

There is no clear doctrine of a resurrection after death in the teaching of the prophets although such a belief was current in the time of Jesus (when the Sadducees were identified as the party who did not believe in resurrection) but there are certainly some references that indicate a belief that the dead would rise again. Notable among these is Ezekiel's vision of the valley of bones where the dried skeletons of those who had been slaughtered by the enemy were brought to life by the power of the living God.

The most explicit reference to the resurrection of the dead in the prophetic writings is found in Isaiah 26.19 where it is said, 'But your dead will live, their bodies will rise. You who dwell in the dust; wake up and shout for joy. Your dew is like the dew of the morning; the earth will give birth to her dead.'

Additionally, there is a clear reference to a resurrection from the dead in Isaiah 53: the Servant of the Lord who bears the iniquities of his sinful people and actually 'poured out his life unto death and was numbered with the transgressors,' is given by God 'a portion among the great' (53.12). Clearly he could only be given such a portion among the great, after having poured out his life unto death, if he was raised from the dead. Thus there is a clear expectation of resurrection in this period.

Judgment of the Nations

Among the post-exilic prophets there arose the belief that the

111

day would come when God, who is a God of justice, would not only fully restore Israel to her former glory after she had suffered for her sins, but would also punish the nations of the world for their sinfulness. Joel makes this teaching explicit:

> In those days and at that time, when I restore the fortunes of Judah and Jerusalem, I will gather all nations and bring them down to the Valley of Jehoshaphat. There I will enter into judgment against them concerning my inheritance, my people Israel, for they scattered my people among the nations and divided up my land (Joel 3.1,2).

God would not allow wickedness to triumph nor the violence of men to hold sway over the nations for ever. His justice and righteousness would be seen by all peoples and he would overcome his enemies.

There are numerous passages where the prophets foresee a day of judgment or a time when God will call all the nations to account for their actions. Zephaniah sees a time coming when God will act internationally to bring the nations together for a time of judgment. 'I have decided to assemble the nations, to gather the kingdoms, and to pour out my wrath upon them, all my fierce anger. The whole world will be consumed by the fire of my jealous anger. Then I will purify the lips of the peoples, that all of them may call on the name of the Lord and serve him shoulder to shoulder' (Zep 3.8,9).

World-wide Destruction

The time of judgment of the nations was seen to be such a momentous event of world-wide significance that it became linked with a time of cosmic destruction. Just as God had had to take Israel and Judah, his own covenant people, through a time of tremendous suffering to purge away their sinfulness, so the day would come when God would extend this principle to all the nations of the world.

Malachi sees God sitting like a refiner and purifier of silver

112

on the day of judgment (3.3). He foresaw God burning up all
the evil, 'Surely the day is coming; it will burn like a furnace.
All the arrogant and every evildoer will be stubble, and that
day that is coming will set them on fire, says the Lord
Almighty' (4.1).

The scenes of world-wide destruction are most vividly
described in Isaiah 24, where it is envisaged that the whole
earth will be completely laid waste and most of the earth's
inhabitants will be burnt up. The prophet foresees a destructive power being loosed on the earth, so great as actually to
shake and break up the crust of the earth (24.19).

What the prophet sees are scenes of destruction similar to
those of an international nuclear conflict, which he says will
take place because, 'The earth is defiled by its people; they
have disobeyed the laws, violated the statutes and broken the
everlasting covenant. Therefore a curse consumes the earth;
its people must bear their guilt' (24.5,6).

Similar scenes of world-wide destruction are described by
Zechariah, who says, 'Their flesh will rot while they are still
standing on their feet, their eyes will rot in their sockets, and
their tongues will rot in their mouths' (Zec 14.12). This was
what happened to the people of Hiroshima when the first
atomic bomb was dropped. The present nuclear arsenal
possessed by the nations, with bombs many times more
powerful give new significance to these prophecies of world-
wide destruction. They are now being seen by many
commentators not simply as apocalyptic symbolism but as
events that may take place in our own lifetime.

Zechariah went on to describe how the world-wide destruction would affect all living creatures in a manner resem-
bling what modern scientists know as 'the nuclear winter'.
Micah 7.13 says that 'The earth will become desolate because of its inhabitants, as the result of their deeds.' Micah
foresees this time of destruction coming upon the earth after
the restoration of Israel. This is similar to the prophecy of
Joel, who also sees the destruction taking place after the
restoration of Israel.

PROPHECY PAST AND PRESENT

The Reign of God

The experience of the exile taught the prophets that God's purpose in allowing the nation to suffer was for cleansing and purification so that he could use them as his servant to the nations to carry out his purposes of salvation for all peoples. The later prophets foresee God cleansing the nations from their wickedness in order to fulfil his final purpose of establishing his reign throughout the world. This is most clearly expressed in Isaiah 65 and 66 although it was foreshadowed at a much earlier time in Micah 4 and Isaiah 2. There it is said that in the last days God will establish his reign of justice and peace. He will settle the disputes for strong nations and 'they will beat their swords into ploughshares and their spears into pruning hooks. Nation will not take up sword against nation, nor will they train for war any more' (Mic 4.3 and Is 2.4).

In Isaiah 65 the prophet looks forward to the creation of 'new heavens and a new earth'. He foresees a time of great rejoicing when God will create a new Jerusalem and will wipe away tears and the sound of weeping and crying will be heard no more.

When God establishes his reign upon the earth the whole of nature will be harmonised.

> 'The wolf and the lamb will feed together, and the lion will eat straw like the ox, but dust will be the serpent's food. They will neither harm nor destroy in all my holy mountain,' says the Lord (Is 65.25).

The vision describing the reign of God in Isaiah 66 is that of new heavens as well as a new earth and a time when 'all mankind will come and bow down before me, says the Lord'. It will be a time when the enemies of God will be destroyed and when he will gather all the nations to see his glory (66.17–24).

In Ezekiel 38 and 39 scenes of international conflict are described. In the picture presented, God leads the nations unwillingly, by putting hooks in their jaws to fight against

114

Israel and meet their final destruction amid the mountains of Israel. The multitude of slain bodies of the enemy nations will be buried in a valley that will be sealed off.

The outcome of these horrific scenes will be that God will display his glory among the nations (Eze 39.21). He will intervene in the great international conflict in the Middle East that Ezekiel foresees and will overcome those who conspire to attack Israel so that his authority is finally established over all the nations of the world. God will then complete the re-gathering of Israelites from around the world so that he can show himself 'holy through them in the sight of many nations' (Eze 39.27) and thus establish his world-wide reign of glory upon the earth.

CHAPTER SEVEN

THE PROPHET AT PRAYER

Prayer was essential to the prophetic ministry. It came naturally to the prophets and was the life-blood of their ministry. Prayer was their principal means of communication with God and lay at the heart of their personal relationship with God.

There are numerous examples in the Bible of the prophets at prayer. These often give us penetrating glimpses into the devotional life of the prophets. They also reveal something of the deep emotion experienced by men who closely identified with the message they were charged to declare. On one occasion Jeremiah cried out to God, 'Think of how I suffer reproach for your sake ... Why is my pain unending, and my wound grievous and incurable?' (Jer 15.15–18).

Among the fragments of prayer in the writings of the prophets and the historical records of Israel are to be found many of the different aspects of prayer, such as praise, adoration, invocation, confession, supplication and intercession.

Prayer was endemic to the prophetic ministry. It was through prayer that the prophets learned to enter the presence of God, to take their requests before him, to listen to him and to receive the word of the Lord. It was, of course,

117

receiving the word of the Lord that was the major task of the prophetic ministry.

The prophets, no doubt, each had their own particular way of entering the presence of God, but praise and remembering the deeds of the Lord are often to be found on their lips. From such a time of prayer they often flowed easily and naturally into prophecy. A good example is found in Isaiah 25 where the opening words of prayer are:

> O Lord, you are my God; I will exalt you and praise your name, for in perfect faithfulness you have done marvellous things, things planned long ago.

Still in the context of praise the prophet refers to some of the deeds of the Lord through which his name is exalted, 'Therefore strong peoples will honour you.' He then flows smoothly into prophecy:

> On this mountain the Lord Almighty will prepare a feast of rich food for all peoples . . . On this mountain he will destroy the shroud that enfolds all peoples, the sheet that covers all nations; he will swallow up death for ever. The Sovereign Lord will wipe away the tears from all faces . . . (Is 25.1–8).

Intercession

Although praise and adoration were often upon the lips of the prophets, it was intercessory prayer that was most closely associated with the ministry they exercised. There is a real sense in which they were the intercessors of Israel, pleading with God on behalf of the nation. Jeremiah, on one occasion, reminded the Lord how he had been faithful in this area of ministry, 'Remember that I stood before you and spoke on their behalf to turn your wrath away from them' (Jer 18.20).

Isaiah was outstanding among the intercessors of Judah. His ministry began with the cry, 'Woe to me for I am ruined.' Forty years later a similar cry was heard on the prophet's lips. This time it was not for himself, but against the Assyrian invader who was ravishing the land and slaughtering his countrymen: 'Woe to you, O destroyer.' Isaiah's indignation and his sense of outraged justice was almost impossible to express in mere words.

Sennacherib, the invader, was not merely an evil tyrant whose merciless cruelty had become a byword throughout the nations, but he was not even honourable to his own word. Sennacherib was a treacherous traitor who had received heavy tribute from Hezekiah but despite this he had broken his pledge not to attack Jerusalem. Hezekiah had stripped the gold and silver from the doors and doorposts of the Temple and had sent thirty talents of gold and 300 talents of silver (800 talents of silver and many of the priceless Temple furnishings according to Assyrian records). This still did not prevent Sennacherib sending a further threatening letter to Hezekiah saying that when he had dealt with Egypt he would return and destroy Jerusalem.

Isaiah was outraged at this treachery, 'Woe to you, O traitor, you who have not been betrayed! When you stop destroying, you will be destroyed; when you stop betraying, you will be betrayed' (Is 33.1). This time the enemy had gone too far. 'Where is that chief officer? Where is the one who took the revenue?' (33.18). The Lord himself would deal with these treacherous tyrants. 'You will see those arrogant people no more, those people of an obscure speech, with their strange incomprehensible tongue' (33.19).

Isaiah did not wait to be consulted as he had done a few months earlier when the field commander had come and shouted his threats in Hebrew so that all the people on the wall could hear and understand. On that occasion Hezekiah had sent a message to Isaiah seeking guidance (2 Kg 19.1–7). This time, Isaiah did not hesitate. He immediately sent a message of encouragement to Hezekiah and shortly afterwards he joined the king in the Temple for intercession and waiting upon the Lord. Sennacherib's letter was probably received in Jerusalem simultaneously with the news of the crushing defeat inflicted upon Egypt at Eltekeh following which most of the political leaders in Jerusalem who belonged to the pro-Egypt party left the city and fled (Is 22.3).

Isaiah had been warning against trust in Egypt. 'Woe to those who go down to Egypt for help, who rely on horses . . . but do not look to the Holy One of Israel, or seek help from the Lord. . . . The Egyptians are men and not God; their horses are flesh and not spirit' (Is 31.1,3). He had also prophesied that 'Assyria will fall by a sword that is not of man; a sword, not of mortals, will devour them' (31.8).

Now that he had been proved right in the first part of his prophecy, Isaiah was concerned to encourage the king not to be anxious over the desertion of his fainthearted politicians whose policies Isaiah had always opposed. Jerusalem was better off without them. Now, stripped of all hope in man, there was no alternative but for king and people together to turn to God and put their trust solely in him. This was the policy Isaiah had always advocated. Now he was free to intercede to the Lord with singleness of heart, 'O Lord, be gracious to us; we long for you. Be our strength every morning, our salvation in time of distress.' He declared his total confidence in the power of the Lord, 'At the thunder of your voice, the peoples flee; when you rise up, the nations scatter' (Is 33.2,3).

The account given in 2 Chronicles 32.20 of king and prophet standing together in the Temple crying out to God in prayer is one of the most poignant in the history of Israel. Hezekiah, whose reign had begun with Holy Spirit revival sweeping through the city of Jerusalem (2 Chr 30.23–31.1) and Isaiah, the greatest of all the prophets of the old covenant, joined together in intercession, crying out to God to defend his name against the Assyrian emperor who had uttered such blasphemy against him; 'Just as the gods of the peoples of the other lands did not rescue their people from my hand, so the god of Hezekiah will not rescue his people from my hand,' Sennacherib had boasted (2 Chr 32.17). The very portals of heaven shook as king and prophet cried out in unison! There was no power on earth that could stand against such intercession. The sword of the Lord swept through the all-conquering army of Assyria. Decimated by plague, the tattered remnant of Sennacherib's once proud world-conquering force 'withdrew to his own land in disgrace' (2 Chr 32.21).

There was also a negative side to the intercessory ministries of the prophets. The strength of their intercession tended to reduce the universality of prayer in the lives of ordinary men and women throughout the nation. The religious life of the people consisted mainly in bringing tithes and offerings as instructed in the Law, and participating in feasts, fasts and the varying customs of religious festivals. Intercession, in particular, was regarded as the task of leadership. In the early history of Israel this was mainly the responsibility of the prophets. During the period of the monarchy and the centralisation of worship, at Jerusalem in the south and Bethel in the northern kingdom the task of interceding for the people fell to the priests. The task was, however, shared by the kings in the case of those who loved the Lord.

An example from the earlier days of Israel of the prophets praying for the people is found in 1 Samuel 7. During the period of the Judges, in the early days of the settlement in Canaan, people lapsed into idolatry, particularly worshipping the local gods of the Canaanites. Samuel rebuked them and told them to get rid of the foreign gods and Ashtoreths and to commit themselves solely to the Lord. God would then deliver them out of the hands of the Philistines.

Samuel assembled all the people and said that he would intercede with the Lord on their behalf. The people observed a day of fasting and performed various religious rituals and confessed their unfaithfulness to God.

> They said to Samuel, 'Do not stop crying out to the Lord our God for us, that he may rescue us from the hands of the Philistines.' . . . He cried out to the Lord on Israel's behalf and the Lord answered him (1 Sam 7.8,9).

David and Solomon were outstanding among the kings of Israel in interceding on behalf of the nation. Many of the psalms are a testimony to David's faithfulness in carrying out this responsibility. Solomon's great prayer at the dedication of the Temple (2 Chr 6) is a beautiful example of intercessory prayer.

Jehoshaphat also led the nation in prayer when faced with a united army of neighbouring states that threatened to overwhelm Judah. He brought all the people together and led the intercession. His prayer was answered through the prophet Jahaziel who brought a word from the Lord that gave both encouragement and clear direction for the battle (2 Chr 20).

We may conclude, therefore, that intercession under the Old Covenant was largely vicarious. It was the prerogative of the leaders who prayed on behalf of the people. It was Jeremiah who foresaw that under the New Covenant every believer would have a personal relationship with God (Jer 31.31–34). Every believer would thus be able to undertake the prophetic task of intercession which under the Old Covenant was the responsibility of those in anointed ministries.

Praying for the Nation

The prophets were strong patriots; they loved the nation and they loved the land, although their primary loyalty was to God. The whole of the prophetic tradition from Moses to Malachi is founded on the concept of a *covenant relationship* between the nation and God. That covenant demanded absolute loyalty to God from the people in return for God's protection and loving care over the nation.

The prophets believed that God was the one and only true God and that all other gods were but worthless idols who were not gods at all. They believed God to be in control of the whole universe and that he held the destinies of the nations in his hands. Yet his particular commitment was to Israel and it was upon the basis of this commitment that they were able to make their pleas to God in times of distress. Jeremiah used the covenant relationship with God in precisely this way:

> For the sake of your name do not despise us; do not dishonour your glorious throne. Remember your covenant with us and do not break it. Do any of the worthless idols of the nations bring rain? Do the skies themselves send down showers? No, it is you, O Lord our God. Therefore our hope is in you, for you are the one who does all this (Jer 14.21,22).

If there is one theme common to all the prophets it is their demand for absolute loyalty to God. Idolatry was the besetting sin of the nation from the time Moses left them to climb Mount Sinai and receive the commandments through to the exile in Babylon. In each generation, both Israel and Judah whored after other gods. In each generation the prophets warned of the consequences of idolatry, pleaded with the people, reminded them of the covenant which required loyalty in return for blessing and protection. They called upon the people to turn away from following after other gods and return to the Lord, and they interceded with God on behalf of the nation. It was their great love of the nation plus their loyalty to God that caused the prophets much suffering and gave a note of urgency to their message.

The prophets wept over the sins of the nation. They could see clearly where idolatry and faithlessness were leading. Isaiah actually saw the trail of destruction left by the advancing Assyrian army. 'Your country is desolate, your cities burned with fire; your fields are being stripped by foreigners right before you, laid waste as when overthrown by strangers' (Is 1.7). This was happening because the people had 'forsaken the Lord', they had 'spurned the Holy One of Israel and turned their backs on him' (1.4). The prophet pleaded with the people:

> Why should you be beaten any more? Why do you persist in rebellion? Your whole head is injured, your whole heart afflicted. From the sole of your foot to the top of your head there is no soundness—only wounds and welts and open sores not cleansed or bandaged or soothed with oil (1.5,6).

Jeremiah lived through a similar experience a hundred years later as he saw the Babylonian armies devastating the country and leaving a trail of blood and death as they marched towards Jerusalem. 'If I go into the country,' he said, 'I see those slain by the sword; if I go into the city I see the ravages of famine' (Jer 14.18).

Jeremiah has often been labelled the prophet of doom and gloom; yet what else could he do when faced with the stark reality of the situation that he saw more clearly than anyone else in his day? He was accused of being unpatriotic by the political and religious leaders in Jerusalem who hated the message he was bringing. Yet it would be a complete misrepresentation of the prophet and his ministry if we did not note the heartbreak in the message. The words of warning and the pronouncement of judgment upon a sinful generation were wrung from him with tears.

> Let my eyes overflow with tears night and day without ceasing; for my virgin daughter—my people—has suffered a grievous wound, a crushing blow (Jer 14.17).

The tears in Jeremiah's eyes he saw as representing God's own weeping for his people, his 'virgin daughter' who had suffered such a grievous wound and a crushing blow. But her wounds were the result of her own prostitution, her unfaithfulness, her adultery with foreign gods, even to the detestable practices of child sacrifice.

Jeremiah's heart was breaking in the face of the unresponsiveness of the people and what he knew would happen to them in the near future. Their only hope was in God so in his intercession he cried out the more urgently to the Lord—

> Have you rejected Judah completely? Do you despise Zion? Why have you afflicted us so that we cannot be healed? We hoped for peace but no good has come, for a time of healing but there is only terror (14.19).

In the next verse we see the extent to which Jeremiah identified with the nation of which he was a part and which he loved so dearly. He actually identified with the sins of the nation. Although he of all men in Jerusalem was probably the least guilty of sin he saw himself as part of a sinful generation who had rejected God so he cried out:

O Lord, we acknowledge our wickedness and the guilt of our fathers; we have indeed sinned against you. For the sake of your name do not despise us (14.20,21).

This identification with sin is not to be compared with the vicarious suffering for sin undertaken by the Messiah and referred to in Isaiah 53:

Surely he took up our infirmities and carried our sorrows . . . He was pierced for our transgressions, he was crushed for our iniquities . . . and by his wounds we are healed . . . the Lord has laid on him the iniquities of us all.

The prophet was here foreseeing the redemptive purposes of God being worked out through the suffering and death of the Messiah. But this must not be confused with the identification of the prophets with the sins of the nation.

The great prayer in Daniel 9 is the classic prayer of the prophet who fully identified with the nation. Although he personally was not one who had deliberately forsaken the way of the Lord he nevertheless saw himself as part of a rebellious generation. He prayed:

O Lord, the great and awesome God, who keeps his covenant of love with all who love him and obey his commands, we have sinned and done wrong. We have been wicked and have rebelled; we have turned away from your commands and laws. We have not listened to your servants the prophets, who spoke in your name to our kings, our princes and our fathers and to all the people of the land. Lord, you are righteous, but this day we are covered with shame . . . Our sins and the iniquities of our fathers have made Jerusalem and your people an object of scorn . . . Give ear, O God, and hear; open your eyes and see the desolation of the city that bears your name . . . O Lord, listen! O Lord, forgive! O Lord, hear and act! For your sake, O my God, do not delay, because your city and your people bear your Name (Dan 9.4–19).

125

Praying with Understanding

The prophets sometimes used prayer to argue with the Lord. There was nothing disrespectful about this. Indeed, a mark of all the genuine prophets was their sense of awe in the presence of the Almighty God. As Moses took off his shoes in the presence of the Lord, so all the prophets had a strong sense of the holiness of God before whose presence they stood in reverential awe and holy fear.

This 'fear of the Lord' did not, however, prevent them from questioning God in order to understand his nature and his ways. This was part of the prophet's quest for discernment which was essential if he was to be the mouthpiece of God to the nation and rightly to interpret the signs of the times and to declare the whole counsel of God to the people.

The book of Habakkuk is a good example of the prophetic method of arguing a difficult matter before the Lord. He had a genuine desire for enlightenment hence the stream of questions: 'Why do you make me look at injustice? Why do you tolerate wrong?' (1.3). 'Why do you tolerate the treacherous? Why are you silent while the wicked swallow up those more righteous than themselves?' (1.13). 'Was your wrath against the streams? Did you rage against the sea?' (3.8).

Jeremiah also tried to work out answers to incomprehensible problems in the same way. On one occasion he cried out to God, 'You are always righteous, O Lord, when I bring a case before you. Yet I would speak with you about your justice; why does the way of the wicked prosper? Why do all the faithless live at ease?' (Jer 12.1).

Jeremiah's belief in the sovereignty of God was so strong that he could not conclude that it was an accident that the wicked escaped summary judgment. He hastened to add, 'You have planted them and they have taken root; they grow and bear fruit.' Of course, God knew that evil men were prospering and he allowed it to happen, but why? The prophet saw the hypocrisy of the wicked who outwardly were

126

very religious, so in prayer he continued, 'You are always on their lips but far from their hearts.'

At this point the whole tone of Jeremiah's prayer changed. He was utterly convinced of God's justice and righteousness. Therefore he knew that the wicked could not escape punishment for ever. He saw how close the nation was to disaster with the approaching Babylonian onslaught. He knew that unless the people repented and totally put their trust in the Lord disaster was inevitable. He knew that within the perfect will of God the wicked who were in leadership positions and were misleading the people, would be held accountable to God. He therefore took it as part of the responsibility of the prophetic ministry to pray into being what he knew to be the will of God. In his intercession he actually called for judgment swiftly to be brought upon these unfaithful shepherds who were misleading the sheep.

> Drag them off like sheep to be butchered! Set them apart for the day of slaughter! How long will the land lie parched and the grass in every field be withered? Because those who live in it are wicked, the animals and birds have perished. Moreover, the people are saying, 'He will not see what happens to us' (Jer 12.3,4).

Creative Prayer
Readers who are unfamiliar with the prophetic ministry may find it hard to understand how Jeremiah could utter such a prayer. Taken out of context it is certainly startling. But the task of the prophet was to discern the will of God and then *to pray it into being*. It is here that revelation and intercession combine.

Jeremiah knew that it was not a bit of use praying, 'Peace, peace', if God was saying, 'There is no peace'. It was the false prophets who spoke of peace when God was warning of coming destruction. The true message was, 'Repent, or disaster will befall you.' Jeremiah realised that if you pray for something that is not God's intention, you actually put yourself against God. Hence the need for revelation to give clear direction to intercession.

It was the urgency of the situation, the imminence of disaster, that caused Jeremiah to include such a violent plea in his intercession. He saw what was going to happen to the nation and that the people would be like sheep dragged off to be butchered by the Babylonians because they were being misled. So in order to prevent the national disaster he actually prayed for the leaders to be swiftly removed.

Ezekiel spoke in similar terms about the wicked leadership through whom the people were being misled, 'Because my flock lacks a shepherd and so has been plundered and has become food for all the wild animals . . . I am against the shepherds and will hold them accountable for my flock' (Eze 34.8–10).

Once the prophet had discerned the will of God in the circumstances of the day, his greatest desire was to see God's will accomplished. Hence 'praying into being' the will of God was a regular part of the prophetic responsibility. Elijah was told by God that there would be a drought for three years. At the end of the three years he was told to call together the king, the people and the false religious leaders. He was told to initiate a confrontation and that God would send down fire upon the altar that he built. He was also told that at the conclusion, when the prophets of Baal had been destroyed and the people had acknowledged their loyalty to God, the drought would be broken. At each stage Elijah 'prayed into being' the will of God. He prayed for the drought, he prayed for fire to come down and consume the sacrifice on the altar, and he prayed for the rain to fall, although he had already prophesied that this would happen. The prophetic task was to proclaim the word of God in faith and to pray it into being in the perfect timing of the Lord.

Jeremiah did this with the prophecies he was given concerning the eventual downfall of Babylon. He had said that the Babylonian empire would last for seventy years but at the end of that time he knew that in the sovereignty of God

Babylon would be overthrown. God would use the ruthless cruelty of the Babylonians just so long as it suited his purpose but then he would discard them.

> Babylon was a gold cup in the Lord's hand; she made the whole earth drunk. The nations drank her wine; therefore they have now gone mad. Babylon will suddenly fall and be broken. . . . The Lord will carry out his purpose, his decree against the people of Babylon. . . . Babylon will be a heap of ruins, a haunt of jackals, an object of horror and scorn, a place where no-one lives (Jer 51.7,8,12,37).

Because he knew that he would not live to see the fulfilment of the word he had been given, Jeremiah wrote down the prophecies and then handed the scroll to Seraiah who was taken captive to Babylon with king Zedekiah. The prophet instructed Seraiah, 'When you get to Babylon, see that you read all these words aloud. Then say, "O Lord, you have said you will destroy this place, so that neither man nor animal will live in it; it will be desolate for ever"' (51.62).

Here we see that although the prophet had already prayed about the word of the Lord in private, that prayer had to be spoken aloud together with the words of prophecy in order to seal the word of the Lord. When he had carried out all that Jeremiah had instructed, Seraiah was to tie a stone around the scroll and throw it into the river Euphrates as a further prophetic act and to say, 'So will Babylon sink to rise no more because of the disaster I will bring upon her. And her people will fall' (51.64). The prophets believed that power was released when the word of God was declared aloud; it would not 'return void', it would accomplish the purpose of God.

Praying for Guidance
The prophets used prayer to seek guidance for their ministry, for the actions they should undertake, for the words they should speak and for the advice they should give. There was

one very significant occasion on which Jeremiah was asked to advise the people and the remaining leaders in Judah whether or not they should go to Egypt. Jerusalem had been destroyed by the Babylonians following Zedekiah's revolt and the second wave of captives had been taken into slavery. Those who remained in the land were mostly poor peasants and Nebuchadnezzar had appointed Gedaliah as governor of Judah leaving a small garrison of his soldiers with him at Mizpah. Gedaliah was of the family of Shapham who had been good friends to Jeremiah for a number of years. In the following months people who had been in hiding all over Judea rallied to Gedaliah along with survivors (and no doubt deserters) from Judah's vanquished army. Unfortunately, just as some semblance of organised social and economic life was beginning to develop under Gedaliah's leadership, Ishmael, who was of royal blood, staged a coup and assassinated Gedaliah together with the Babylonian garrison.

Ishmael's coup was short-lived; he was quickly overcome by Johanan, who was evidently a senior army officer and a supporter of Gedaliah. Ishmael and his conspirators fled the country and Johanan, together with a large company of the survivors, began to trek south planning to go to Egypt because they feared for their lives once the Babylonians heard that there had been yet another revolt in Judah. They stopped at a village near Bethlehem just south of Jerusalem and consulted Jeremiah.

The question was, should they stay in the land of Judah and face possible retribution from the Babylonians or should the entire remnant make their way to Egypt as refugees? They begged the prophet to pray for them, 'Pray that the Lord your God will tell us where we should go and what we should do' (Jer 42.3). Jeremiah replied, 'I will certainly pray to the Lord your God as you have requested; I will tell you everything the Lord says and will keep nothing back from you.' In return, the people promised they would act in accordance with everything the Lord said to Jeremiah, 'Whether it is favourable or unfavourable, we will obey the

Lord our God, to whom we are sending you, so that it will go well with us.'

Jeremiah carried out his promise to come before the Lord in prayer, 'Ten days later the word of the Lord came to Jeremiah' (42.7). It took Jeremiah ten days of faithful and urgent intercession to receive the word of the Lord. Guidance was not always received spontaneously or without effort. The prophets often had to wait patiently for God to speak to them.

Jeremiah was not a young man at the time of this incident. He was at least sixty years of age and had been exercising the ministry of the prophet for forty one years. He was an experienced intercessor; he had many times been in the presence of the Lord; he knew how to listen and how to weigh what he was hearing and seek confirmation that he was rightly receiving the word of the Lord. Yet it took Jeremiah *ten days* before the word of the Lord came to him. Seeking guidance was never easy or automatic, even for the greatest of the prophets.

Another example of the prophet at prayer seeking guidance is also to be found in Jeremiah on the occasion when his cousin Hanamel came to him while he was imprisoned in Jerusalem asking the prophet to buy a family field in his home village at Anathoth. Jeremiah had already received forewarning of Hanamel's visit and clearly saw it as a sign from the Lord so he duly signed the deed of transfer, paid the money, had the documents witnessed and placed in a sealed jar. He then sought the Lord in prayer for the significance of this transaction.

It needs to be remembered that the Babylonians were already laying siege to the city of Jerusalem and Anathoth was in enemy-occupied territory. No-one was buying and selling land so in prayer Jeremiah sought an explanation as to why God should tell him to buy a field that it was impossible to possess. His prayer is one of the great classics of Scripture. It begins with praise, affirmation of confidence in God, remembers God's mighty deeds in the past; then moves into the contemporary situation and finally lays before the Lord the question for which guidance was sought.

> Ah, Sovereign Lord, you have made the heavens and the earth by your great power and outstretched arm. Nothing is too hard for you. You show love to thousands but bring the punishment of the father's sins into the laps of their children after them. O great and powerful God, whose name is the Lord Almighty, great are your purposes and mighty are your deeds. Your eyes are open to all the ways of men; you reward everyone according to his conduct and as his deeds deserve. You performed miraculous signs and wonders in Egypt and have continued them to this day, both in Israel and among all mankind, and have gained the renown that is still yours. You brought your people Israel out of Egypt with signs and wonders, by a mighty hand and an outstretched arm and with great terror. You gave them this land you had sworn to give to their forefathers, a land flowing with milk and honey. They came in and took possession of it, but they did not obey you or follow your law; they did not do what you commanded them to do. So you brought all this disaster upon them.
>
> See how the siege ramps are built up to take the city. Because of the sword, famine and plague, the city will be handed over to the Babylonians who are attacking it. What you said has happened, as you now see. And though the city will be handed over to the Babylonians, you, O Sovereign Lord, say to me, 'Buy the field with silver and have the transaction witnessed' (Jer 32.17–25).

The Prophetic Silence

We have already noted that the prophets were great intercessors who loved their nation and continually pleaded with God on behalf of the people, even to the point of identifying with the sins of their generation. So long as the prophets were praying for the nation there was hope. The most devastating sign of judgment was when the prophet ceased to intercede. When the 'prophetic silence' descended upon the nation the fate of that generation was sealed.

Three times Jeremiah was told to stop praying for the

132

nation. 'So do not pray for this people nor offer any plea or petition for them; do not plead with me, for I will not listen to you' (Jer 7.16). That word was received in the context of God's anger at the blatant idolatry of the people. 'In the towns of Judah and in the streets of Jerusalem' the whole population was worshipping Queen Ishtar, the goddess of Babylon, who was also known as the Queen of Heaven. 'The children gather wood, the fathers light the fire, and the women knead the dough and make cakes of bread for the Queen of Heaven' (Jer 7.18). Ishtar was a fertility goddess whose worship included a variety of detestable sexual practices including male and female shrine prostitution and even child sacrifice. In the same chapter Jeremiah describes this in two or three sentences, 'They have set up their detestable idols in the house that bears my Name and have defiled it. They have built the high places of Topheth in the Valley of Ben Hinnom to burn their sons and daughters in the fire' (7.30,31).

In the same context of condemning idolatry the second instruction to cease praying for the people was received.

> You have as many gods as you have towns, O Judah; and the altars you have set up to burn incense to that shameful god Baal are as many as the streets of Jerusalem.
>
> *Do not pray for this people* nor offer any plea or petition for them, because I will not listen when they call to me in the time of their distress (11.13,14).

The third instruction to cease praying for the nation came in the context of a condemnation of lying prophets, 'False visions, divinations, idolatries and the delusions of their own minds' (14.14). The word Jeremiah received on this occasion was:

> Then the Lord said to me, '*Do not pray for the well-being of this people*. Although they fast, I will not listen to their cry; though they offer burnt offerings and grain offerings, I will not accept them. Instead, I will destroy them with the sword, famine and plague' (14.11).

133

Another example of the prophetic silence is found in Amos 7 where the prophet is given three visions, each relating to a time of devastation coming upon the nation. In the first picture Amos saw a swarm of locusts stripping the countryside and he cried out, interceding on behalf of the nation, 'Sovereign Lord, forgive! How can Jacob survive? He is so small!'

Amos' intercession was heard and God said this would not happen. Then in the second picture he saw judgment by fire falling upon the land and burning everything up. Again Amos cried out in passionate intercession, pleading for the nation, 'Sovereign Lord, I beg you, stop! How can Jacob survive? He is so small!' Once again the plea of the prophet was heard and God said this would not happen.

The third picture was of the Lord standing by a wall with a plumb line in his hand. This was accompanied by the word, 'Look, I am setting a plumb line among my people Israel; I will spare them no longer.' Amos knew now it was useless to plead. God himself was coming to judge his people. The prophet was silent. Judgment swiftly followed. The end of Israel was in sight.

Prayer was the lifeline of the prophets and was at the heart of their relationship with God. They were the intercessors of the nation. So long as they were praying the forces of destruction were held at bay. When they ceased to pray the 'prophetic silence' descended upon the land. The fate of a rebellious generation was sealed. Judgment was inevitable.

CHAPTER EIGHT

THE MESSAGE OF THE PROPHETS

To attempt to summarise the message of the prophets in a
single chapter is a task fraught with difficulty. The prophets
were individuals and the message of each bears different
characteristics. They most certainly did not speak with one
voice. Thus it is not possible in a few pages to give a summary
outline of the message of the prophets. They were men of
their times and the message they brought reflected contemporary conditions both within Israel and in international
affairs. The ministry of the prophets took place over a period
of many hundreds of years from the time of the Judges to the
Maccabees. During this period there was considerable development in the understanding of God, of his ways and his
purposes, all of which makes a simple summary of the
message of the prophets impossible.

It is, however, possible to trace certain themes that provide common ground for the prophets and may thereby be
regarded as representative of the thinking of the prophets
and basic to their message. These themes are particularly to
be found in the work of the great writing prophets from
the eighth century to the early post-exilic period. It is
these themes we shall attempt to outline briefly in this
chapter which will necessitate mentioning some scripture
passages already noted in earlier chapters.

The Nature of God

All the prophets began their ministries with an understanding of the nature of God that provided the foundation of their calling and the cornerstone of the convictions that underlay the message that they proclaimed.

God of Law

In the first place, and of paramount importance, the prophets saw God as a God of law. He was not a capricious God like the false gods of the nations worshipped by the peoples among whom the Israelites had settled. He was reliable, totally dependable and consistent. It was this self-consistency in the nature of God that provided the sure foundation for the ministry of each of the prophets. They knew that what God called 'good' on one occasion he would still call 'good' a hundred years later. And what he declared to be evil would be evil for ever.

The prophets knew that God did not act in an arbitrary manner like the capricious despots, the Baals of the Canaanites and the evil gods of the surrounding nations. God was a God of law whose ways were predictable and whose word was unchangeable. It was from this understanding of God that the prophets derived their concept of the faithfulness of God; his utter dependability and the certainty that once he had declared his word he would fulfil it.

Jeremiah gives powerful expression to this dependability of God when he declares his conviction concerning the eventual restoration of Israel. Despite the destruction of Jerusalem, despite the tragedy of the exile, despite the faithlessness of the people, there would come a time of complete restoration when God would fulfil the terms of his covenant with the nation. 'This is what the Lord says; if you can break my covenant with the day and my covenant with the night . . . then my covenant with David my servant can be broken' (Jer 33.20,21). God would never reject the nation he had chosen, that was as certain as the fixed laws of nature which he himself had established. 'If I have not established

136

my covenant with day and night and the fixed laws of heaven and earth, then I will reject the descendants of Jacob and David' (33.25,26). It was this self-consistency and dependability of God that enabled the prophet to predict with confidence what God would do in different situations and to know what he was saying to them so that they could declare his word with confidence.

God of Love

The prophets knew God not only to be consistent and reliable but to be a God who loved his people. Hosea was the first to make this a major feature of his teaching and he did so out of his own bitter experience of an unhappy marriage to an unfaithful wife. Hosea loved his wife dearly despite her running after other lovers and he saw God using this to teach him something of his divine nature and of his own long-suffering love for the people whom he had chosen to be his own but who were unfaithful to him.

> The Lord said to me, 'Go, show your love to your wife again, though she is loved by another and is an adulteress. Love her as the Lord loves the Israelites, though they turn to other gods and love the sacred raisin cakes' (Hos 3.1).

Hosea believed that God would never forsake Israel because of his great love for her. 'I will betroth you to me for ever; I will betroth you in righteousness and justice, in love and compassion' (2.19). He expresses the tenderness and compassion of God in the most beautiful terms and perceives God as a loving Father caring for a small child.

> It was I who taught Ephraim to walk, taking them by the arms; but they did not realise it was I that healed them. I led them with cords of human kindness, with ties of love (11.3,4).

Hosea sees the love and justice of God presenting a dilemma for him. Justice demanded punishment, abandoning the faithless nation to its fate; but love demanded compassion. And God was not a man driven by legalism. With God love is predominant.

How can I give you up, Ephraim? How can I hand you over, Israel? . . . My heart is changed within me; all my compassion is aroused. I will not carry out my fierce anger, nor devastate Ephraim again. For I am God, and not man—the Holy One among you. I will not come in wrath (11.8,9).

In the lofty thought of the great post-exilic prophecies of Isaiah 54 some 200 years after Hosea, the prophet speaks of God's great love for the shattered city of Jerusalem in the unforgettable words of verse 11: 'O afflicted city, lashed by storms and not comforted, I will build you with stones of turquoise, your foundations with sapphires. I will make your battlements of rubies, your gates of sparkling jewels, and all your walls of precious stones.' This is preceded by the declaration that although God momentarily removed his covering protection because of the wickedness of the people, in his great love he will again have compassion.

'For a brief moment I abandoned you, but with deep compassion I will bring you back. In a surge of anger I hid my face from you for a moment, but with everlasting kindness I will have compassion on you,' says the Lord your Redeemer. '. . . Though the mountains be shaken and the hills be removed, yet my unfailing love for you will not be shaken nor my covenant of peace be removed' (54.7–10).

A later development of this thought showed God actually suffering through the suffering of his people which he had allowed to come upon them. 'In all their distress he too was distressed, and the angel of his presence saved them. In his love and mercy he redeemed them' (Is 63.9). The love of God was not just something theoretical; it was to be seen in the deeds of the Lord. 'I will tell of the kindnesses of the Lord, the deeds for which he is to be praised . . . the many good things he has done for the house of Israel, according to his compassion' (63.7). It was through the tangible expression of his love in his deeds that 'he became their Saviour' and actually demonstrated his great love.

138

THE MESSAGE OF THE PROPHETS

God of Mercy

The love of God was seen to be linked with his mercy. It was part of the nature of God to have mercy upon those who really deserved punishment for their sinfulness. Micah, an eighth-century contemporary of Isaiah, foresaw the coming storm that would engulf Israel and Judah because of the wickedness of her people. Everywhere in the two nations he saw injustice, deceit, bribery and corruption, divination and idolatry. In both nations he saw 'her leaders judge for a bribe, her priests teach for a price, and her prophets tell fortunes for money. Yet they lean upon the Lord and say, Is not the Lord among us? No disaster will come upon us' (Mic 3.11). The prophet declared in no uncertain terms that disaster would befall both nations and even 'Jerusalem will become a heap of rubble' (3.12).

But Micah knew the mercy of God which he linked with God's willingness to forgive sin.

> Who is a God like you, who pardons sin and forgives the transgression of the remnant of his inheritance? You do not stay angry for ever but delight to show mercy. You will again have compassion on us; you will tread our sins underfoot and hurl all our iniquities into the depths of the sea. You will be true to Jacob, and show mercy to Abraham, as you pledged on oath to our fathers in days long ago (Mic 7.18–20).

It was because the prophets themselves had experienced the forgiveness of sins and they saw in times past how eager God had been to forgive the iniquities of his unfaithful people, that they were able to plead with the nation. It was on the basis of God's mercy that they were able to call upon the people to turn away from their sinfulness knowing that God in his mercy was eager to forgive and to restore the nation to its place in a right relationship with himself.

In Jeremiah's teaching, even though the outlook for Jerusalem was becoming increasingly desperate, the people had only to acknowledge their guilt and God would immediately change the whole situation in his loving mercy.

139

> Return, faithless Israel, declares the Lord, I will frown on you no longer, for I am merciful, declares the Lord. I will not be angry for ever. Only acknowledge your guilt—you have rebelled against the Lord your God. . . . Return, faithless people, declares the Lord, for I am your husband (Jer 3.11–14).

God of Justice

Justice is a theme that runs right through the prophets. They knew God to be a God of justice. Jeremiah saw justice as such a basic element in the nature of God that anyone who claimed to know him should be aware of it.

> Let him who boasts boast about this; that he understands and knows me, that I am the Lord, who exercises kindness, justice and righteousness on earth, for in these I delight, declares the Lord (Jer 9:24).

Isaiah also boldly declares that God is a God of justice and he links this with his mercy and his desire to show compassion to his sinful and rebellious people.

> Yet the Lord longs to be gracious to you; he rises to show you compassion. For the Lord is a God of justice (Is 30.18).

In the teaching of the prophets there is no contradiction in linking God's compassion with his justice. But this throws into sharp relief the difference between the Hebrew understanding of justice and our western concept. Modern western thought is derived from the Roman concept of justice which is legalistic and based on retribution. Roman justice demands that the punishment fits the crime. Thus for God to be merciful and have compassion upon a sinful people would be a denial of his justice which demands punishment. Retributive justice cannot be satisfied until the full price has been paid for the wrongdoing.

In contrast the Hebrew concept of justice was rooted in *relationships* and based upon mercy. The just man was one who was in a right relationship with God and with his neighbours. Hence love and mercy long to have compassion upon the penitent sinner and restore him to a right relationship with the one from whom he is estranged by reason of his wrongdoing. That wrongdoing breaks harmonious relationships which are based upon love and trust. This is what Isaiah meant when he said that God 'looked for justice, but saw bloodshed; for righteousness, but heard cries of distress' (5.7). God was looking for right relationships among his people but he saw only violence and oppression.

If God were to allow disaster to come upon his people by withdrawing his protection and leaving them exposed to their enemies, God would be perfectly justified in so doing, for the people had broken the right relationships that he demanded and they had accepted as part of the covenant relationship. In fact Isaiah saw that for God to allow the disaster of destruction and exile to come upon his people (5.13) who turned the moral law upside down and called 'evil good and good evil' (5.20) would actually *be a demonstration to the world of his justice, ie* his demand for right relationships.

> The Lord Almighty will be exalted by his justice, and the holy God will show himself holy by his righteousness (5.16).

This understanding of God's justice lay at the heart of the covenant he had established between Israel and himself. The covenant was based upon right relationships. Sin broke that relationship and it could only be restored through the repentance of the sinner and the forgiveness of God. 'For I, the Lord, love justice; . . . and make an everlasting covenant with them' (Is 61.8).

God of Holiness

Just as the justice of God demanded that he allowed disaster to come upon his rebellious people, so, according to Ezekiel's teaching, the holiness of God's nature demanded that he should restore his people to the land he had given them. Ezekiel said that God had poured out his wrath upon the people because 'they had shed blood in the land and because they had defiled it with their idols' (36.18). Hence he had 'dispersed them among the nations'. But this had led to

141

God's holy name being profaned among the nations because they were saying, 'These are the Lord's people, and yet they have had to leave his land' (36.20). Therefore God was going to re-gather his people from all the countries where he had sent them. He would cleanse them from the impurities of their idols and give them a new heart and put a new spirit in them (36.25–26). The reason he would do this was not because the people deserved it:

> This is what the Sovereign Lord says: It is not for your sake, O house of Israel, that I am going to do these things, but for the sake of my holy name, which you have profaned among the nations where you have gone. I will show the holiness of my great name which has been profaned among the nations. . . . when I show myself holy through you before their eyes (36.22,23).

Holiness, for the prophets, meant that God was not like man; 'For my thoughts are not your thoughts, neither are your ways my ways, declares the Lord' (Is 55.8). God was wholly other than man. He was the one before whom men trembled. In Moses' day the people had even been afraid to go near the mountain where he had communicated with Moses. All the prophets speak of God as 'the Holy One of Israel'. This phrase is used scores of times throughout the prophetic literature.

Isaiah's experience of the holiness of God at the time of his call into the prophetic ministry never left him. 'Holy, holy, holy is the Lord Almighty' were the words that filled his mind and led to his confession of uncleanness; he, a mere sinful mortal, had come into the presence of the holy God who was unapproachable by sinful men and entirely set apart from the profane things of this world. In his prayer at the time of Sennacherib's threat to Jerusalem Isaiah referred to the Lord as being exalted and dwelling on high (33.5).

Although references to the holiness of God are found in the eighth-century prophets (see Amos 2.7 and Hosea 11.9) it was Ezekiel who laid great emphasis upon the holy nature of

God. In his vision of the rebuilt Temple Ezekiel saw a clear distinction being made between things for common use and holy things, *ie* things set apart for use exclusively in worship (see 42.13–20). In his vision of the final conflict between God and the nations Ezekiel sees God's purpose in intervention as being to establish the holiness of his name among the nations. 'I will make known my holy name among my people Israel. I will no longer let my holy name be profaned, and the nations will know that I the Lord am the Holy One in Israel' (Eze 39.7).

God of Faithfulness

All the prophets speak of the faithfulness of God. Of his reliability and dependability there could be no doubt. His word was his bond. When the Lord spoke he would fulfil his word. He would carry out that which he had declared. This was the first revelation that Jeremiah received at the beginning of his ministry; he saw the branch of the almond tree as signifying that God was watching to see that his word would be fulfilled (Jer 1.12).

The charge that Hosea was told to bring against Israel was that 'there is no faithfulness, no love, no acknowledgment of God in the land' (Hos 4.1). Nevertheless, despite the faithlessness of Israel, God remained faithful so that the word the prophet was given to declare was, 'I will betroth you in faithfulness' (2.20). Hosea saw the faithlessness of Israel in contrast to the faithfulness of God as an incredible tragedy. God had loved Israel since she was a child, fed her, healed her, protected her and cared for her in every way but,

> Ephraim has surrounded me with lies, the house of Israel with deceit, and Judah is unruly against God, even against the faithful Holy One (11.12).

It was because the prophets were convinced of the faithfulness of God that they were able to continue to declare his good purposes for the nation even in the face of tragedy. Hence Jeremiah was able to inform the exiles in Babylon

143

with great confidence that God would watch over them and prosper them even in a foreign land, and also that the day would come when God would bring them back to the land of Judah. His confidence in the faithfulness of God was such that he knew God had good plans for his people, 'plans to prosper you and not to harm you, plans to give you hope and a future' (Jer 29.11). Jeremiah's confidence in the faithfulness of God to fulfil his word was such that he could already foresee the towns of Judah and the streets of Jerusalem that were deserted being once more filled with 'the sounds of joy and gladness' and the people bringing thank-offerings to the house of the Lord saying 'Give thanks to the Lord Almighty for he is good; his love endures for ever' (33.11).

Isaiah foresaw that the full purposes of God would only be fulfilled through a messianic figure. One of the qualities he foresaw in the Messiah was that of faithfulness. He said, 'Righteousness will be his belt and faithfulness the sash round his waist' (Is 11.5). The faithfulness of the Messiah was later developed in the servant songs where the servant of the Lord was faithful even unto death. 'He was oppressed and afflicted, yet he did not open his mouth. . . . He was cut off from the land of the living . . . though he had done no violence.' The servant was given the highest status by God 'because he poured out his life unto death' and 'he bore the sins of many' (Is 53). The faithfulness of the servant of the Lord is seen as a reflection of the nature of God himself.

Summary
We have looked at the nature of God as revealed through the teaching of the prophets because it is the foundation of the message they declared. It is not possible to appreciate the revelation of the word of God through the mouths of the prophets without first having a clear picture of the nature of God in their understanding. Their teaching of the requirements of God and their confidence in declaring the word of God for their times stemmed from this understanding.

They saw him as a God of law, a God of love, a God of

144

mercy, a God of justice, a God of holiness, and a God of faithfulness.

Lord of Nature

All the prophets saw God as the Lord of nature. He was in control of all natural phenomena. He sent the rain or withheld the rain, he sent the thunder and the lightning, the storm and the drought. Whatever happened in nature was the direct action of God and a major part of the prophets' task was to interpret to the understanding of the people what God was doing through nature. The prophets, therefore, took careful note of what was happening around them in the natural order of things so that they could understand what God was doing and receive revelation of his word to the people.

Although we have already referred to Amos 4 it is relevant here to note that this passage provides us with a classic example of the way the prophets used natural phenomena to interpret and to declare the word of the living God. 'I gave you empty stomachs in every city and lack of bread in every town' (Am 4.6).

Amos continued in the same vein through a catalogue of events that must all have been well known to his hearers. He spoke of God withholding the rain and how people 'staggered from town to town for water'. He described graphically the agricultural problems they had encountered through crop disease, blight and mildew. He referred to a plague of locusts that had devoured the fig harvest and the olive trees. He referred to plagues that had come upon the people and to some enormous catastrophe that reminded him of the events at Sodom and Gomorrah. His objective was to interpret each of these events as a warning from God of danger facing the nation and to call for repentance and turning to God. Amos could not have given this powerful message unless he had complete confidence in God's absolute control as Lord of nature.

Jeremiah similarly used natural phenomena to bring a

message from God. But there is an interesting development here since Jeremiah assumes that this teaching is so well known that the people ought to be able to interpret for themselves the message of God from the occurrences in nature. It was God's normal pattern to give regular seasons and in this way he blessed the people when they were in a right relationship with him. When he was displeased with the nation this regular pattern in nature was disturbed.

Jeremiah accused the nation of being 'foolish and senseless people, who have eyes but do not see, who have ears but do not hear'. They should have been able to understand what God was saying to them through what was happening in nature.

> But these people have stubborn and rebellious hearts; they have turned aside and gone away. They do not say to themselves, 'Let us fear the Lord our God, who gives autumn and spring rains in season, and who assures us of regular weeks of harvest.' Your wrong doings have kept these away; your sins have deprived you of good (Jer 5.21–25).

The teaching that God is the Lord of nature reaches its height in the pure monotheism of the central chapters of Isaiah where God is declared to be the creator of all things who 'has measured the waters in the hollow of his hand'. God had marked off the heavens with the breadth of his hand; he 'weighed the mountains on the scales' (Is 40.12).

According to the prophet's teaching God was the one who sat 'enthroned above the circle of the earth' and who 'stretches out the heavens like a canopy' (40.22). His confidence in God was such that he was able to declare that 'the Lord is the everlasting God, the creator of the ends of the earth' (40.28).

This teaching reaches its height in chapter 45 where God is shown to be totally in control of the world of nature where he and he alone is the almighty and sovereign God.

> I am the Lord, and there is no other; apart from me there is no God. . . . From the rising of the sun to the place of its setting men

146

may know there is none besides me. I am the Lord, and there is no other. I form the light and create darkness, I bring prosperity and create disaster; I, the Lord, do all these things (Is 45.5–7).

Lord of History

All the prophets regarded God as the Lord of history. From the earliest prophets of Israel onwards they consistently taught that God was in control of the destiny of Israel and that his power was sufficient to guarantee the protection of the nation provided the people were faithful to him. The gods of the other nations were powerless before the God of Israel. Although God's primary interest was in the nation Israel, when Israel became involved with other nations God exercised his authority over them. This was the teaching of some of the earliest prophets as, for example, when Samuel called the people together and made his farewell speech.

Samuel made the people stand before him while he confronted them with what he called the evidence of all the righteous acts performed by the Lord for the nation. He reminded them that it was God who had brought their forefathers out of Egypt and settled them in the land.

> But they forgot the Lord their God; so he sold them into the hands of Sisera, the commander of the army of Hazor, and into the hands of the Philistines and the king of Moab, who fought against them. They cried out to the Lord and said, 'We have sinned; we have forsaken the Lord and served the Baals and the Ashtoreths. But now deliver us from the hands of our enemies, and we will serve you.' Then the Lord sent Gideon, Barak, Jephthah and Samuel, and he delivered you from the hands of your enemies on every side, so that you lived securely (1 Sam 12.9–11).

Samuel's speech clearly shows his view of history. God was more powerful than the Baals; he was able to save his people when they cried out to him and thus he was able to direct the course of their history. The prophet Nathan reflects the same view of history in bringing the word of the

147

Lord to David as recorded in 2 Samuel 7.5–16 and 1 Chronicles 17.4–14.

The eighth-century prophets Amos and Hosea both refer to God having brought the nation up out of Egypt (Am 2.10 and Hos 12.9;13.4). Amos also refers to the neighbouring nations around Israel and warned that God will punish them for their wickedness. Clearly he believed that God not only controlled the destiny of Israel but also the surrounding nations. Nearly two centuries later Jeremiah recognised God's authority over both Assyria and Babylon. He said, 'Therefore this is what the Lord Almighty, the God of Israel, says: "I will punish the king of Babylon and his land as I punished the king of Assyria"' (Jer 50.18). Jeremiah saw that God controlled the history of many nations for he spoke of the way God would destroy Babylon by stirring up an alliance of great nations against them (Jer 50.9). Isaiah also had seen God's ability to call for nations far away to come and do his bidding in bringing judgment against his own rebellious people. 'He lifts up a banner for the distant nations, he whistles for those at the ends of the earth. Here they come swiftly and speedily!' (Is 5.26). But it is not until the exile that the understanding of God as universal Lord of history in control of all the nations became fully explicit, although there are hints of this in Isaiah's reference to God shaking the nations 'in the sieve of destruction' (Is 30.28) and in Jeremiah's reference to God as 'king of the nations' in the rather uncharacteristic poem of chapter 10 (10.7).

In Isaiah 40 the sovereignty of God is spelt out in such terms that

> . . . the nations are like a drop in a bucket; they are regarded as dust on the scales . . . Before him all the nations are as nothing; they are regarded by him as worthless and less than nothing (Is 40.15,17).

This teaching lays the foundation for God calling Cyrus to accomplish his purpose of overthrowing Babylon and releasing the captives so that the remnant of the nation could return to Judah. Even though Cyrus did not know him or acknowledge his name, God had the power to take hold of him and use him to subdue the nations and thereby to carry out his purposes (Is 45.1–5).

The experience of the exile and the fulfilment of prophecy in the overthrow of Babylon and the return of the remnant to rebuild Jerusalem laid the foundation for the later prophets to look forward to the day when God would establish his authority over all the nations as sovereign Lord of history, which is the picture presented in such passages as Zechariah 14.

God of Ethical Requirements

The prophets spoke with one voice against ritual excesses. The unnamed prophet of 1 Kings 13 went to Bethel to declaim against the whole sacrificial system in the northern kingdom of Israel as instituted by Jeroboam. In the prophetic tradition ritualistic sacrifices on the high places that were practised throughout the land were synonymous with idolatry.

Amos is scathing in his denunciation of religious ritual.

I hate, I despise your religious feasts; I cannot stand your assemblies. Even though you bring me burnt offerings and grain offerings, I will not accept them. Though you bring choice fellowship offerings, I will have no regard for them. Away with the noise of your songs! I will not listen to the music of your harps (Am 5.21–23).

Amos' concern was for justice and righteousness rather than the mere outward show of religion. 'Let justice roll on like a river,' he cried, 'and righteousness like a never failing stream!' To Amos the whole religious sacrificial system was a sign of syncretism and unfaithfulness to God. It had crept into Israel's religion during the early years of settlement in Canaan and had never been thoroughly purged despite the protests of the prophets in each generation. As far back as Joshua the clear warning had been given not to worship the

149

Canaanite Baals and Ashtoreths or disaster would come upon the nation (see Joshua 24.14–24).

Amos questions whether any of the current sacrificial practices were to be traced back beyond the settlement in Canaan. He asks, 'Did you bring me sacrifices and offerings for forty years in the desert, O house of Israel?' (5.25). The answer clearly anticipated is, No! If we look back to the time when Moses presented the Law to the people we can see the force of the question Amos raises. Exodus 34.22 says, 'Celebrate the feast of weeks with the first fruits of the wheat harvest, and the feast of ingathering at the turn of the year.' This must refer to a future period as it clearly was not possible for Israel during Moses' lifetime. The Israelites did not grow wheat throughout the period of their wanderings in the wilderness, neither could they possibly have observed a great end-of-the-year harvest festival. The previous verse says, 'Six days you shall labour, but on the seventh day you shall rest; even during the ploughing season and harvest you must rest.' Most Israelites would not have seen a plough until they had crossed the Jordan and begun to settle among the Canaanites and to learn the ways of an agricultural and settled pastoral people. It took them a long time to learn these skills and for many years they did not even know how to make a plough, as the Philistines were the only blacksmiths (see 1 Sam 13.19–21).

It was the local people, the Canaanites, Amorites and others, who taught Israel how to till the soil. Along with these agricultural practices they taught them the requirements of the local gods who controlled the land, its fertility and rainfall. It is to this period that we may trace most of the sacrificial ritual that was current religious practice throughout Israel and Judah in the eighth century during the ministry of Amos. Hence he could declare scathingly, 'You have lifted up the shrine of your king, the pedestal of your idols, the star of your god—which you made for yourselves' (5.26).

The end-of-the-year great harvest festival was probably

what Amos was referring to when he said, 'I hate, I despise your religious feasts.' This became largely associated with the fertility cults of Ashtoreth, or the Asherah poles. They were predominantly sex cults and included both male and female shrine prostitution. These practices all became incorporated into the religion of Israel and Judah. Manasseh, for example, even introduced these practices into the Temple. They were later cleared out in Josiah's reform (see 2 Kings 23.4–7; for the practices in the northern kingdom see 2 Kings 17.7–20). These idolatrous practices included child sacrifice as part of the fertility rites which were roundly condemned by the prophets.

Jeremiah is representative of the prophets' anger at the disgusting sacrificial practices that had crept into the syncretistic worship of the nation when he spoke with horror about what he saw in Jerusalem.

> The people of Judah have done evil in my eyes, declares the Lord. They have set up their detestable idols in the house that bears my Name and have defiled it (Jer 7.30).

He saw the whole nation as being guilty, because everyone was involved in idolatry, even the children who gathered wood so that their fathers could light a fire for the women to make cakes for the Queen of Heaven.

The prophets, however, were not simply against ritual practices, their major concern was to present the true requirements of God which were ethical. Micah states clearly the contrast between current religious practices in the late eighth century and the true ethical requirements of God.

> With what shall I come before the Lord and bow down before the exalted God? Shall I come before him with burnt offerings, with calves a year old? Will the Lord be pleased with thousands of rams, with ten thousand rivers of oil? Shall I offer my firstborn for my transgression, the fruit of my body for the sin of my soul? He has showed you, O man, what is good. And what does the Lord require of you? To act justly and to love mercy and to walk humbly with your God (Mic 6.6–8).

Hosea sums up the same thoughts in a single sentence, 'For I desire mercy, not sacrifice, and acknowledgment of God rather than burnt offerings' (Hos 6.6). Jeremiah brought a similar word from God, 'What do I care about incense from Sheba or sweet calamus from a distant land? Your burnt offerings are not acceptable; your sacrifices do not please me' (Jer 6.20).

It was not simply that the prophets disliked the disgusting practices of animal sacrifice, the detestable practices of ritual fornication or even the unthinkable horror of human sacrifice; their opposition to the whole sacrificial system was because their thinking about God was on an entirely different plane. To the ordinary Israelites sin was the neglect of ritual, but to the prophets it was the *violation of moral law*. This had the effect of severing the relationship between God and his people through the breaking of the covenant that he had established with them and into which they had voluntarily entered.

It was on these moral grounds that the prophets set about exposing the evil practices of the nation. 'The sins of Ephraim are exposed and the crimes of Samaria are revealed,' cried Hosea. 'They practise deceit, thieves break into houses, bandits rob in the streets; but they do not realise that I remember all their evil deeds' (Hos 7.1,2). Amos thundered against the merchants who were cheating with dishonest scales and the bribery and corruption that ran from top to bottom of society (Am 8.4–6). Jeremiah echoed the same demand for justice as Amos and other eighth-century prophets had done—

> This is what the Lord says; Do what is just and right. Rescue from the hand of his oppressor the one who has been robbed. Do no wrong or violence to the alien, the fatherless or the widow, and do not shed innocent blood in this place (Jer 22.3).

Ezekiel's description of what constituted a righteous man in chapter 18 is very informative since it is almost wholly ethical. According to the prophet such a man would shun idolatry, not commit adultery or other sexual perversions; would refrain from oppression, robbery and lending money at excessive interest; he would give to the hungry and the poor and would keep the law of the Lord. According to Ezekiel the requirements of righteousness are purely ethical, with no mention of ritual or sacrifice which, during the exile which was the period of Ezekiel's ministry, would have been impossible.

For a post-exilic view of the requirements of God the emphasis in Isaiah 58 is very largely ethical. Again there is no mention of sacrifices of any kind. The ritual that is here under scrutiny is not the blood of bulls and goats but religious fasting. The question the returned exiles were asking of God was 'Why have we fasted and you have not seen it? Why have we humbled ourselves and you have not noticed?' (Is 58.3). The prophet answered the question by outlining the ethical failures of those who exploited their workers, who quarrelled and fought and thought that one day of fasting and symbolic humbling by lying on sackcloth was pleasing to God.

> Is that what you call a fast, a day acceptable to the Lord? Is not this the kind of fasting I have chosen; to loose the chains of injustice and untie the cords of the yoke, to set the oppressed free and break every yoke? Is it not to share your food with the hungry and to provide the poor wanderer with shelter—when you see the naked, to clothe him? . . . If you spend yourselves on behalf of the hungry and satisfy the needs of the oppressed then your light will rise in the darkness. . . . Your people will rebuild the ancient ruins and will raise up the age-old foundations; you will be called Repairer of Broken Walls, Restorer of Streets with Dwellings (58.6–12).

The final exhortation in chapter 58 is about keeping the Sabbath. It would thus appear that the exile cleansed the nation of many of the detestable practices introduced to them when they entered Canaan and against which the prophets uniformly warned. In the immediate post-exilic period the emphasis was simply upon fulfilling the law in

153

regard to Sabbath observance and right ethical behaviour with the strong emphasis upon justice and caring for the needy. Gone are the prophetic warnings against idolatry. Sin in the post-exilic period had become more subtle!

God of Universal Morality
The opening chapters of Amos contain an incredible pronouncement. Amos says:

> This is what the Lord says: 'For three sins of Moab, even for four, I will not turn back my wrath. Because he burned, as if to lime, the bones of Edom's king, I will send fire upon Moab that will consume the fortresses of Kerioth' (Am 2.1,2).

Although the prophets did not hesitate to make pronouncements about other nations, for Amos to say that God would punish Moab for a wicked act against Edom was quite startling. The Israelites gathered at Bethel listening to the prophet would have applauded enthusiastically all his pronouncements recorded in chapter 1 where he spoke judgment against the neighbouring nations whom they hated. But his pronouncement against Moab would have been received with, at best, incredulity.

Amos' pronouncement against Moab represents a great leap forward in the concept of God as a God of universal morality. It was a well established part of the prophetic ministry to speak of God bringing judgment upon other nations for their cruelty to Israel just as he had punished the Egyptians who had chased after the fleeing slaves when he brought his people out of that land of oppression. But it was an entirely new thought for God to punish a nation for a wicked act against another nation where it had no bearing upon Israel whatsoever. Amos was seeing God as one who was concerned with moral standards among all the nations and whose jurisdiction was not bounded by the borders of Israel and Judah. There can be little doubt that this prophecy would not have been greeted with much enthusiasm, particularly if we compare it with the pronouncements of

Obadiah who demonstrates the fierce hostility that both Israel and Judah felt towards Edom. Amos chooses to ignore this and declares that God will punish Moab for her cruelty to Edom's king.

Many of the prophets made pronouncements against other nations. Indeed, most of the prophets demonstrate their belief that there will come a day when God will judge all nations. Nahum prophesied against Nineveh, Zechariah chapter 9 speaks about the judgment God will bring upon the neighbouring states surrounding Israel and Isaiah devotes considerable time to words against Assyria, Babylon, Moab, Syria, Cush and Egypt (Isaiah chapters 10 to 23) and Jeremiah refers to a day when God will punish all the nations.

> 'The days are coming,' declares the Lord, 'when I will punish all who are circumcised only in flesh—Egypt, Judah, Edom, Ammon, Moab and all who live in the desert in distant places. For all these nations are really uncircumcised, and even the whole house of Israel is uncircumcised in heart' (Jer 9.25,26).

The figure of the Messiah as depicted in Isaiah 11 and upon whom the Spirit of the Lord will rest, shows him as one who will judge righteously. His jurisdiction is foreseen to be not only over Israel but 'with justice he will give decisions for the poor of the earth. He will strike the earth with the rod of his mouth; and with the breath of his lips he will slay the wicked' (11.4). Similarly, in the Servant Songs the Servant of the Lord is seen as one who will establish justice far beyond the borders of Israel, 'In faithfulness he will bring forth justice; he will not falter or be discouraged until he establishes justice on the earth. In his law the islands will put their hope' (Is 42.4). And in 51.4 there is the declaration that God's justice 'will become a light for the nations'. He would one day establish himself as the God of universal morality.

God of the Covenant

The covenant established by God with Israel from the time of Moses and solemnly renewed under Joshua's leadership towards the end of his life (Joshua 24) was the basis of the relationship between God and the nation. It was this relationship that lay at the heart of the ministry of the prophets. They continually reminded both leaders and people that their forefathers had entered into this solemn covenant which bound the nation for all time to God. The relationship involved mutual obligations. Provided the nation was faithful to God in carrying out his commands he would watch over them, protect them and provide for them.

The history of Israel from Moses to the exile, generation after generation, could be written in a series of sayings such as 'And Israel departed from the covenant with the Lord their God and served other gods and the Lord handed them over to the Philistines/Amorites/Midianites/Syria/Egypt/Assyria/Babylon who oppressed them, and the people cried out to the Lord their God, and the Lord heard them and he raised up Samuel/Jephthah/Gideon/David/Hezekiah etc, and the Lord delivered them out of the hands of their enemies.'

The prophets knew God as the God of covenant who was faithful in all his dealings with his people. Time and again throughout their history he had forgiven them and although they were faithless he remained faithful. In his great love and mercy he continually called the people back to him and re-established the broken relationship through his willingness to forgive.

Hosea catalogued the idolatry and faithlessness of the people in his day which he saw as breaking the covenant with God and thereby placing the nation in imminent danger.

> Put the trumpet to your lips! An eagle is over the house of the Lord because the people have broken my covenant and rebelled against my law. Israel cries out to me, 'O our God, we acknowledge you!' But Israel has rejected what is good; an enemy will pursue him (Hos 8.1,2).

Similarly, Jeremiah reminded the people of the terms of the covenant and the dire consequences of breaking them. He was commanded by God to say:

This is what the Lord, the God of Israel says; cursed is the man who does not obey the terms of this covenant—the terms I commanded your forefathers when I brought them out of Egypt, out of the iron smelting furnace. I said, obey me and do everything I command you, and you will be my people, and I will be your God. . . . From the time I brought your forefathers up from Egypt until today, I warned them again and again, saying, 'Obey me'. But they did not listen or pay attention . . . So I brought on them all the curses of the covenant (Jer 11.3–8).

Jeremiah continued to warn that the idolatry in the nation in his day was breaking the terms of the covenant and the inescapable result would be disaster (11.10–13).

Out of the bitter experience of exile Ezekiel looked forward to the time when God would re-establish his covenant and make it an everlasting covenant (Eze 16.59–63). Following his vision of the restored nation rising again out of the valley of dry bones he received the prophecy that the new and everlasting covenant that God would establish with Israel would be a covenant of peace. 'I will make a covenant of peace with them; it will be an everlasting covenant. . . . I will be their God and they will be my people' (Eze 37.26,27).

The theme of an everlasting covenant of peace is reiterated in the unforgettable words of Isaiah 54.10:

Though the mountains be shaken and the hills be removed, yet my unfailing love for you will not be shaken nor my covenant of peace be removed, says the Lord, who has compassion on you.

It was this promise that provided the firm foundation for the ministries of the later prophets through all the difficult years of the post-exilic period.

It was, however, Jeremiah in the bitter days just prior to the destruction of Jerusalem and the exile in Babylon who received the sublime revelation of the new covenant that God would one day establish with his people. Of all the prophets of ancient Israel Jeremiah's ministry was the most tragic. Yet there was none more faithful to God. His was a lonely ministry full of suffering and the bitterness of being despised and rejected by the people of his day. His was a lonely life, at times even barred from worship in the Temple. In the whole of the Old Testament there is no more poignant passage than Jeremiah's cry to God in chapter 20. He lived in a world alone with his God, learning to stand in his presence and to shut out the world that he might listen more attentively.

For forty years Jeremiah saw the disaster coming upon the land but time and again it was delayed. He lived in a day when the authenticity of the prophet was attested mainly by the fulfilment of his predictions. Jeremiah himself believed this, which increased the agony of his suffering, and it is reflected in chapter 20. But it was this bitter pain of spirit that led him to one of the greatest advances in understanding spiritual truth. Again and again throughout the history of Israel they had broken the covenant with God through deliberate rebellion, although it had never been broken on God's side. In his own lifetime he had seen the reforms of Josiah carried through, based on the book of the covenant, but the hope it engendered was short-lived and the people soon returned to the most detestable practices of idolatry. What was needed was a new form of covenant, not based upon a book or upon ritual sacrifice, but a covenant that would enter so deeply into the hearts and minds of men as to make it as impossible for man to break as for God.

Jeremiah saw that a mere written covenant was worthless whether it was written on a scroll or on solid stone; the new covenant had to be written deep within the spirit of each individual. Hence his sublime prophecy, 'I will put my law in their minds and write it on their hearts, I will be their God and they will be my people' (Jer 31.33). Jeremiah could not have known that it would be 600 years before this prophecy would be fulfilled and just as the old covenant had been sealed through the blood of a lamb without spot or blemish so the new covenant was to be sealed by the one who said, 'This is my blood of the new covenant which is shed for many.'

The Purposes of God

In this chapter we have been reviewing the teaching of the prophets and in this final section we shall attempt to summarise briefly the purposes of God as revealed through the message of the prophets. We have already noted the development of the message of the prophets over the years and inevitably the purposes of God are revealed most clearly in the writings of the later prophets who were able to draw upon all that God had revealed to his servants over the centuries and were also able to look back over the history of the nation and interpret the deeds of the Lord. We have already noted that the prophets learned much about the purposes of God through his actions in dealing with his people and with the surrounding nations.

Remnant and Restoration

The exile in Babylon following the destruction of Jerusalem was not only a turning point in the history of the nation, it was a watershed in religious experience. The destruction of the Temple and the separation from the land, were shattering blows, but they had the effect of proving unmistakably that the God of Israel was not confined to a small piece of land where he exercised jurisdiction like the local Baals and false gods of the Gentile nations. The discovery that he could be worshipped in a foreign land, that his presence was with them, that he could still speak to his people through prophets such as Ezekiel who lived and ministered among the exiles, was a major step forward in religious experience and in the understanding of the nature and purposes of God.

Even before the exile the word 'remnant' was being freely used by the prophets. They saw that the destruction of the nation was inevitable in the face of their persistent idolatry and rebellion against God who would not defend an unholy nation. In the early days of his ministry Isaiah saw Assyria as the major threat and in chapter 11 he looked beyond the destruction to the time when God would send a Saviour and he would regather the 'exiles of Israel' and would 'assemble

159

the scattered people of Judah from the four quarters of the earth'. He said 'There will be a highway for the remnant of his people that is left from Assyria as there was for Israel when they came up from Egypt' (Is 11.12,16).

Jeremiah realised that destruction and exile in Babylon were inevitable but he too looked forward to a time of restoration when God would bring back his people, 'I myself will gather the remnant of my flock out of all the countries where I have driven them' (Jer 23.3). Micah also had spoken of a remnant surviving (see Micah 5.7,8).

The prophets were able to declare with confidence that God would not allow the whole nation to be destroyed, despite the sinfulness of the people, because of his covenant with their forefathers. That covenant was as sure and fixed as the natural laws governing day and night; it was established by the word of God and he would never break it (see Jeremiah 33.19–26). But it was the bitter experience of suffering during the exile itself that brought about the understanding of the way God would work out his purposes through a remnant. This remnant of the people would be cleansed from their sinfulness, from the contamination of foreign gods. It would be a remnant that had learned the bitter lessons of rebellion and whose trust would now be solely in the Lord their God. They would be holy unto him.

It is interesting to note that in one major respect this expectation of the cleansing of the nation through the exile was totally fulfilled, that is in respect of idolatry. Prior to the exile the attention of all the prophets throughout their ministries was largely occupied by combating idolatry and its effects. They continually had to stand against the evil practices of sacrificing to the local Baals, Ashtoreths and their associated evil practices. After the exile there is no mention of such idolatrous practices. The post-exilic prophets had other problems to concern them but idolatry was no longer a besetting sin of the nation. In this respect they were cleansed and the prophecy that a purified remnant would return to the land was fulfilled. Thus it was foreseen that the returning exiles would be called 'the holy people, the redeemed of the Lord' (Is 62.12), and that they would come back with great joy. 'The ransomed of the Lord will return. They will enter Zion with singing; everlasting joy will crown their heads' (Is 51.11). This joy would be that of a cleansed and renewed people. To them God would say;

> See, I have refined you, though not as silver; I have tested you in the furnace of affliction (Is 48.10).

Light to Gentiles
God's purpose in bringing this cleansed and purified remnant back to the land and back into the full blessings of the covenant relationship with himself was so that he could work out his purposes through them:

> The sun will no more be your light by day, nor will the brightness of the moon shine on you, for the Lord will be your everlasting light, and your God will be your glory (Is 60.19).

God's intention had always been that he would reveal himself to the nations through that nation he had called into a covenant relationship with himself. Now, through the purified remnants, he would be able to accomplish that purpose by using them to relay and reflect the light of his glory to all the nations.

The idealised Israel was to be the Servant of the Lord. To them he made the promise:

> I, the Lord, have called you in righteousness; I will take hold of your hand. I will keep you and make you to be a covenant for the people and a light for the Gentiles, to open eyes that are blind, to free captives from prison and to release from the dungeon those who sit in darkness (Is 42.6,7).

The fact that this prophecy was not fulfilled through the whole company of returning exiles but through a remnant of one, in the person of the Messiah, does not invalidate the prophecy. The Servant of the Lord in the central chapters of

Isaiah is capable of both interpretations, as an idealised group or as an individual Messianic figure.

The same phrase, 'a light for the Gentiles', occurs in chapter 49 where it more clearly refers to the servanthood of the nation and in particular to the restored remnant, although once again it is capable of interpretation in the single representative person of the Messiah.

> It is too small a thing for you to be my servant to restore the tribes of Jacob and to bring back those of Israel I have kept. I will also make you a light for the Gentiles, that you may bring my salvation to the ends of the earth (49.6).

The fact that this prophecy is set firmly within the context of the return from Babylon and the restoration of Israel is an indication of God's original intention and desire in choosing Israel to reveal himself to all the nations through them and to communicate his word through them to the whole world.

Universal Knowledge of God
God's clear intention was to radiate knowledge of himself throughout the world and in order to accomplish this he had chosen a nation that was capable of reaching the sublime heights of spiritual understanding that was attained by the prophets and is particularly reflected in the central and later chapters of Isaiah. In chapter 56 God's objective in communicating his salvation to others is clearly announced. That salvation is to include foreigners who love the Lord and are faithful to him. They will actually be given a place within the Temple and 'foreigners who bind themselves to the Lord to serve him, to love the name of the Lord and to worship him' would be allowed to enter into the joy of the Lord in his house of prayer which 'will be called a house of prayer for all nations' (Is 56.3–8).

There is an interesting prayer of confession in the song of praise in Isaiah 26 which most scholars assign to a late date since it also contains references to the resurrection of the dead which did not enter the religion of Israel until well into the post-exilic period. The prayer is clearly that of a people who have experienced the suffering of exile and the joy of being restored to their own land.

> Lord, you establish peace for us; all that we have accomplished you have done for us. O Lord, our God, other lords besides you have ruled over us but your name alone do we honour.... Lord, they came to you in their distress; when you disciplined them, they could barely whisper a prayer.

The confession then follows that they were like a woman in labour who cried out in pain but who did not give birth to a healthy child.

> We have not brought salvation to the earth; we have not given birth to people of the world (Is 26.12–18).

God's purpose in re-gathering his people was so that all the nations of the world would see his glory and recognise that he had fulfilled his word and kept his covenant with his own people. Through them, this cleansed and purified remnant, he would communicate the knowledge of his nature, the understanding of his purposes and his great salvation to all the nations of the world.

Judgment of the Nations

It is an unpleasant but unavoidable fact that the subject of judgment occurs largely throughout Scripture. Even in the teaching of Jesus he speaks more of judgment than he does of love. He makes only two or three direct references to the love of God (John 3.16; 14.23 and possibly Luke 11.42) whereas he makes scores of references to judgment, to trials and tribulations and to a future time of turmoil and destruction coming upon the world.

The belief that God would one day establish his justice throughout the world brought the prophets to the understanding that all nations would be judged by God. They were constantly aware of the evil of mankind, the violence in the very nature of man, the cruelty of nation to nation. The situation of Israel and Judah as tiny buffer states in central Palestine en route between Egypt in the south and the great empires of the north, brought successive invasions and great suffering upon the people to whom the prophets ministered. In their understanding of the sovereignty of God nothing happened without his allowing it even if it was not part of his perfect will and his best intention for his people. Because of their sinfulness he allowed the nation to suffer but the day would come when he would punish those whom he used to discipline his own people. God would punish the Gentile nations for their arrogance, cruelty and shedding of innocent blood.

But the prophets saw that the problem of man's violence and wilful rebellion against God was universal. If God had so much trouble in disciplining his own people how much greater was the problem with nations of unbelievers. The Spirit of God began to make it clear to the prophets that things would get much worse before they could get better. Hence there was revealed to some of the prophets pictures of the most fearful destruction that would occur among the nations before God would eventually intervene and carry out his ultimate purposes for the good of mankind.

Reference has already been made in chapter 6 to scenes of world-wide destruction in Isaiah 24 whereby the crust of the earth is split and the whole world is shaken (v19). The whole world is said to be engulfed in flames so that most of the 'earth's inhabitants are burned up, and very few are left' (v6). The reason given for this world-wide scene of destruction is that the people of the world have polluted the earth by their disobedience to natural law. They thereby bring a curse upon themselves that consumes the whole earth (vv5,6).

Similar scenes of destruction are portrayed in Zechariah 14 where it is said that the whole land of Judah, except for Jerusalem, becomes desert 'like the Arabah' (v10). Ezekiel, in the same way as Zechariah, foresees the destruction of the nations occurring following their attack upon Israel. In chapters 38 and 39 he outlines a confederate force of nations attacking Israel resulting in widespread destruction and vast numbers of dead. He says, 'For seven months the house of

Israel will be burying them in order to cleanse the land.' Many of the dead appear to be dangerous to touch so that men have to go through the land and when they see a human bone they set up a marker beside it so that it can be removed to a particular valley where the gravediggers will bury all the contaminated bodies. This has led some biblical scholars to conclude that Ezekiel is referring to the effects of modern chemical or germ warfare. This interpretation should be approached with caution since the vision shows the destruction of the enemy occurring through the direct intervention of God.

Universal Peace

Following the time of violence and destruction among the nations there will be universal peace, according to both Zechariah and Ezekiel. This accords with the vision of universal peace recorded by both Micah and Isaiah (Mic 4 and Is 2). Both these prophets foresee the time coming when God will exalt Jerusalem among the nations. Many nations will go to Jerusalem, seeing it as the source of true revelation of God; 'The law will go out from Zion, the word of the Lord from Jerusalem.' And at that time God will settle the disputes of strong nations and,

> They will beat their swords into ploughshares and their spears into pruning hooks. Nation will not take up sword against nation nor will they train for war any more (Mic 4.3 and Is 2.4).

Isaiah foresaw this time of universal peace being established in the Messianic age when God would raise up his servant 'from the stump of Jesse' and having subdued the wicked he will bring into harmony the whole of natural creation so that in that day:

> The wolf will live with the lamb, the leopard will lie down with the goat, the calf and the lion and the yearling together; and a little child will lead them. . . . They will neither harm nor destroy on all my holy mountain, for the earth will be full of the knowledge of the Lord as the waters cover the sea (11.1–9).

165

A similar scene of universal peace is described in Isaiah 65 where God eventually intervenes to create 'a new heaven and a new earth' where the former things are not remembered and where weeping and crying and suffering 'will be heard no more'. Again it is foreseen that 'the wolf and the lamb will feed together, and the lion will eat straw like the ox . . . They will neither harm nor destroy on all my holy mountain, says the Lord' (Is 65.17–25).

God's Final Authority
The objective in God's guiding the destiny of the nations and his intervention in human affairs to judge the nations, to quell the violence and wickedness of men and to establish universal peace, is ultimately to establish his final authority over all creation. In doing this he will ensure that his purposes of communicating his justice and his salvation to the ends of the earth are finally carried out.

There is no loftier vision given to the prophets under the old covenant of God carrying out his ultimate purposes and establishing his final authority over the whole created order and the rebellious nations of mankind than is given in Isaiah 45. In verse 6 it is said that God will be known throughout the entire world as the one and only God.

> So that from the rising of the sun to the place of its setting men may know there is none besides me. I am the Lord, and there is no other (v6).

The purpose of God revealing himself in all his glory and establishing his authority among men is so that every human being will acknowledge him as Lord of all creation.

> By myself I have sworn, my mouth has uttered in all integrity a word that will not be revoked; before me every knee will bow; by me every tongue will swear. They will say of me, 'In the Lord alone are righteousness and strength' (Is 45.23,24).

166

PART 2

PROPHECY IN THE EARLY CHURCH

CHAPTER NINE

PROPHECY AND THE NEW COVENANT

Prophecy played a significant part in the life of the New Testament church. It was exercised both as a ministry and as one of the gifts of the Spirit. There are, however, major differences between prophecy in the Old Testament and prophecy in the New Testament. We shall note below four of the outstanding differences.

Covenant Relationship

In the Old Testament Israel was a nation in a covenant relationship with God. This covenant formed the essential basis for prophecy in that it was a relationship with God into which Israel had *voluntarily* entered. That covenant implied mutual obligations and it was to these that the prophets continually made reference. Without the covenant there could have been no prophecy for it formed the fundamental basis of the appeal the prophets made to the nation, reminding the people of their heritage and calling them back to their promise of faithfulness to Yahweh. It was upon the certain knowledge of God's faithfulness in keeping his covenant promises that the prophets were able to take their stand in delivering the word of God for their times. They knew him to be a faithful God who kept covenant with his people. They

169

could therefore both demand faithfulness from the nation and promise blessings from God with complete confidence.

After the year 70 AD Israel as a state ceased to exist. It is arguable that the covenant relationship with God had already been destroyed at the time of Israel's rejection of the Messiah and the resultant crucifixion of Jesus. It is, however, incontrovertible that the *evidence* that the covenant relationship between God and Israel no longer existed was provided by the events of 70 AD; the destruction of the city of Jerusalem, the slaughter of at least half-a-million Judeans and the dispersal of the remnant across the Roman Empire. The land was resettled and successive conquering armies incorporated it into their empires for nearly 1,900 years.

In the New Testament, the concept of covenant is extended beyond Israel. Even before the destruction of the old nation of Israel the newly formed church, consisting of believers in the Messiahship of Jesus, saw themselves as the true inheritors of the covenant and the promises originally given to Israel. Paul was writing to *Gentiles* in Galatia when he said, 'Now you, brothers, like Isaac, are children of promise' (Gal 4.28).

He reasoned that the promise given to Abraham and his seed related to Christ and that through Christ they had been extended to all who were believers in Christ Jesus, 'What was promised, being given through faith in Jesus Christ, might be given to those who believe' (Gal 3.22). Paul declared that all believers in Messiah Jesus, whether Jew or Gentile, entered into a new relationship with God, as sons of God, and therefore became the seed of Abraham and therefore heirs of the promise. 'You are all sons of God through faith in Christ Jesus . . . If you belong to Christ, then you are Abraham's seed, and heirs according to the promise' (Gal 3.26–29). Paul saw himself and those who preached the gospel as 'ministers of a new covenant' (2 Cor 3.6) established by God through faith in Christ Jesus.

It was therefore *the church* that was in a new covenant relationship with God; a covenant, not written upon stone,

170

but written in the hearts of the believers, as promised in Jeremiah 31.31. They, therefore, were the true inheritors of the promise of God to pour out his Spirit upon his people. The promises given through the prophets to the Israel of the old covenant had now been inherited by the people of the new covenant, Jew and Gentile alike, male and female, slave and free, since all human distinctions were irrelevant among believers where the only qualification was faith in Christ (Ga 3.28).

Israel and the Church

In the Old Testament, prophecy was to Israel. A second major difference between prophecy in the Old Testament and in the New Testament was that under the old covenant, prophecy was to the nation Israel. Even those words of the prophets that were directed towards other nations were apparently delivered to the people of Judah and Israel, or simply spoken aloud by the prophets in much the same way as they addressed the mountains of Israel, or as Ezekiel spoke the word of God into the valley full of dry bones. There is no evidence of any of the prophets actually going to Edom, or to Moab or Syria, or Egypt and actually delivering the word of the Lord to any of the leaders of those nations. Ezekiel prophesied in Babylon, but he spoke to the Israelites in captivity there, and as far as we know he did not address the Babylonians although he was in an ideal position to do so. Elisha was sent to anoint Ben Hadad as the next king of Syria, but it is quite possible that he met him in Israel. In any case this was a private ceremony and there is no evidence that he addressed the Syrian people. The nearest we get to such an action is in the story of the reluctant Jonah going to Nineveh. But this account, which many scholars believe to be allegorical, clearly has a strong spiritual message to convey to Israel. It is in line with some of the sayings of Jesus to the towns of Galilee that if the mighty things done in them had been performed in Sodom and Gomorrah then the people would have repented.

The prophets of the old covenant were called by God

to prophesy to the nation whom God had called into that special relationship with himself and when words were given that were directed towards other nations they were spoken to Israel so that they should understand God's purposes in the world. The reason why God revealed to Israel his thoughts concerning other nations was so that they would understand what he was doing and thereby be able to fulfil their servanthood and thus be used to carry out the purposes of God.

In the New Testament, prophecy under the new covenant was to *the church* not to any particular nation. The believers who formed the church were drawn from many nations and races. Through belief in Christ that had brought them into the new relationship with God they had entered a new relationship with each other. Although humanly speaking they were from many nations and therefore not a nation at all, yet in Christ they had become a single united people.

> You are a chosen people, a royal priesthood, a holy nation, a people belonging to God, that you may declare the praises of him who called you out of darkness into his wonderful light. Once you were not a people, but now you are the people of God (1 Pet 2.9,10).

That last sentence is one of the most sociologically significant statements in the whole New Testament. God has, in Christ, created a community out of diversity. He had brought together those who were divided by race, language, nationality, culture and social rank. It was to them that divine revelation was given. Prophecy in the New Testament, therefore, was not spoken to any one nation or race but to this new community of believers, who once had nothing in common, but who had now been brought together by their common faith in Christ.

Guidance

In the Old Testament, prophecy was to guide Israel. Prophecy under the old covenant was given by God for the specific purpose of guiding the nation, particularly in times of crisis, so that they would be enabled to fulfil the purposes of God. We have already established that prophets were not appointed by men but were called by God and were given divine revelation to enable them to carry out their task. Where it was necessary for them to see into the future and to understand the consequences of the present policy being followed by the leaders of the nation, they were given this understanding. It was given them so that they could rightly proclaim the word of God to call the nation back from apostasy into the centre of the divine will so that through them God could work out his purposes to bring all the nations into a right relationship with himself and to harmonise the whole of his natural creation.

In the New Testament, prophecy had a similar purpose, to give guidance and clear direction to the believers to enable the church to carry out the mission of Christ. Where it was necessary for the believers to know the consequences of their own actions or the policies being followed by the nations, the divine revelation was given, so the mission of Christ should not founder. The Acts of the Apostles clearly records the spread of the gospel from city to city and from province to province as being directed by the Spirit, *ie* by prophetic revelation.

Thus the church, as the inheritor of the promise of the Spirit, was able to fulfil the purposes of God to bring light to the Gentile nations and to carry the message of God's salvation to all the nations of the world though the revelation of divine truth was prophetically give.

Contrasting the Old and the New
In the Old Testament, prophecy was an individual ministry. Under the old covenant it was given by God to outstanding individuals. They were the great men and women of faith who were called into special relationship with God and were privileged to stand in the council of the Lord to receive the revelation of divine truth that they proclaimed to the nation. Through the anointing of the Spirit of God upon their lives they were not only enabled to receive the word but also given the power to deliver it. Their delivery was

directed by God. When the Spirit of the Lord came upon them they performed actions of prophetic significance or they spoke words of prophetic insight under the direction of the Spirit of God that could be recognised and respected even by those who hated and rejected the word.

In the New Testament, prophecy, by contrast, was for *everyone*. The Spirit of God was not simply to be seen in the lives of great individuals, as under the old covenant, but now was to be seen in the lives of all believers. It was the whole company of believers together at Pentecost who received the Holy Spirit and wherever the gospel was proclaimed those who became true believers received the Holy Spirit.

When we come to examine the practice of prophecy in the New Testament church in more detail we shall note that, while all the believers were able to exercise the gift of prophecy, there were some whose major ministry was that of the prophet. For the moment we simply want to emphasise that in contrast to the old covenant, under which individuals were given the Spirit of God to enable them to proclaim the word of the living God, under the new covenant this privilege was given to all— all the believers received the Holy Spirit. He enabled them to be his witnesses, to proclaim the word of God to the nations.

In the New Testament we see the fulfilment of God's intention that the whole company of believers should be a prophetic people, his witnesses in the world, in order to fulfil the Great Commission of Jesus to go into all the world and make disciples of all nations. This was a fulfilment of God's declared intention that had been revealed to the prophets many years earlier. We note below four steps that led to this fulfilment.

The Vision

Moses was the first prophet to the nation of Israel, and he was the first to see the possibility of what eventually happened at Pentecost and began to become a reality in the New Testament church. In Numbers 11 there is the record of Moses wilting under the burden of leadership when the whole nation was groaning under the hardship of life in the desert. Moses was instructed to bring together seventy of Israel's leaders who would share the task of leadership with him. God said to him:

> I will come down and speak with you there, and I will take of the Spirit that is on you and put the Spirit on them. They will help you carry the burden of the people so that you will not have to carry it alone (Num 11.17).

Moses reported this to the people and the seventy elders met with Moses at the special tent reserved for the worship of God. While they were standing there the Spirit of the Lord came upon the elders and 'when the Spirit rested upon them they prophesied . . .' (v25). At this point the Hebrew text is unclear since the same form of the verb could mean a single action or a present continuous tense; hence the different renderings 'but they did not do so again' or 'and they continued to do so' in different translations of the Bible.

The account concludes with the fact that two of the elders, Eldad and Medad, had remained in the camp but the Spirit of God had nevertheless come upon them and they had actually prophesied in the camp; *ie* in the common place, not in the place set apart for holy activities. Joshua regarded this as blasphemy and appealed to Moses to stop them instantly. But Moses, in his greater wisdom, perceived the great significance of this and expressed a prophetic wish that was not fulfilled until the Day of Pentecost more than a thousand years later. 'Are you jealous for my sake?' he asked. 'I wish that all the Lord's people were prophets and that the Lord would put his Spirit on them!' (v29).

The Promise
Moses' wish was given the force of prophecy and pronounced as a direct promise from God through the great prophet of the Exile who wrote chapters 40–59 of Isaiah. From the pen of the one who foresaw the servanthood of Messiah and the message of redemption through suffering there came the promise to those who were suffering the humiliation and pain of slavery and banishment from the land of their fathers.

This is what the Lord says—your Redeemer, the Holy One of Israel: 'For your sake I will send to Babylon and bring down as fugitives all the Babylonians' (Is 43.14).

The promise spoke of God doing something entirely new but this was not the mere act of saving the people from slavery; after all, God had already done that when he overthrew the Egyptians and released his people. The prophet referred to that great act of salvation in the past that was the high spot in the history of Israel, and he rudely said 'Forget it!' 'Forget the former things; do not dwell on the past. See, I am doing a new thing!' (vv18,19).

The new thing God was preparing to do was not simply to make 'a way in the desert and streams in the wasteland' in order to bring the people from Babylon back to the land of Israel, for they were still a faithless people. 'You have not called upon me, O Jacob, you have not wearied yourselves for me, O Israel.' Instead they were a people who had burdened God with their sins and wearied him with their offences (vv22,24). But God was one who forgives, who cleanses his people and who blots out the sins of the past.

A new day would dawn for the people of God. Then the new thing that he promised would come to pass.

For I will pour water on the thirsty land, and streams on the dry ground; I will pour out my Spirit on your offspring, and my blessing on your descendants (Is 44.3).

Thus the new thing God was promising to the exiles would not be fulfilled immediately. It would be fulfilled through the *descendants* of the exiles. God was beginning to prepare the way for that day by bringing them back to the Promised Land, but the promise of the Spirit being poured out was for a later generation, the offspring of those who had been through the terrible experience of exile and slavery, who had been purified from idolatry, redeemed of the Lord, brought back to Israel where God had promised to send his Messiah to lead his people into a new and right relationship with himself the living God.

176

PROPHECY AND THE NEW COVENANT

As Jeremiah had seen, this would be a new relationship that would be the establishment of a new covenant written into the hearts of the people, a covenant that could not be broken like the pieces of stone upon which the old covenant had been written. The new covenant would signify, not a legal bonding, but a spiritual relationship between God and his people (Jer 31.31–34).

The Prophecy

The prophet Joel elaborated the same theme and saw it in an eschatological setting. The date of Joel's ministry in Israel is completely unknown, although there are literary indicators of a post-exilic date and it is that view that is adopted in out present arrangement. The words of Joel are almost too well-known to repeat them here, but it is important to notice exactly what Joel did say concerning the promise of God to pour out his Spirit.

> I will pour out my Spirit on all people. Your sons and daughters will prophesy, your old men will dream dreams, your young men will see visions. Even on my servants, both men and women, I will pour out my Spirit in those days. I will show wonders in the heavens and on the earth, blood and fire and billows of smoke. The sun will be turned to darkness and the moon to blood before the coming of the great and dreadful day of the Lord. And everyone who calls on the name of the Lord will be saved; for on Mount Zion and in Jerusalem there will be deliverance, as the Lord has said, among the survivors whom the Lord calls (Joel 2.28–32).

Joel speaks of the outpouring of the Spirit of God taking place after some kind of holocaust experience which brings devastation upon the nation like an army of locusts spread across the land. He foresaw a time of blessing when God would repay 'for the years the locusts have eaten' and he twice repeated the promise of God, 'Never again will my people be shamed' (2.25–27). The murder of six million Jews in the Nazi concentration camps was undoubtedly a 'shaming of the people'. So if this interpretation is correct

177

PROPHECY PAST AND PRESENT

the fulfilment of Joel's prophecy has to be after 1945. It would appear, therefore, that the fulfilment of the prophecy concerning the outpouring of the Spirit of God upon all people has yet to take place.

The Fulfilment
Why then did the apostle Peter quote the Joel prophecy to the Jerusalem crowd on the Day of Pentecost? There were no apocalyptic signs in the heavens on that day, although the sun was turned to darkness on Good Friday and very probably, as a consequence, the moon appeared to be blood-red that night. But the second coming of the Lord Jesus did not take place on the Day of Pentecost; unless it is held that the coming of the Holy Spirit was the return of Jesus. One is then faced with the question: Why then did the belief in a second coming of Christ persist throughout New Testament time, long after the Day of Pentecost?

Peter's reason for quoting Joel was not because the prophecy was totally fulfilled at Pentecost but that it began to be fulfilled on that day. Peter specifically relates the events of that day to the prophecy of Joel. But it is important to note the context. Luke says that Peter cited Joel to the Jerusalem crowd to account for the behaviour of the believers—a group numbering about 120, according to Acts 1.15—who were all together in one place on the Day of Pentecost when the Spirit of God came upon them. They made such a noise that a crowd gathered around them. Despite the fact that many visitors from other parts of the world heard the word of God proclaimed in their own languages, the believers were charged with drunkenness. It was in the face of *this charge* that Peter quoted the Joel prophecy.

The essence of Peter's declaration was that these men and women were not drunk—they were *prophesying!*

It was indeed a remarkable event; a crowd of people, 120 strong, spilling out into the narrow streets of Jerusalem, over-flowing with spiritual ecstasy from the outpouring of the Holy Spirit they had collectively experienced, and speaking in strange tongues. Some were shouting and praising God, others began immediately to fulfil the Great Commission of Jesus to proclaim the gospel and make disciples of all nations. They began to declare the word of the Lord to the numerous overseas visitors, Jews of the dispersion, in the city for the festival. They declared themselves to be witnesses to the resurrection of Messiah Jesus. The great excitement in their voices and the strange message they conveyed convinced some of the scoffers that these people were simply a bunch of drunks. Peter silenced the crowd and reminded them of the prophecy of Joel that most of them would have known in its messianic/eschatological significance.

Peter's interpretation certainly indicated that a new day had dawned. It was *the beginning* of a new age. God was doing a new thing. It was beginning that very day. Peter's emphasis was not upon eschatological signs, but upon the fact that the believers were prophesying. They were not drunk, they had been anointed with the Holy Spirit to declare the word of the Lord with power. This was *prophesying!* The believers were the mouthpiece of God, declaring the counsel of the Lord. They were not like the great individual prophets of the old covenant; this was the new thing God had promised, 'Your sons and daughters will prophesy, your young men will see visions, and your old men will dream dreams.'

The Spirit of God would be poured out on all believers without regard to sex, or age, or social status. Men and women would prophesy, young and old would receive revelation, free men and slaves—yes 'even on my servants, both men and women, I will pour out my Spirit in those days'. At this point, in order to ram home the message, Peter added some words to the prophecy of Joel, '*and they will prophesy*'.

Peter deliberately added those words to emphasise the point he was making. It was the anointing of the Holy Spirit that was responsible for the phenomenon the crowd was seeing—simple unlettered people from all walks of life,

179

both male and female, were prophesying in the streets of Jerusalem declaring the word of the living God. The reason they were doing this was because they were witnesses to the resurrection of the Lord Jesus. Peter declared:

> God has raised this Jesus to life, and we are all witnesses of the fact. Exalted to the right hand of God, he has received from the Father the promised Holy Spirit and has poured out what you now see and hear (Acts 2.32,33).

These remarkable events in the streets of Jerusalem changed the lives of three thousand people on that day who repented and were baptised. Peter promised them, 'You will receive the gift of the Holy Spirit. The promise is for you and your children and for all who are far off—for all whom the Lord our God will call' (Acts 2.38,39).

The happenings on the Day of Pentecost, the birthday of the church, the first day of a new age, were a remarkable testimony to the power of prophecy. The prophets of ancient Israel would have rejoiced to see that day. Under the anointing of the Holy Spirit the power of God was given to declare the word of the Lord with such authority that it pierced to the heart of a vast crowd, three thousand of whom made a specific response. With such a multitude being baptised, perhaps at the pool of Siloam, in the heart of Jerusalem, the whole city must have been shaken. The events of that day must have seemed to the authorities who had crucified Jesus six weeks earlier as though the whole city had been turned upside down. Such was the power of prophecy.

The Holy Spirit was God's birthday gift to the church to enable the believers to carry out the Great Commission of Jesus to go to all the world and make disciples of all nations. The church was to be God's prophetic people declaring his word to all the nations in their own tongues. Even the Gentiles were now able to hear 'the wonderful works of God'. The wish of Moses had come true, all the people were prophets; God had put his Spirit upon the whole company of believers in Messiah Jesus.

CHAPTER TEN

THE TEACHING OF JESUS

The definition of prophecy we gave in chapter one is consistent with its use throughout the Bible. The link between prophecy and revelation was firmly established through the ministry of the prophets of ancient Israel. Their authority was not derived from their power as orators or from their charismatic personalities. Their authority was rooted in their claim to be the bearers of the word of God, *ie* to be in possession of divinely revealed truth.

Throughout the New Testament, prophecy and revelation are linked in the same way as we find them in the Old Testament. Prophecy was still being exercised in Israel at the time of the birth of Jesus. Luke's account of the Nativity is followed by the presentation of Jesus in the Temple where he was twice prophesied over. Simeon, a 'righteous and devout' believer who was 'waiting for the consolation of Israel' (a standard rabbinic description of the Messianic Age) was a man of prophetic insight to whom the Holy Spirit had revealed that he would not die until he had seen the fulfilment of God's promise to send Messiah.

Having given thanks for the fulfilment of this promise he saw in the infant Jesus the one who was to bring salvation, to open the eyes of the Gentiles to the truth of God and to lead Israel into the glory of her national destiny. But he also foresaw that 'this child is destined to cause the falling and rising of many in Israel', a phrase that has often been interpreted in individualistic terms but is more likely to have referred to the fall of the whole nation of Israel who would only rise to a fully restored relationship with God through Jesus.

The prophetess Anna, who also was an elderly devout believer spending most of her time in worship and prayer, saw the fulfilment of messianic promise in the infant Jesus and gave thanks to God and prophesied over him. She was one who was 'looking forward to the redemption of Jerusalem', another messianic phrase indicating that Jerusalem was agog with expectation of the fulfilment of prophecy and many devout believers were watching for the revelation of divine truth. The way was thus prepared for the ministry of John the Baptist who was widely held to be a prophet, and subsequently for the ministry of Jesus. But, as always, the message was perceived only by those who had eyes to see and ears to hear.

Jesus himself gave no specific teaching on prophecy except to warn about the dangers of false prophets and to offer some practical advice on how to recognise the false prophet; 'Watch out for false prophets. They come to you in sheep's clothing, but inwardly they are ferocious wolves. By their fruit you will recognise them' (Mt 7.15,16). Jesus, however, did give a considerable amount of teaching to his disciples on revelation. Both by his words and by his personal example he gave a great deal of teaching on the communication of divine truth to man which is the prerequisite of prophecy. We have already noted that prophecy involves the two-fold task —that of *receiving the word of God* and of *delivering the word*, or being 'the mouthpiece of God'. Jesus gave teaching on both these aspects which we shall now examine.

Receiving the Word
We will consider Jesus' teaching on receiving the word in three parts. Listening to the Father; Seeing what the Father is doing; Perceiving the signs.

THE TEACHING OF JESUS

Listening to the Father

Jesus was a great listener. As a boy, on his first visit to Jerusalem for his Bar Mitzvah, he was fascinated by everything to do with the Temple. He simply could not tear himself away from it and was so engrossed in listening to the teaching of the Rabbis that he was not even conscious that Mary and Joseph, together with the other pilgrims from Galilee, had already set off in their caravan for the northern region. This ability to listen became the bedrock of his prayer life.

Prayer, for Jesus, was not a public exhibition as it was for many of the Pharisees who on their way to prayer sometimes had a man precede them blowing a horn. Neither was prayer, for Jesus, the repetition of many words. His instructions were to go away privately and quietly seek the presence of the living God whom he taught his disciples to call 'Father'. He said:

> When you pray, go into your room, close the door and pray to your Father who is unseen. Then your Father, who sees what is done in secret, will reward you. And when you pray, do not keep on babbling like pagans, for they think they will be heard because of their many words (Mt 6.6,7).

Prayer was the lifeline of Jesus' ministry. Even though he was busy teaching and healing late into the night he still began praying before daybreak. 'Very early in the morning, while it was still dark, Jesus got up, left the house and went off to a solitary place, where he prayed' (Mk 1.35). Luke similarly records that it was Jesus' regular habit in the midst of the most demanding period of his Galilean ministry to get away alone for prayer.

> The news about him spread all the more, so that crowds of people came to hear him and to be healed of their sicknesses. But Jesus often withdrew to lonely places and prayed (Lk 5.15,16).

Before undertaking any new phase of ministry, Jesus took time to pray it through with the Father. Hence we find him spending a whole night in prayer before calling all his

183

followers together and choosing twelve of them for their special role as apostles; *apostolous*, literally 'the ones sent'.

> One of those days Jesus went out into the hills to pray, and spent the night praying to God. When morning came, he called his disciples to him and chose twelve of them, whom he also designated apostles (Lk 6.12,13).

Jesus sometimes prayed in private, that is away from the crowds, but with his disciples (Lk 9.18) and sometimes he just took two or three of them up into the hills to be with him during his time of prayer, as at the Transfiguration (Lk 9.28ff). Just before the Crucifixion he spent time praying with his disciples the beautiful prayer that is recorded in John 17. Then, in the Garden of Gethsemane, he took three of them on one side to pray with him but even they fell asleep and heard only a few words of his urgent supplication (Mt 26.37ff).

The prayer life of Jesus was central to his mission and ministry because for Jesus, as for the prophets of the old covenant, prayer and revelation were inseparably linked. It was through prayer that the prophets learned to receive the word of the Lord, and it was through prayer that Jesus communicated with the Father, listened to him and then carried out his will. Even in Gethsemane, although he asked to be spared the agony of crucifixion, he nevertheless affirmed, 'Yet not what I will, but what you will' (Mk 14.36).

Jesus had learned perfect obedience to the Father. He had resisted the onslaught of the enemy at the beginning of his ministry and his own testimony was that he only did what the Father told him to do; 'I do nothing on my own but speak just what the Father has taught me . . . for I always do what pleases him' (Jn 8.28). Again and again Jesus emphasised that he spoke only what he had already received from the Father. 'Whatever I say is just what the Father told me to say' (Jn 12.50). 'The words I say to you are not just my own. Rather, it is the Father, living in me, who is doing his work' (Jn 14.10).

184

THE TEACHING OF JESUS

Jesus emphasised the importance of prayer for him. It was through listening to the Father that he received the word he was to proclaim publicly. 'What I have heard from him I tell the world' (Jn 8.26). Again and again he emphasised his own powerlessness to do anything on his own. He gave all the glory to the Father. His duty was to listen attentively, to be obedient and to speak exactly the words that the Father gave to him.

> By myself I can do nothing; I judge only as I hear, and my judgment is just, for I seek not to please myself but him who sent me (Jn 5.30).

In addition to his public ministry of proclaiming the word of God to the nation, Jesus also spent much time teaching his own followers, both the twelve and the wider company of disciples, *eg* the seventy whom he sent out on a mission to heal the sick and proclaim the good news. They had to be carefully instructed before being sent on a mission. There are many examples in the gospels of Jesus explaining the Scriptures to his disciples as he did after the resurrection on the road to Emmaus, 'And beginning with Moses and all the prophets, he explained to them what was said in all the Scriptures concerning himself' (Lk 24.27).

This instruction of the disciples was an important part of the mission of Jesus. He revealed the Father to them so that they would be able to continue his ministry after he was no longer with them. The disciples learned at first-hand how Jesus received from the Father through listening in prayer. This prepared them for doing the same when they no longer had his physical presence with them.

Jesus promised never to leave his followers alone but, just as the Father had given him a task to carry out and also communicated the very words to be spoken, so Jesus would ensure that the same thing happened for his followers. 'I will ask the Father, and he will give you another Counsellor to be with you for ever—the Spirit of truth' (Jn 14.16). The disciples would be able to continue the ministry of Jesus in

185

the world through the ministry of the Holy Spirit, the Counsellor.

The Holy Spirit would enable them to receive from the Father in the same way as Jesus and the prophets of the old covenant. The difference would be that the Holy Spirit would be given not only to one or two outstanding individuals but to all believers! 'If anyone loves me, he will obey my teaching. My Father will love him, and we will come to him and make our home with him' (Jn 14.23). This was not just an overnight lodging that Jesus was promising but a permanent dwelling. I and my Father, he promised, will be with you for ever through the Holy Spirit who will come to you after I am gone. 'Unless I go away, the Counsellor will not come to you; but if I go, I will send him to you' (Jn 16.7).

Numerous times Jesus spoke of the Holy Spirit as 'the Counsellor', a phrase reminiscent of Jeremiah 23 in which the prophet spoke of 'standing in the council of God'. It was the Holy Spirit who enabled the prophets to receive the counsel of the Lord and it was precisely this that Jesus was promising for all believers. The Holy Spirit would teach them all things (Jn 14.26), he would confirm and witness to the ministry of Jesus (Jn 15.26), he would convict the world of guilt in regard to sin (Jn 16.8). The Counsellor would guide the believers into all truth, and he would actually even reveal the future where it is necessary for the mission of Christ (Jn 16.13).

This interpretation is consistent with the ministry of the Holy Spirit under the old covenant where the future was never revealed simply to give privileged information to a small élite or merely to satisfy curiosity. The prophets received revelation concerning the future where it was essential for the effective communication of the word of God to give clear direction to the nation or where they were glimpsing the ultimate purposes of God.

In addition to speaking of the Holy Spirit as the Counsellor, Jesus also referred to him as 'the Spirit of truth' (Jn 14.17; 15.26; 16.13). His clear teaching was that the Holy

Spirit would not, and could not, mislead the believer. That is not to say that the believer could not be misled by failing to hear the Holy Spirit correctly. Jesus' teaching was that whoever truly loves him and obeys his commands would be loved by the Father and would receive the Counsellor, the Spirit of truth, who would guide him into all truth. Thus the prerequisite of receiving divine truth is a personal experience of the Lordship of Jesus and an overwhelming love for him and obedience to him that would lead to faith in him. Jesus promised 'Anyone who has faith in me will do what I have been doing' (Jn 14.12). But Jesus' own testimony was that he only did what he received from the Father. Through the ministry of the Holy Spirit this ability to hear from the Father was to be extended to all believers.

Jesus' teaching on listening to him is found in John 10, where he uses the simile of the shepherd and the sheep. He taught that the sheep recognise the voice of the shepherd and follow him because they know his voice, but they will not follow a stranger; they would, in fact, run away from him. Jesus said that he knew his own sheep just as the Father knew him and the sheep would be attentive to his voice—they would listen and be obedient when he spoke to them.

Seeing What the Father is Doing
Jesus' own testimony was that he did only what the Father instructed him to do. He spoke the words that he received from the Father and he did the things that he saw the Father *doing*. He emphasised his own powerlessness without the Father and ensured that all the glory for his ministry was given to the Father. He said, 'The Son can do nothing by himself.' He went on to testify:

> He can do only what he sees his Father doing, because whatever the Father does the Son also does. For the Father loves the Son and shows him all that he does (Jn 5.19,20).

The question arises as to what Jesus meant by his statement that the Father 'shows him all that he does'. Did it

187

mean that Jesus received guidance from the Father through pictorial communication as did the prophets of the old covenant? The answer is: Yes, he certainly did; but this is not the whole answer.

Jesus received pictures of divine revelation as, for example, on the occasion of his sending out a large company of disciples whom he had trained to preach the gospel. They were to heal the sick and to proclaim the nearness of the kingdom of God. When they returned to Jesus and joyfully reported that even evil spirits submitted to them in his name Jesus told them that while they had been out on their mission he had received a picture revealing the significance of what they were doing. He said, 'I saw Satan fall like lightning from heaven' (Lk 10.18). He added that he had given them power to overcome all the power of the enemy and then he broke into a prayer of thanksgiving to the Father who had revealed these things to those who had the trust of little children and hidden them from the worldly-wise and learned. Jesus added, 'No-one knows who the Father is except the Son and those to whom the Son chooses to reveal him' (Lk 10.22).

Revelation of divine truth, in the teaching of Jesus, was strictly governed by his own authority. It was to be communicated through the Holy Spirit who would be given only to those who loved him and were obedient to his commands.

Jesus himself received direction from the Father not simply through pictures that were brought into his mind during the times he spent alone with the Father in prayer. Because of his own special relationship with the Father, as only-begotten Son, who had been with the Father from the beginning of creation (Jn 1.2), he knew the whole counsel of the Father. He understood the immediate will of the Father because he knew the ultimate purposes of God. He was able to watch the whole panoramic scene of events unfolding in his day with understanding in the context of the working out of God's purposes to bring the knowledge of his nature and purposes and the message of his redemption to all the nations. Jesus understood the Father's intention to use Israel as a springboard for the communication of this knowledge to all people—as a light to the Gentiles.

Because of his special relationship with the Father, Jesus was able to perceive the significance of all the Father was doing both in Israel and worldwide to prepare the way for the coming of the Holy Spirit upon those who entered the new relationship with the Father through himself and for the gospel going out beyond the borders of Israel. Jesus saw how the whole of Israel was buzzing with excitement concerning their expectation of the coming of Messiah. His mother had no doubt told him the words that Simeon and Anna had spoken over him as a baby when she and Joseph had presented him in the Temple.

Jesus also perceived the significance of the international situation that in the perfect timing of the Father was preparing the way for the gospel; a common language, Greek, was understood by many nations; a common political system, the Roman Conquest had broken down national barriers and prepared the way for the gospel to travel rapidly across national frontiers throughout the Middle East and Europe. The Romans had built roads for swift travel and international communication. God was using Caesar, just as he had used Cyrus five centuries earlier, to carry out his purposes through one who did not acknowledge him as Lord.

Jesus also saw the Father doing in the heavenlies what he was to do on earth; to proclaim release for the captives, to bring good news of God's redemptive purposes to the poor and the oppressed, to heal the sick and bring deliverance to those in bondage to the power of the enemy. The Father was breaking that power in the heavenlies so Jesus began to do on earth what he saw the Father doing in the spiritual realms. 'As long as it is day,' he declared, 'we must do the work of him who sent me. Night is coming, when no-one can work. While I am in the world, I am the light of the world' (Jn 9.4). In doing the work of the Father he brought divine light into the world by revealing the purposes of God through doing what the Father told him to do.

The understanding Jesus possessed of what the Father was doing not only caused him to rejoice but also brought him great sorrow. When he saw the blindness of those who refused to receive the revelation of truth that he brought and who failed even to perceive the clear spiritual signs the Father had sent alongside the earthly ministry and mission of his Son, Jesus experienced great sorrow. When he looked into the future and saw what was coming upon the people of Jerusalem because of their spiritual blindness and rejection of all the signs sent to them by the Father including his own Son, Jesus wept.

> O Jerusalem, Jerusalem, you who kill the prophets and stone those sent to you . . . Look, your house is left to you desolate . . . They will not leave one stone on another, because you did not recognise the time of God's coming to you (Lk 13.34,35; 19.44).

Perceiving the signs
In chapter five we defined a sign in biblical language as 'an object or event, either natural or of human originating, that has spiritual significance'. We saw how the prophets regularly perceived a message from God through everyday objects that confronted them such as an almond tree (Jer 1.11) or a basket of ripe fruit (Am 8.1) or a cooking pot (Eze 24.3). Jesus did the same. He looked at a fig tree and perceived in it a significant message from the Father (Mk 11.20), he saw the little children the people were bringing for a blessing and perceived the deep truth concerning the way the kingdom is received (Mark 10.13), he perceived the messianic significance of the praises of the Palm Sunday crowds, 'If they keep quiet, the stones will cry out' (Lk 19.40).

Jesus also perceived the significance of the crowd of Samaritan villagers who came out to him in response to the testimony of the woman at the well. Even the disciples did not understand the significance of this but Jesus saw it as a sign of the coming kingdom. The Holy Spirit had not yet come upon them and they were spiritually blind. 'Open your eyes and look at the fields!' he said. 'They are ripe for

190

harvest' (Jn 4.35). We have already noted Jesus' reaction when the crowd of disciples came back from a mission rejoicing at the things that had happened in his name. Jesus saw these as a sign of the kingdom and gave thanks to the Father but he also realised that these signs were only perceived through faith. The wise and learned who relied upon human intellect did not see them.

Both Matthew and Mark record the Pharisees coming to Jesus immediately after the feeding of the four thousand and demanding a sign, a request that Jesus outrightly refused. Four thousand people had just witnessed a miraculous sign and here were these faithless leaders demanding a special sign from heaven! Without faith in God it was impossible for them to understand the significance of any sign. It was unbelief that blinded their spiritual eyes. In fact John frankly state that 'even after Jesus had done all these miraculous signs in their presence, they still would not believe in him' (Jn 12.37).

Signs, then, were for *believers*, not for unbelievers. They were perceived only by those whose eyes were opened by faith in God, hence the significance of Jesus' reply to the question put to him by Judas in John 14.22, 'Why do you intend to show yourself to us and not to the world?' At first sight Jesus' reply is not an answer at all. He stated, 'If anyone loves me, he will obey my teaching. My Father will love him, and we will come to him and make our home with him. He who does not love me will not obey my teaching.' His meaning was that anyone who did not love him and obey his teaching would not receive the Holy Spirit according to his promise is John 14.15. 'If you love me, you will obey what I command. And I will ask the Father, and he will give you another Counsellor, to be with you for ever.'

Jesus' answer to Judas was that he would reveal himself only to those who have the Holy Spirit because without the Holy Spirit it is impossible to receive divine revelation—the Spirit is the means through which the Father communicates with men. The Spirit is given to those who love and obey

Jesus and who therefore have faith in God through Christ.

In the teaching of the Gospels Jesus himself was a sign. This is especially brought out in John's Gospel where there is special emphasis laid upon miraculous signs as evidence of the messiahship of Jesus. Simeon was the first to perceive that Jesus himself would be a sign to the nation (Lk 2.34). John expressed this in theological terms in his prologue, 'The Word became flesh and lived for a while among us. We have seen his glory' (Jn 1.14). The fact that Jesus was the actual physical embodiment of the word of God was the ultimate expression of a spiritual sign.

When the Spirit of God came upon the prophets they spoke the word of God, but on certain occasions the word was expressed through them, not with words, but actually in their lives. Hosea is a good example of this when he was instructed to marry a woman who would prove faithless and run after other lovers. The suffering her faithlessness brought into the prophet's life was an embodiment of the word he proclaimed of the suffering of God due to Israel's faithlessness. Hosea's continuing love for his wife expressed the unbreakable love of a God who could not give up his people and whose mercy and forgiveness was freely offered.

Ezekiel, at one time, similarly expressed in his own life the word he was given to speak. It was on the occasion of the death of his wife that he was told not to grieve or to go into mourning; when the people asked him for an explanation of his behaviour he was to interpret his actions as a sign from the Lord.

Spiritual signs could also be contained in prophetic actions. We have seen this time and again in the ministry of the prophets as, for example, when Jeremiah smashed a jar in the presence of the elders of the nation and used it as a prophetic sign to demonstrate the word of the Lord, 'I will smash this nation and this city just as this potter's jar is smashed and cannot be repaired' (Jer 19.11). Many more examples of prophetic actions that were spiritual signs to the nation could be given; as, for example, when Micah went about barefoot and naked and actually rolled in the dust of the streets of Jerusalem to symbolise the humiliation that was coming upon the nation that refused to hear the word of the Lord and to turn to him in repentance, love and obedience.

Jesus also undertook prophetic actions as signs to the nation. He did this when his righteous anger boiled over causing chaos in the courts of the Temple as he 'overturned the tables of the money-changers and the benches of those selling doves, and would not allow anyone to carry merchandise through the temple courts' (Mk 11.16).

Jesus also discerned spiritual significance in events that occurred in his own day in much the same way as the prophets had done. For it to be a sign the event did not have to be a direct act of God. It could be a man-originated event or even simply an accident. God could use anything upon which the attention of the community or nation was focused in order to convey a message to his people, that is, to those with eyes to see and ears to hear. Many in the nation were so spiritually blinded that even when the sign was interpreted for them they could not perceive, or did not want to know, the message. Sometimes they deliberately stopped their ears and rejected the message.

Jesus' use of signs is well illustrated in Luke 13. He had just been rebuking the people (Lk 12.54) for their lack of spiritual perception.

> When you see a cloud rising in the west, immediately you say, 'It's going to rain,' and it does. And when the south wind blows, you say, 'It's going to be hot,' and it is. Hypocrites! You know how to interpret the appearance of the earth and the sky. How is it that you don't know how to interpret this present time?

Luke records that some of the crowd began asking him questions about some Galileans who had been murdered by Pilate. Jesus immediately rejected the suggestion that this was a direct judgment from God. He went on to illustrate his point by interpreting a sign. He referred to a tragedy that had evidently recently happened in Jerusalem when a tower at Siloam had collapsed and eighteen people had died in the rubble. All Jerusalem was talking about it. Jesus rejected the suggestion that God had sent it as a judgment but he saw it as a warning sign:

> Those eighteen who died when the tower in Siloam fell on them—do you think they were more guilty than all the others living in Jerusalem? I tell you, No! But unless you repent, you too will all perish (Lk 13.4,5).

The accident probably happened through shoddy workmanship, faulty materials or even error in design. It was a man-made accident; a failure of technology. It was in no sense an act of God although he knew it would happen. In God's ultimate sovereignty it could be said that he *allowed* it. Possibly no-one was interceding for Jerusalem or for the safety of those eighteen who died, or they might have been protected when the inevitable accident caused by the carelessness of men occurred.

Jesus used the event as a sign to warn the people of Jerusalem that as those eighteen had suffered, so would be the fate of the whole city of Jerusalem and all its inhabitants unless they turned to God. The only hope for the people lay in repenting of their evil ways and seeking God's loving protection by righteous living and holy consecration.

Signs, therefore, in Jesus' teaching and practice were either physical things or events that had a spiritual significance. Their message, however, was only perceived by those who had eyes to see and whose hearts were open to God.

Delivering the Word
The two-fold task of prophecy consisted in receiving the word from God and delivering the word of God to men. In this chapter we have been noting Jesus' teaching on receiving divine revelation; we now need to consider his teaching

on delivering the word of God to men under the direction and power of the Spirit.

Prophetic Action

The discovery and translation of the Dead Sea Scrolls has revealed what many scholars consider evidence of a closer association between early Christianity and the Qumran Community than had hitherto been recognised. If there is in fact a connection between 'the Teacher of righteousness' referred to in the Qumran texts and the person of Jesus this could shed new light on some of the teaching and prophetic activity of Jesus. There is a strong case for recognising an association between John the Baptist and the Qumran community who also practised a similar ritual of baptism which was associated with repentance and cleansing from sins.

If the future publication of further evidence from the scrolls strengthens this connection it would shed additional light upon the record in John's Gospel of Jesus' prophetic action in cleansing the Temple soon after his baptism by John in the Jordan. The Qumran community were known to have considerable reservations about some of the activities in the Temple which would be in line with the attitude of Jeremiah and the tradition of the eighth-century BC prophets of Israel and could well be a reflection of Jesus' own prophetic words and actions in relation to the priestly leadership of Israel in his own day.

The Great Commission

Jesus himself delivered the word of God both through the spoken word and through his deeds in much the same way as the prophets. We have noted that they sometimes expressed the word they were given in actions and we have noted that in the teaching of John's Gospel Jesus actually was 'the word made flesh'; the physical embodiment of the word of God.

In his earthly ministry Jesus spoke of the way of salvation through his proclamation of the gospel, but he also accomplished it through his action in going to the Cross and in rising from the dead. Jesus not only forgave sins by

195

the word he spoke but he was also the *means* of forgiveness. He not only showed the way of righteousness through his teaching, he *was* the way to the Father.

It was Jesus' clear intention that his disciples, and all those who believed in him in subsequent generations, should continue the work he began in his earthly ministry. 'I tell you the truth,' he emphasised, 'anyone who has faith in me will do what I have been doing. He will do even greater things than these, because I am going to the Father' (Jn 14.12). These words were said in the context of Jesus' promise to send the Holy Spirit upon his disciples. That promise was clearly extended to all believers and did not just apply to the twelve. Jesus specifically prayed for future generations of believers.

> My prayer is not for them alone. I pray also for those who will believe in me through their message, that all of them may be one, Father, just as you are in me and I am in you. May they also be in us so that the world may believe that you have sent me (Jn 17.20,21).

Jesus prayed that he and the Father would dwell in future generations of believers so that the world would believe the mission he had been sent to accomplish, the message of which was given to the believers to deliver. Jesus expressed this task in the form of a command that we know as 'the Great Commission'. It is, in fact, both an injunction and a promise, and although it was given first to the eleven disciples in Galilee it was understood and accepted by the New Testament church as a commission directed to the whole company of believers.

> Therefore go and make disciples of all nations, baptising them in the name of the Father and of the Son and of the Holy Spirit, and teaching them to obey everything I have commanded you. And surely I am with you always, to the very end of the age (Mt 28.19,20).

Luke gives a shortened version of the Great Commission, that 'repentance and forgiveness of sins will be preached in his name to all nations, beginning at Jerusalem' (Lk 24.46). Luke reports Jesus as saying that the disciples were to be witnesses, not only of the person and teaching of Jesus but also to the events of his death and resurrection. He then reminded them of what the Father had promised, *ie* the Holy Spirit, and warned them to stay in the city until they had received his power (Acts 1.4–8).

The Strategy for Mission

Jesus not only commissioned the believers with a task but promised them the power to enable them to fulfil it. In Acts 1.8 he gave them the strategy for carrying out the Great Commission:

> You will receive power when the Holy Spirit comes on you; and you will be my witnesses in Jerusalem, and in all Judea and Samaria, and to the ends of the earth.

That strategy became the plan of action followed by the believers in the New Testament church and recorded through the book of Acts.

There were thus three strands Jesus gave to the believers for carrying out the Great Commision.

First, *they were to wait for the power of the Holy Spirit* to come upon them to ensure that they did not go in their own strength or try to carry out the mission of Christ through the mere exercise of human intellect and human wisdom.

Secondly, *they were to be personal witnesses to Jesus*, to teach what he taught, to declare the message of his Crucifixion and Resurrection, but to do this in terms of personal witness. Thus the message was to be founded upon the believers' own personal experience of the risen Christ.

Thirdly, *they were to start where they were* and then work out; to begin in Jerusalem on home ground, then move out into Judea where the culture and language were identical even though the people might not be known personally to them. They were then to go to Samaria, where the language was the same but the culture was different and they would be breaking barriers of tradition and tribal identity. Finally, they were to continue to move outward to other nations where there was no identity of culture or language, nationality or tradition and where the gospel would be breaking all the human barriers. They would only be able to fulfil this task through the power of the Holy Spirit.

The Great Commission has never been rescinded. Neither has the promise of the Holy Spirit to believers in the Lord Jesus. The Great Commission to make disciples and teach them to obey the Lord Jesus is still the primary task of the church. The three-fold strategy for fulfilling the Great Commission given at the Ascension, and the Holy Spirit given to the church at Pentecost, were the cornerstones of the mission of the New Testament church. These stemmed directly from the teaching of Jesus. They defined the task and the means of its fulfilment that was followed in the early church throughout the period for which we have records.

There is nothing in the New Testament to suggest a change occurred either in the task or the strategy of mission. Neither is there one word in the New Testament to suggest that the presence of Christ in his church or the power of the Holy Spirit would be withdrawn at any particular point in time. The specific promise of Jesus was to be with his people always, right to the end of the age, which must mean until the coming of the Son of Man in his glory.

The task of the church was therefore defined by Jesus as being to declare the word of God to the nations which, within the narrower confines of the nation Israel, had been the task of the prophets under the old covenant. This was the prophetic task given to the body of believers and foretold hundreds of years before by the prophets who foresaw the outpouring of the Holy Spirit upon all those with whom God would establish his new covenant. It was for the fulfilment of this prophetic task that Jesus commissioned his church and empowered them with the gift promised by his Father; the Holy Spirit, the Counsellor, the Spirit of truth through whom divine revelation would be given to the disciples and to successive generations of believers.

198

CHAPTER ELEVEN

THE TEACHING OF PAUL

Paul's teaching on prophecy is closely linked to his understanding of revelation. Divine truth, in Paul's experience,
was not received as an intellectual process. It was received
through the direct action of God in communicating with his
people through the Holy Spirit. It was through revelation
that Paul first encountered the Lord Jesus on the road to
Damascus according to his own testimony given to King
Agrippa, 'We all fell to the ground, and I heard a voice
saying to me in Aramaic, "Saul, Saul, why do you persecute
me?"' (Ac 26.14).

Similarly, Paul claimed the gospel he preached was not
received through the teaching of others but by divine revelation. In writing to the Galatians he stated explicitly, 'The
gospel I preached is not something that man made up. I did
not receive it from any man, nor was I taught it; rather, I
received it by revelation from Jesus Christ' (1.12).

Revelation played an important part in Paul's ministry.
His original 'sending out' from Antioch on the first missionary journey together with Barnabas came about through
revelation (Ac 13.2); the direction of his missionary journeys
from place to place was directed by the Holy Spirit, as when
he received the vision of the man of Macedonia calling him to
begin preaching in Greece (Ac 16.9); and even his personal

visits to the other apostles were determined by revelation, 'I went in response to a revelation' he told the Galatians (2.2). More importantly, Paul saw the gospel that was being proclaimed through the whole church as having been given by God through revelation. It was a mystery that had been 'hidden for long ages past, but now revealed' (Rom 16.25), 'God has revealed it to us by his Spirit' (1 Cor 2.10); the gospel that was proclaimed through the church was 'the mystery of Christ which was not made known to men in other generations as it has now been revealed by the Spirit to God's holy apostles and prophets' (Eph 3.5).

This revealed truth concerning the purposes of God which had been given to the apostles and prophets in the church set the standard of truth to be proclaimed in the churches for all time. God had appointed the apostles and prophets as the foundation of the church 'with Jesus Christ himself as the chief cornerstone' (Eph 2.20). Together with all the believers in the Lord Jesus who were 'members of God's household' they formed a building that was 'a holy temple in the Lord' which had become 'a dwelling in which God lives by his Spirit' (Eph 2.19–22). Through the Holy Spirit, God continually unfolded his will and plans for the church to fulfil his purposes to carry the gospel of salvation through Christ to the whole of mankind.

This continuous revelation that came about through the presence of the Holy Spirit in the church demanded the utmost care in handling. Already there were false prophets and false teachers troubling the church. There had to be authoritative standards as a yardstick for measuring truth; there had to be diligence in testing that which purported to be revelation; and there had to be order and discipline surrounding the receiving and discernment of revelation. It was even more important now that the Holy Spirit had been given to all believers than in the times of the Old Covenant.

Paul's teaching was directed towards the practical responsibilities of handling revelation within the churches. He knew that God could speak through any one of the believers, as he had done in Antioch during a time of worship when the Spirit had said, 'Set apart for me Barnabas and Saul for the work to which I have called them' (Ac 13.2). There is no record of this word having been given by any of the 'pillars of the church'. In fact the record in Acts suggests that there were no apostles present; this was the local body of believers at worship, some of whom were prophets, and the Lord spoke to Paul and Barnabas through them. It was this experience that actually commissioned Paul and Barnabas to embark on the first missionary journey. Therefore Paul had every reason to encourage believers in all the churches to prophesy, to listen to what the Spirit was saying, to test carefully what they were hearing, to throw out anything that was false, and to hold fast to that which was good (1 Th 5.19,20).

Despite the spiritual chaos and disorder in the church at Corinth Paul nevertheless urged the brothers to 'be eager to prophesy' although he hastened to add 'but everything should be done in a fitting and orderly way' (1 Cor 14.39,40). Paul's great concern was that the Spirit should not be suppressed, which would prevent the church from receiving clear guidance and instruction from the Lord, but he wished to guard the church against deception. For this reason the standard of truth had been given to the apostles and prophets in the church and no-one should go beyond this (1 Cor 4.6). He continually warned against going beyond the teaching of the apostles, 'So then, brothers, stand firm and hold to the teachings we passed on to you, whether by word of mouth or by letter' (2 Th 2.15).

Paul's teaching on prophecy is largely pragmatic, drawn from him by the demands of what was actually happening in the churches. He knew that every Spirit-filled believer could receive a word from the Lord. Men and women, young and old, slave and free were one in Christ and could hear from God through the Holy Spirit, but there was grave danger of the church being misled if revelation was not rightly handled. Corinth was a prime example and, because of the situation in this church, Paul gave his most detailed teaching on the subject in writing to them. Someone had been heard actually cursing Jesus while supposedly speaking under divine inspiration. Paul demolished this firmly by saying it was impossible for anyone 'speaking by the Spirit of God' to say 'Jesus be cursed' (1 Cor 12.3). This was clearly a throw-back to the pagan practices that surrounded the church in Corinth and from which some of the Christians had scarcely departed. The demonic forces in the old pagan religions still exercised an influence in some of the new believers and they fought against the Holy Spirit. There was great danger of the whole church being deceived. In dealing with this problem in the list of nine gifts Paul gave, it is intentional that the gift of prophecy is followed by the gift of 'distinguishing between spirits'. Paul perceived that God gave gifts to the fellowship that were appropriate to meet their specific needs.

He recognised that there are three sources from which words may be spoken into the church even during periods of prayer and worship. They are:

> from the Spirit of God;
> from the human spirit;
> from evil spirits.

It was vital in the Corinthian situation that there should be the ability to distinguish between spirits so that anything that was not of God could be sifted out, even if it was not emanating from evil spirits but simply coming from the human mind as the product of a fertile human imagination.

Paul's chief concern was with the health and correct functioning of the church, which comprised a multitude of individuals with different natural talents and spiritual gifts. He saw them as many members making up a whole in the same way as there are many parts of a human body. Each part has its separate function but is necessary for the health, well-being and correct functioning of the whole body. His statement in 1 Corinthians 12.12 that 'the body is a unit, though it is made up of many parts' is basic to his doctrine of the church. He might have been expected to conclude with the statement, 'So it is with the church' but instead he said, 'So it is with *Christ*'.

The believers were not simply members of a brotherly fellowship or human organisation; they actually formed the *body of Christ* in the world and were indwelt by the Spirit of Christ. They were therefore to be directed by the Holy Spirit. Hence the need for clear discernment of what the Spirit was saying to the church.

Paul gives three lists of gifts, each performing different functions within the body. Prophecy is the only one that appears in all three lists.

> The first is *a list of ministries* given in Ephesians 4.11;
> the second is *a list of natural talents* or natural abilities given in Romans 12.6–8;
> the third is *a list of spiritual gifts* or, more accurately, 'spiritual manifestations', given in 1 Corinthians 12.7–11.

Our concern in looking at each of these three lists is to examine Paul's teaching on prophecy.

The Ministry of Prophecy

> It was he who gave some to be apostles, some to be prophets, some to be evangelists, and some to be pastors and teachers, to prepare God's people for works of service, so that the body of Christ may be built up until we all reach unity in the faith and in the knowledge of the Son of God and become mature, attaining to the whole measure of the fulness of Christ (Eph 4.11–13).

Paul emphasises that the fivefold division of ministries in the early church was of *God's ordering*. They were not the appointments of men; it was God who summoned each individual into ministry. The human activity was to respond to the call of God. Those who were called by God into ministry were given specific gifts appropriate to that ministry. This is because the ministries were a *function* rather than a *status* within the church. This function is stated in

Ephesians 4.12, 'to prepare God's people' and for the building up of the body of Christ. Thus the ministries were given to *the church* not to the world. They were intended to equip the church 'for works of service', to do the work of Christ in the world.

Paul sees the ministries all functioning together to build up the church to maturity so that it may be the expression of the fulness of Christ in the world. In order to achieve this Paul perceives the need for the church to 'reach unity in the faith'. In this he may be echoing the prayer of Jesus in John 17 where he specifically stated that he was not praying for the world (v9) but for his disciples and all those who would believe through them, *ie* the church, so that they 'may be brought to complete unity' in their witness to the world and their expression of the love of Christ through the fellowship of believers (v23).

Clearly the ministries did carry status within the church although this was not the purpose of the ministry. They were ministries of service but those who held these appointments were honoured within the church, not for themselves, but as a way of honouring the Giver of the ministry gifts. Inevitably the more carnally minded believers would covet the ministry gifts for the honour accorded them and the status thereby attained within the church. Paul alludes to this in 1 Corinthians 12.28ff where he says that 'in the church God has appointed first of all apostles, second prophets, third teachers'.

Paul is not necessarily referring to a hierarchy of status at this point. Commentators are divided in their interpretation, but the most likely explanation is that he was speaking chronologically. The first to be appointed were the apostles and their continuing function was to spearhead the mission of the church. Literally they were those who were 'sent out' to proclaim the gospel and to plant churches. They were closely followed, and in New Testament times were often accompanied by, prophets.

The task of the prophets was to hear from God, to discern

what the Spirit was saying to the churches, to give direction to the mission of Christ, to perceive danger and give appropriate warning, to interpret the signs of the times so that the 'now' word of God could be received by the church. Their ministry was thus to be the ears and eyes of the church, to put the sword of the Spirit into the hand of the church so that the whole body of believers would be rightly equipped with the word of God to meet the changing demands of the situation of mission from place to place and from time to time. The prophets were essential for the effective equipping of the church for the carrying out of the Great Commission (Mt 28.19) to proclaim Christ to the nations.

Thirdly, according to Paul, God appointed teachers in the churches whose function was to teach the faith, to ensure every believer possessed a grasp of sound doctrine. Their task was to study the word of God through the Scriptures of the old covenant and through the writings of the apostles under the new covenant (that were already becoming available to the churches) and to teach them effectively to the new believers. The ministry of the teacher was to incorporate the new believers into the body of Christ and to establish them firmly in the faith.

The other two ministries from the list in Ephesians 4.11, those of evangelist and pastor, or possibly pastor/teacher, were not seen as part of the pioneering work of the church but as the ministry functions within established churches. The evangelists were responsible for equipping the church for evangelistic outreach and the pastors acted as shepherds of the people caring for the needs of the believers, encouraging and comforting them in the faith. Thus the ministries dovetailed to equip the church to carry out the work of Christ in the world.

The Gift of Prophecy
Natural Talent

We have different gifts, according to the grace given us. If a man's gift is prophesying, let him use it in proportion to his faith. If it is serving, let him serve; if it is teaching, let him teach; if it is encouraging, let him encourage; if it is contributing to the needs of others, let him give generously; if it is leadership, let him govern diligently; if it is showing mercy, let him do it cheerfully (Rom 12.6–8).

In this passage Paul returns to the metaphor of the body that he first used when writing to the church at Corinth. Just as the human body has different parts each with a different function, so those who are in Christ 'form one body and each member belongs to all the others' (v5).

Paul's emphasis here is on humility. He pleads with the believers not to think of themselves more highly than they ought but rather to think of themselves 'with sober judgment'. They should cease to conform 'to the pattern of this world' and allow God to renew their minds through Christ. An essential part of this renewal would be the recognition that the natural abilities they possessed were not human achievements in which they could take personal pride but were gifts from God.

These natural talents, part of the human endowments from birth that were developed over the years, should be seen not according to the pattern of worldly values but as part of God's special gifting to the body of Christ, into which each believer had been incorporated, to equip the church for its task. The believer would only be able to evaluate rightly his natural gifts after his mind had been renewed by Christ.

The natural gift of prophesying was expressed through prophetic preaching. Paul probably had in mind men such as Apollos with an outstanding gift of oratory. Once this man's natural ability as a speaker had been taken in hand by Priscilla and Aquila, who carefully taught him the faith, he became one of the outstanding expository preachers of the church in New Testament times and acquired a powerful following in the church of Corinth.

Paul also noted that there was a natural gift of teaching that enabled those who had this ability to communicate clearly in such a way that even complex ideas could be grasped by simple believers. In the same way some had a talent for encouraging others, for building up faith or for serving, quietly getting on with the tasks in hand without fuss; or for giving, or for exercising leadership.

Prophesying as a natural talent had to be exercised according to the amount of a believer's faith. The prophetic preacher, when expounding the Scriptures or the doctrine of the apostles, would often find himself speaking prophetically in applying the word of God to the needs of the church. This was a function of the Holy Spirit within him as he perceived the significance of the word he was expounding as a direct word from God into the contemporary situation. Such a word would give encouragement to the believers, it would build their faith, increase their understanding of the purposes of God and it would give specific direction to the immediate needs of the fellowship of believers for the task facing them.

Thus the natural talent of the orator, when seen as a gift from God and combined with faith and exercised under the direction of the Holy Spirit, became a powerful instrument in equipping the church for the task of ministry in the world.

Paul, however, had a strong word of warning for those exercising natural ability as prophetic preachers that they should not get so carried away in eloquence that they went beyond established doctrine. He specifically named Apollos when applying this lesson to the church at Corinth: 'I have applied these things to myself and Apollos for your benefit, so that you may learn from us the meaning of the saying, "Do not go beyond what is written." Then you will not take pride in one man over against another' (1 Cor 4.6).

The gifted preacher's task was to apply established doctrine to the contemporary situation in such a way that it became the 'now' word of the living God. But he was not to go beyond teaching approved by the apostles. This was the safeguard to keep the church from deviating into heresies and cultic practices.

PROPHECY PAST AND PRESENT

Spiritual Gifts

> Now to each one the manifestation of the Spirit is given for the
> common good. To one there is given through the Spirit the
> message of wisdom, to another the message of knowledge by
> means of the same Spirit, to another faith by the Spirit, to
> another gifts of healing by that one Spirit, to another miraculous
> powers, to another prophecy, to another the ability to dis-
> tinguish between spirits, to another the ability to speak in diff-
> erent kinds of tongues, and to still another the interpretation of
> tongues. All these are the work of one and the same Spirit, and
> he gives them to each one, just as he determines (1 Cor
> 12.7–11).

Spiritual gifts, or literally 'spirituals' (*pneumatiká*) or manifestations of the Spirit, were the evidence of the working of
the Holy Spirit within the body of Christ. These different
manifestations of the Spirit were available to all believers
and were given by God to meet the needs of the fellowship for
the mission of Christ at any particular time. Paul emphasises
that all believers have received the Holy Spirit, 'For we were
all baptised *with* one Spirit into one body whether Jews or
Greeks, slave or free' (12.13). In this instance the Greek
preposition *en* should not be translated 'by' but 'with', which
brings this verse into line with the witness of the Gospels and
Acts that Jesus is the baptiser. The Holy Spirit is the *power*
with which the believer is baptised.

Paul emphasises that it is the one Spirit at work within the
body of believers who manifests himself in different ways.
'To one there is given through the Spirit the message of
wisdom, to another the message of knowledge . . .' but these
spiritual gifts cannot be gained by merit or grasped by force,
they are given by God to whom he wills. In this sense they are
gifts rather than *attainments*.

Paul's teaching on the use of the gift of prophecy needs to
be seen in relation to the situation in the church of Corinth
where the members were contentious, loveless and status-
seeking; while in worship they were noisy, shallow and
overly concerned with the experiential. Paul's concern in

208

emphasising unity in the body—that all are one in Christ —was to stress that the gifts are not given for individual exaltation but for the benefit of the whole body. Each one should rejoice in the manifestations of the Spirit in others because as the gifts were multiplied in each fellowship so the whole body grew in maturity.

Paul is consistent in his teaching on this subject in all his writings. A good example is seen in his prayer for the Ephesians where he is not praying for individuals, as could be interpreted from English translations, but for the *whole fellowship*, that together with other groups of believers they would grasp the incredible love of Christ; and 'that you (*plural*) may be filled to the measure of all the fulness of God'. Clearly no individual could receive all the fulness of God, but through the presence of the Holy Spirit the whole church could, for in belonging to Christ we belong to each other and together we form the body of Christ.

In Corinth there was no such unity or understanding of what it meant to be 'in Christ'. There were party factions; there was the 'Paul party', the 'Apollos party', the 'Peter party' and, of course, there were those who were above party faction who saw themselves as the 'Jesus people' claiming not to follow men but to follow Christ! (1.12). There was sexual immorality among them (5.1), quarrelling and taking law suits against each other (6.1), there was disorder in worship and even drunkenness at the eucharist (11.21). Despite all that was wrong in the life of the fellowship the Corinthians were still proud and boastful of their spiritual attainments. Paul not only dealt firmly with the things that were blatantly wrong but also cut them down to spiritual size by declaring that he could not even address them 'as spiritual but as worldly—mere infants in Christ' (3.1). Thus in his teaching on the spiritual gifts in chapters 12 to 14 the strong emphasis is upon the gifts being given by God for the sake of the *whole fellowship of believers*—to build up the body. This can be done only as each member has an understanding of the nature of the body of Christ, its interacting members

209

with their different functions each fulfilling a vital part in the life of the body.

Paul concludes chapter 12 with a series of rhetorical questions 'Are all apostles? Are all prophets? Are all teachers? . . .' Clearly the intended answer is 'No'. These questions are followed by the charge 'But you are eagerly desiring the greater gifts' (1 Cor 12.31). Unfortunately the Greek verb *zeloō* has the same form, *zeloute*, in the second person plural present indicative, the second person plural present subjunctive, and the second person plural present imperative. Thus it could mean 'you are eagerly desiring' or 'you have been eagerly desiring' or the command 'eagerly desire!' In the context of this letter the last alternative is the least likely. Paul would not have encouraged these people to seek after the greatest gifts if he was referring to *ministry* gifts. That was precisely what they *were* doing and why he was rebuking them so severely throughout this letter. If *zeloute* is an imperative, as it undoubtedly is in 14.1, then Paul must be referring to spiritual gifts rather than the ministry gifts. According to Paul in 14.1, prophecy is the greatest gift. What the Corinthians were seeking or 'earnestly desiring' was the more spectacular gifts to give themselves the highest status—and in their understanding of spiritual things 'speaking in tongues' was the greatest gift that they all wanted to exercise. Hence the chaotic situation when all the house fellowships in Corinth came together for worship and they all wanted to give their individual performances! (14.26).

This was why Paul laid such stress upon the supremacy of love. You Corinthians, he said, are eagerly desiring the greater gifts but I will show you the most excellent way of all, the way of love. But note, love is not a gift; it is a *fruit* of the Spirit (Gal 5.22). Without love the believer speaking in tongues is like a clanging cymbal, and those exercising the gifts—even the gift of martyrdom—are nothing without love. Love is the only thing that never fails and is everlasting. Even prophecy and tongues will become irrelevant when we see the Lord Jesus face to face.

Clearly it is the second coming of Christ that Paul has in mind when he speaks of perfection coming (1 Cor 13.10), not the fixing of the canon of Scripture by the Council of Carthage in 397 AD. Such a concept would not have entered Paul's mind. Yet this latter is the view taken by some commentators who attempt to use this verse to support their belief that spiritual gifts ceased at the end of the New Testament period. But the text does not bear such an interpretation and there is certainly no other statement in the New Testament even remotely suggesting that the Holy Spirit would be withdrawn from the church at any time before the second coming of our Lord.

Paul's teaching is that the presence of the Holy Spirit in the church distributes gifts among the believers which must be used in the context of love; hence his statement at the beginning of chapter 14, 'Follow the way of love and eagerly desire spiritual gifts, especially the gift of prophecy.' Paul's preference for prophecy above all the gifts is because it edifies, or builds up the church. It strengthens, encourages and comforts the believers (14.3).

Paul is here speaking about the exercise of the gift of prophecy within the local church—a gift open to every believer. Clearly he is not speaking about the ministry of the prophet, nor even the natural talent of the gifted expository preacher. The ministries were the appointments of God, and not everyone could be a gifted preacher. There would have been even greater chaos in Corinth if they had all tried to become great preachers! In urging them all to prophesy Paul is referring to something quite distinctive. Michael Green's definition of prophecy in this context provides a helpful basis for understanding what Paul was urging upon the members at Corinth; 'A word from the Lord through a member of his body, inspired by his Spirit and given to build up the rest of the body.' (Michael Green, *To Corinth with Love*; Hodder).

Tongues and Prophecy
Paul takes care to distinguish between tongues and

prophecy. A tongue, he says, is spoken to God not to men (14.2) hence a tongue is always a form of prayer. Paul underlines this in verses 13–17 where he specifically associates speaking in a tongue with *prayer*, although the interpretation of a tongue may reflect God's response to the tongue (see page 215).

By contrast Paul describes prophecy as speaking to men (14.3). It is a word *from* God to men conveying what the Spirit is saying to the churches.

In Corinth the gift of tongues was being grossly misused for self-glorification. It was a mindless exercise (v14) which indicated to Paul how immature the Corinthian Christians were; they were mere babes in Christ who had to be fed with milk and not with the meat of the gospel. They had barely left behind their pagan practices which were full of exuberant and exotic forms of worship including speaking in tongues; indeed tongue-speaking was very common in the Greek mystery cults from which many of the Christians in Corinth had been delivered.

Paul takes the view that the main value in speaking in tongues is personal and individual. In public worship he would much prefer those who possessed this gift to keep quiet and speak to themselves and to God (v28) and not disturb the whole church with their unintelligible prayers, to which other believers could not even say 'Amen' (v16).

Effects of Prophecy

Paul's strong advocacy of prophecy was because his chief concern was with the growth and strengthening of the church, and he knew the key part which the gift of prophecy played in this function. He noted in 1 Corinthians 14 a number of beneficial effects when prophecy was exercised correctly, with love and humility, and a real concern for others within the body of Christ. Three of these effects are listed in 14.3 and are of considerable significance in understanding the use of the gift of prophecy in the churches of the New Testament period. The NIV translates these, 'strengthening, encouragement and comfort'.

Strengthening

The word used here is *oikodomen* which means to build up and comes from the verb *oikodomeō* which literally means 'to build a house'. Hence the significance of prophecy for Paul as contributing towards the building up of the household of believers through the communication of the word of God into the fellowship.

Encouragement

The word used here is *paraklēsin* which comes from the same root as the term *Paraclēte* which in John's Gospel is the term used by Jesus for the Holy Spirit (Jn 14.16,26; 15.26; 16.7). The Paraclete whom Jesus promised to send after his physical presence was no longer with the disciples was to be their Counsellor and Advocate; literally, one called in to be alongside another to give assistance and support, particularly through instruction or pleading the cause of another.

Clearly Paul sees this as a major function of prophecy which strengthens the life of the local church enabling the members to receive direct guidance from the Lord and facilitating communication through intercession as an advocate with the Father.

Comfort

The word used here is *paramuthian*, which literally means to exercise a gentle influence by speaking words of comfort, consolation or encouragement. The emphasis here is upon gentleness. Paul has in mind the still small voice of the Spirit speaking quietly into the ear of the church particularly during times of stress or persecution.

Paul saw prophecy performing this function of enabling the Spirit to speak directly into stressful situations, scattering the feelings of despair, allaying anxiety and fear and conveying the comfort that comes from the knowledge of the presence of the Lord within his church.

Unbelievers

The fourth effect of prophecy that Paul notes in 1 Corinthians 14 is its effect upon unbelievers. In verses 20–25 he continues the theme of contrasting tongues and prophecy, but this time concentrates upon their effects. Paul quotes from Isaiah 28.11 where the prophet says that because of the rebelliousness of his people God would speak to them through foreign invasion—'the lips of foreigners'; this would be a sign to them, but even this they would reject. In the same way Paul said unbelievers coming into the church and hearing people speak in unknown tongues would not be able to understand what was being said and would reject the word of God.

In contrast, Paul says that if an unbeliever enters the church when everyone is prophesying he will recognise what is being said as coming from God, particularly if there is some revelation concerning his own life that only God could know. He would then fall down exclaiming in the words of Zechariah 8.23, 'God is with you'. It was prophecy that would add a sharp cutting edge to the church's evangelism by bringing a direct word from the Lord into each situation.

Interpretation

The fifth effect of prophecy that Paul notes in 1 Corinthians 14 is to convey to the church a response from God to the exercise of the gift of tongues during worship. Although Paul speaks sternly in this chapter about the misuse of the gift of tongues he does not wish to see the gift totally suppressed. Hence his instruction 'Do not forbid speaking in tongues' (v39). Paul's over-riding concern is with the building up of the church and not with the inflation of individual egos. Tongues were to be allowed during public worship provided there was an interpretation.

It should be noted that Paul is not looking for a *translation* but an *interpretation*. Merely to give a translation of someone's prayer to God was a fairly meaningless exercise. But an interpretation would get to the heart of what was being communicated between the worshipper and God through the ministry of the Holy Spirit. Paul knew that this enabled the Spirit to minister to the believers, to edify, or build up the whole church. Hence his statement in verse 6, 'If I come to you and speak in tongues, what good will I be to you, unless I bring you some revelation or knowledge or prophecy or word of instruction?' In other words the kind of interpretation Paul was looking for would include and centre upon the response of the Father conveyed through the Holy Spirit. The response could come either through the speaker or though someone else. As a message from God it would be regarded as prophecy, and all prophecy, according to Paul's teaching, had to be tested.

Weighing Prophecy

Although this subject will be treated in some detail in chapter 13 it is necessary here to comment upon Paul's statement in 1 Corinthians 14:29 that, 'Two or three prophets should speak, and the others should weigh carefully what is said'. This statement is capable of different interpretations. Did Paul mean only those who were prophets should weigh prophetic revelation, or did he mean that everyone should share in the task of weighing prophecy? Opinion among commentators is divided upon this issue. Paul uses the term *alloi* which usually means 'others of the same kind' but is usually translated simply as 'others'.

In the context of Paul's instructions to the Corinthians in this letter the weight of evidence would suggest that he is appealing to the whole congregation to engage in the task of weighing prophecy. In 14:1 he urges all the believers to prophesy, and in 14:31 he says, 'For you can all prophesy in turn so that everyone may be instructed and encouraged.' It would therefore appear that Paul is looking to the whole body of believers to become a prophetic people who are eagerly listening to what the Holy Spirit is saying to the church. Therefore, Paul is looking for the growth in maturity of the whole body who collectively should be able to discern what is truly coming from the Holy Spirit and that which is spurious. Paul's teaching would suggest that for the right building up of the body it is essential that all the believers should be encouraged to participate in the weighing of prophetic revelation and not simply leave it to one or two who regularly display such manifestations of the Spirit.

This interpretation is strengthened by Paul's statement that, 'If a revelation comes to someone who is sitting down, the first speaker should stop' (v30). This implies that the first speaker who is prophesying is not actually bringing a divine revelation but is engaging in 'prophetic preaching' or expounding the word of God. If a revelation comes to someone whilst the first speaker is speaking, the preacher must give way so that the immediacy of the revelation is not lost. Paul's final instruction in this passage is that, 'The spirits of prophets are subject to the control of prophets' (v32). He makes it clear that he is not referring to anything of an ecstatic nature. Prophecy in this context is divine revelation that comes to the speaker whilst the mind is fully active.

CHAPTER TWELVE

THE PRACTICE OF PROPHECY

Prophecy in the Life of the New Testament Church

Prophetic revelation was a part of the normal experience of daily life in the New Testament church. It was the expression of the presence of the risen Lord in his church. Luke's account of the early days of the church in Jerusalem and the expansion into Judea, Samaria and beyond in obedience to the strategy given by Jesus in Acts 1.8 is vibrant with the presence of the Lord Jesus.

The Resurrection had changed everything for the first disciples. They had actually seen Jesus alive after his death on the tree. It was a fact of their experience. He had met with them, walked with them, talked with them and eaten with them. They had grown used to him disappearing from sight and then reappearing in another place at another time during those heady forty days after the Resurrection. In fact they had grown so used to his appearances that even after the Ascension and his 'final' words to them they still felt him to be near—very near—only just beyond physical sight, sound or touch. Moreover he had promised to send the Holy Spirit and that through the Spirit he would maintain contact with them.

He had kept his word. At Pentecost the Spirit had come —the Lord's gift to his church. From that day they found

217

they could actually communicate with the Lord Jesus through the Spirit as he was poured out into the life of each believer. Peter told the crowds in Jerusalem that the Father had given the Holy Spirit to Jesus and he had poured out the Spirit upon those who received him as Lord and Messiah (Ac 2.33).

It is this experience of the presence of the risen Lord among the believers, watching over his church and directing his work, the mission of Christ, that is the dominant feature of the early history of the church as portrayed in Acts. The Lord of the church spoke to his people through revelation —through prophecy—by the spoken word, by vision, or by dreams and interpretation; exactly as God had spoken to his servants the prophets in former days. Peter was conscious of the link with the prophets of ancient Israel. He believed his generation was actually seeing the fulfilment of the prophecies given to them. He testified in the Temple courtyard that 'All the prophets from Samuel on, as many as have spoken, have foretold these days' (Ac 3.24). Consequently they expected God to be at work in unusual ways, the paranormal became the normal experience of the believers. Luke describes this in a few significant sentences, 'The apostles performed many miraculous signs and wonders among the people . . . People brought the sick into the streets and laid them on beds and mats so that at least Peter's shadow might fall on some of them as he passed by. Crowds gathered also from the towns around Jerusalem, bringing their sick and those tormented by evil spirits, and all of them were healed' (Ac 5.12–16).

The powerful words and deeds of the apostles were the signs and wonders indicating the presence of the Lord in his church and causing even the dead to be raised, as when Peter prayed over the body of Dorcas. 'Then he called the believers and the widows and presented her to them alive' (Ac 9.41). Luke records that this incident became known all over Joppa and was the cause of many people becoming believers. With such convincing evidence of the power of the Lord among

218

them the confidence and expectation of all the people was high. The apostles and leaders especially expected the Lord to communicate with them. Angelic messengers opened prison doors (Ac 5.19; 12.7) and brought messages from the Lord (Ac 8.26; 10.3). Visions also were a common experience as one of the ways in which the Lord communicated with the believers, especially in relation to some new revelation of truth which was to be a milestone in the development of the mission of the church.

It was while Peter was still at Joppa following the raising of Dorcas that both he and Cornelius received visions that led to the Holy Spirit being received by the first Gentile believers. 'The circumcised believers who had come with Peter were astonished that the gift of the Holy Spirit had been poured out even on the Gentiles. For they heard them speaking in tongues and praising God' (Ac 10.45,46).

Paul became a believer through revelation and the personal communication of the Lord. 'He fell to the ground and heard a voice say to him, "Saul, Saul, why do you persecute me?" "Who are you, Lord?" Saul asked. "I am Jesus, whom you are persecuting," he replied. "Now get up and go into the city and you will be told what you must do"' (Ac 9.4–6). Paul spoke of 'other visions and revelations from the Lord' that he received (2 Cor 12.1). He said that he was 'caught up to paradise', and 'heard inexpressible things, things that man is not permitted to tell' (v4).

The Mission of the Church

The mission of the church was directed by the Holy Spirit. The *koinonia*, or fellowship of believers, was not a human institution like the Roman Empire, controlled by men to carry out the will and purposes of men. It was under the control of the Lord of the church who directed its affairs through the Holy Spirit. This direction was received through the practice of prophecy. This may be seen in four major areas of the early church's life and mission. First in the *appointment of leaders*; secondly in the *strategy of mission*; thirdly in *doctrine* and fourthly in *foreknowledge*.

Leaders

Luke tells us that 'In the church at Antioch there were prophets and teachers'; he then goes on to list Barnabas, Simeon called Niger, Lucius of Cyrene, Manaen who was of one of the ruling aristocratic Hebrew families, and Saul. Unfortunately Luke does not say who were prophets and who were teachers but the short description of the commissioning of Barnabas and Paul for apostolic mission work is very illuminating. It shows the significant role of prophecy in the selection of leaders. The church at Antioch was, from the beginning, a mission centre having been founded by Cypriot believers driven out of Jerusalem by the persecution following the death of Stephen. They went there deliberately to take the gospel to the Greeks and the response was so overwhelming that the church at Jerusalem sent Barnabas to Antioch to investigate (Ac 11.19–24).

The church at Antioch was evidently seeking guidance as to the next phase of mission to the Greeks. They had declared a period of fasting and it was while they were worshipping that a prophetic message was received and carefully weighed. The message through the Holy Spirit was 'Set apart for me Barnabas and Saul for the work to which I have called them' (Ac 13.2). Clearly this was a major new development in ministry. Barnabas and Paul had already been chosen to take a gift to the elders of the Judean churches (Ac 11.30) and they evidently preached the gospel from place to place and no doubt encouraged the believers (Ac 12.25) before returning from Jerusalem to Antioch. (This is somewhat difficult to square with Paul's own statement in Galatians 1.22 that he personally was unknown to the churches of Judea.) The church at Antioch did not act immediately to put into effect the prophetic instruction. They did exactly what Paul later laid down as a dictum for the churches in Thessalonica; they weighed and tested it and awaited confirmation. After a further period of fasting and prayer the confirmation came and the whole church then laid their hands on Paul and Barnabas and sent them out on their first major missionary journey.

Timothy, also, was evidently brought into ministry through a prophetic message. As a young man the elders had prayed for him and laid on hands during which there was a prophecy declaring that a certain ministry gift, presumably the gift of teaching, would be given to him. Paul refers to the way Timothy was brought into ministry through prophecy in 1 Timothy 4.11–14 and in 1.18.

Strategy

The strategy for world evangelisation was given by the Lord Jesus to the apostles just before his Ascension. He had repeated his promise to send the Holy Spirit to them and had warned them to stay in Jerusalem until this was fulfilled; he then said, 'You will receive power when the Holy Spirit comes on you; and you will be my witnesses in Jerusalem, and in all Judea and Samaria, and to the ends of the earth' (Ac 1.8). The ever-widening circles of mission were to begin from Jerusalem, moving out through Judea into Samaria and then to all parts of the world. The record in Acts 8 speaks of the believers going throughout Judea and Samaria and recounts how many Samaritans became believers through the ministry of Philip, who then went to Gaza and through the coastal towns preaching the gospel until he reached Caesarea.

Luke's main interest in Acts is in following the mission of Paul but in doing so he notes how the strategy for mission given by Jesus was followed and actually directed by the Lord himself through the Holy Spirit. Prophecy played a major role in this. We have already noted how Paul and Barnabas were commissioned through a prophetic message for the task of mission. In Acts 13.4 Luke records that it was the Holy Spirit who directed them along the route they should take. This probably means that before leaving

Antioch there were prophetic messages indicating the route to be taken for the journey.

Prophecy played a major role in directing the missionary journeys of Paul. Luke records that 'Paul and his companions travelled throughout the region of Phrygia and Galatia, having been kept by the Holy Spirit from preaching the word in the province of Asia' (Ac 16.6). Paul and Silas evidently had a small company of believers with them who no doubt regularly had their times of worship and waiting upon the Lord for guidance. Either a prophetic message or possibly some physical event had evidently kept them from evangelism in Asia so they began to move in the direction of Bithynia. 'But the Spirit of Jesus would not allow them to' (16.7). Hence they made for the town of Troas concluding that the Lord Jesus was about to give them further travel directions to fulfil his original mission strategy. Paul spent the night in prayer during which he received a prophetic revelation. In a vision he saw a Greek in traditional Macedonian dress begging him to 'come over to Macedonia' and bring the gospel (16.9).

This was precisely the kind of direct guidance for which the party was looking. There was no need for further testing. The vision was confirmation of the route they had slowly found themselves being compelled to follow. Now they knew through this revelation that God was opening up a new area of evangelisation into Europe.

Prophetic revelation was important to Paul. He records in Galatians 2.2 how he went up to Jerusalem together with Barnabas and Titus to meet with the leaders of the Jerusalem church (probably for the Council of Jerusalem) but that he went as a result of a revelation. It was important for Paul that everywhere he went he had the assurance that he was being directed by the Holy Spirit.

Doctrine

In Paul's ministry it was not only *where* he preached the gospel that had to be under the direction of the Holy Spirit but of paramount importance was the gospel itself. Paul claimed divine revelation for the message he preached. It was given him, he declared, not through human consultation but as a revelation from God (Gal 1.15,16). 'I did not receive it from any man, nor was I taught it; rather, I received it by revelation from Jesus Christ' (Gal 1.12). Similarly in Ephesians 3.3 he refers to the 'mystery made known to me by revelation' and he concludes his letter to the Romans by referring to the gospel of Jesus Christ 'according to the revelation of the mystery hidden for long ages past, but now revealed and made known through the prophetic writings by the command of the eternal God, so that all nations might believe and obey him' (16.25,26).

Peter similarly speaks of the gospel as having been revealed by God through the Lord Jesus Christ (1 Pet 1.20). This was no doubt of increasing importance in the early church as opposition to the gospel mounted and as confusion arose through the distortions of the gospel by impostors and false teachers. Paul dealt with this in a number of his letters by stating firmly that 'even if an angel from heaven should preach a gospel other than the one we preach to you let him be eternally condemned!' (Gal 1.8).

The revealed nature of truth through the ministry of the Holy Spirit which was the evidence of the presence of the Lord Jesus in his church was the foundation of the doctrine held by the early church. Any changes or new developments in the beliefs and practices of the church had to come directly from the Lord through prophetic revelation. The outstanding example of this is seen in the Council of Jerusalem recorded in Acts 15. The question confronting the church was whether Greek believers should be required to be circumcised and to obey the law of Moses (15.5). The apostles and elders, together with the whole church, sent a letter to the Gentile believers in Antioch, Syria and Cilicia stating that they were not to be burdened with having to obey the law of Moses. The significant statement in the letter was, 'It seemed good to the Holy Spirit and to us not to burden you'

223

(15.28). Behind this simple statement there lies a supreme example of prophecy at work in the New Testament church with the elders discussing the issue and bringing their deliberations before the whole church for prayer and waiting upon the Lord. They were used to hearing directly from the Lord through the ministry of the Holy Spirit in prophetic messages and symbolic revelations. Without this prophetic activity the Council would have been a mere human debate but through the exercise of prophecy they were able to declare that 'it seemed good to the Holy Spirit and to us . . .'.

Foreknowledge
Prophecy was also the means by which the Holy Spirit gave forewarning of future events so that the young church could be prepared to meet special circumstances. The first example of this was a prophecy given in the church at Antioch when one of the leaders of the Jerusalem church, a man called Agabus who exercised the ministry of a prophet, visited the city and spoke in the church. Through the Holy Spirit he 'predicted that a severe famine would spread over the entire Roman world' (Ac 11.28). Luke tells us in parenthesis that this famine actually occurred during the reign of Claudius. The prophecy evidently indicated that the famine would be most severe in the province of Judea. Consequently a decision was taken 'to provide help for the brothers living in Judea' (11.29). Some years later Paul organised a similar collection for the impoverished believers, presumably in Judea, from among the churches of Greece and Asia Minor. The reason why God had given foreknowledge of the coming famine was so that the church could be prepared to meet the problem when the time came.

Similarly, a few years after Paul's death, a warning was given through prophecy of the coming destruction of Jerusalem by the Romans and the widescale slaughter of the people of Judea. This prophetic foreknowledge through an unknown prophet, possibly Agabus, enabled the church in Jerusalem to leave the city and relocate outside Judea at

Pella. When the Jewish revolt against the Romans took place in 68 AD and was followed by the destruction of Jerusalem in 70 AD none of the Christians was in the city. The entire church was saved through prophetic warning.

Paul received numerous prophetic warnings before he went up to Jerusalem for the last time. Luke records that when they landed at Tyre they stayed with the Christians there for seven days. '*Through the Spirit* they urged Paul not to go on to Jerusalem' (Ac 21.4). If the Holy Spirit was in fact speaking through them, as Luke states, then Paul was at fault in ignoring the prophetic forewarning he was given. These warnings were emphasised and confirmed when they reached Caesarea and stayed with Philip the evangelist whose four daughters all prophesied. As if this was not enough to stop the determination of Paul to go to Jerusalem the prophet Agabus arrived in Caesarea a few days later, which surely was no coincidence:

> He took Paul's belt, tied his own hands and feet with it and said, 'The Holy Spirit says, "In this way the Jews of Jerusalem will bind the owner of this belt and will hand him over to the Gentiles"' (Ac 21.11).

The first indication of Paul's projected journey to Jerusalem is in Acts 19.21 at Ephesus where Luke simply says, 'Paul *decided* to go to Jerusalem'. Not that Paul received a vision; or that the Holy Spirit instructed him, but '*Paul decided*'. This contrasts strangely with the way his ministry had been led by prophetic revelation up to this point. The whole record of his journey to Jerusalem speaks of eagerness and determination. He had organised a collection for the believers in Judea and he was determined to take it to them in person. Paul decided to avoid Ephesus despite an earlier promise to return there (Ac 18.21). 'For he was in a hurry to reach Jerusalem, if possible, by the Day of Pentecost' (20.16). He summoned the Ephesian elders to meet him at Miletus and, having told them his plans to visit Jerusalem, he admitted that he had received numerous prophetic warnings *through the Holy Spirit* that prison and hardship awaited him in Jerusalem. Nevertheless, he still felt 'compelled by the Spirit' to go (20.22).

We shall never know whether or not Paul was right to go to Jerusalem. On balance, the prima facie evidence points to Paul having made the wrong decision, although one hesitates to come to such a conclusion in view of Paul's strong conviction of being directed by God to go to Jerusalem. On arrival, however, he does not appear to have taken sufficient note of the warnings. Prophetic warnings cannot be ignored without incurring disastrous consequences. Foreknowledge of danger is only given through the Holy Spirit either so that it may be avoided or that adequate preparation may be made to meet the special circumstances that will arise.

Paul took no action either to avoid the danger by not going to Jerusalem or to take particular care during his visit. Despite the warnings of the Jerusalem elders he was seen openly walking in the streets with Greeks (Ac 21.29). It would appear that despite the fact that according to Paul's own testimony he was 'an apostle to the Gentiles' (Gal 2.9; Rm 11.13) he was determined to have a share in ministry in Jerusalem. He evidently expected his testimony to be the turning point in the evangelisation of the city, but when he had the opportunity to address the crowd the result was disastrous (Ac 22.1-22).

James and the elders of the Jerusalem church reported that many thousands of Jews in and around Jerusalem were believers (Ac 21.20) but the uproar consequent upon Pauls' visit no doubt was a great setback to the gospel in that city. For Paul too the visit was a personal tragedy. It meant the end of his active ministry and he spent the rest of his life in prison. Prophetic foreknowledge is not given to be lightly handled or ignored. Nevertheless, in his letters from prison, Paul does not even contemplate the possibility that his imprisonment might not have been God's purpose for him. He claims, indeed, that it worked out for the furtherance of the gospel (Phil 1.12).

No doubt we would not have had the precious letters Paul wrote from prison if it had not been for his confinement. This, at least, makes his suffering worthwhile from our standpoint!

The Gift of Prophecy

Peter's declaration at Pentecost linking Joel's prophecy with the events of that day was significant for the practice of prophecy through the New Testament period of the church. Joel had said that all the people would prophesy—young and old, men and women, servants and masters—implying that there would be no distinction of age, sex, or social rank in the distribution of spiritual gifts. This became the standard in the community of believers from the first day. They held all things in common and devoted themselves to establishing a community in which belonging to Christ was of greater significance than human distinctions. Paul expressed this in a summary statement to the Galatians:

> You are all sons of God through faith in Christ Jesus, for all of you who were baptised into Christ have clothed yourself with Christ. There is neither Jew nor Greek, slave nor free, male nor female, for you are all one in Christ Jesus (Gal 3.26-28).

This is Paul's definitive statement in regard to relationships within the body of Christ. Among the believers there were to be no distinctions other than the recognition of different spiritual gifts. These produced differences in *function* but not differences in *status*. Paul recognised only two states—those who were sons of God and those who were not. All those who were baptised into Christ were sons of God—not sons and *daughters*, but sons of God 'and heirs according to the promise' (3.29) with an equal share in the inheritance of the spiritual gifts. God had graciously bestowed upon all those who had entered into the new relationship with him through Christ.

227

Paul has often been misunderstood, and his teaching misinterpreted, in regard to the place of women in the churches. This has come about largely because he had to deal with a particularly difficult situation in the church at Corinth where there was a group of married women who were contentious and not only misused the gifts (as did the men also) but actually engaged in arguments during worship and thus destroyed any hope of the Holy Spirit being effective in the life of the fellowship. He told them to be quiet and to discuss spiritual matters with their husbands at home privately and not to interrupt the worship when all the house fellowships came together.

Paul nevertheless told *all the believers* at Corinth that they could prophesy. He did not say that only the men could prophesy. In fact he specifically referred to the women praying and prophesying, although for practical and cultural reasons he preferred them modestly dressed and with some kind of head covering (perhaps to help the carnal men of Corinth to keep their minds on spiritual matters!).

Paul's strict instructions on the right use of the gifts in Corinth have to be seen in the light of the local situation. Despite their pride, their divisions and their blatant carnality, he nevertheless encouraged all the believers to exercise spiritual gifts, especially the gift of prophesy. 'Be eager to prophesy', he said in 14.1 and again in 14.39. But everything had to be done in an orderly fashion, 'You can all prophesy in turn' (14.31), men and women.

The mention in Acts 21.9 of the four unmarried daughters of Philip who all prophesied is an indication of the general acceptance of women prophesying in the early church. Philip, who exercised the ministry of an evangelist, was one of the original seven leaders of the Greek Christian churches recognised by the apostles. The mention of his daughters prophesying does not indicate that they were recognised as prophets in the same way as Agabus. The implication is that they exercised the *gift* of prophecy within the local church at Caesarea. Agabus is mentioned in the very next verse (Ac

228

21.10) and in distinction from Philip's daughters 'who prophesied' he is described as *'a prophet'* who 'came down from Judea.' The ministry Agabus exercised was clearly not confined to the churches of Judea. Indeed, on an earlier occasion he had prophesied in Antioch. He was evidently widely accepted as a prophet among the churches.

This underlined the contrast between the ministry of the prophet and the gift of prophecy. *The prophet exercised a ministry to the whole church, whereas the gift of prophecy was exercised within a local church.* It was the exercise of this gift locally to which Paul was referring when he urged the Corinthians to be eager to prophesy. They could all receive a word from the Lord that was opposite to the local situation and that would bring strength and encouragement to other believers within the fellowship.

The Ministry of Prophecy

We have just been noting the contrast between the gift of prophecy and the ministry of the prophet. Throughout the first two or three centuries in the life of the early church there were prophets like Agabus who travelled from city to city bringing the word of God to the churches. Theirs was an itinerant rather than a localized ministry. It is this wider ministry of the prophet that is examined in this section.

Itinerant Prophets

From the earliest days of the extension of the church beyond Judea there were itinerant prophets exercising ministry among the churches. None of the five men named as being prophets and teachers in the church at Antioch in Acts 13.1 were local Antioch men. They were Barnabas from Cyprus; Simeon called Niger, which means black, probably from Africa; Lucius of Cyrene; Manaen who had been brought up with Herod the Tetrarch, *ie* Herod Antipas, probably from Galilee, and Paul from Tarsus. There were other itinerants who were also known as prophets, such as Judas and Silas who were sent out to the Gentile churches, travelling from place to place with the letter from the Council of Jerusalem, not only reading it but conveying its message in their own words. 'Judas and Silas, who themselves were prophets, said much to encourage and strengthen the brothers' (Ac 15.32).

Jesus spoke of 'prophets and wise men and teachers' being sent who would be persecuted by the Jewish community (Mt 23.34). Similarly, Jesus is reported as teaching on the obligations of hospitality in the Christian community. 'Anyone who received a prophet because he is a prophet will receive a prophet's reward, and anyone who receives a righteous man because he is a righteous man will receive a righteous man's reward' (Mt 10.41). Clearly it was envisaged that there would be travelling prophets and teachers moving among the churches.

Very little distinction was made between prophets, teachers and apostles in the first century AD. In the Acts it is not only the eleven plus Matthias who were spoken of as apostles, but also Paul and Barnabas and, by implication, James (Ac 14.14; 15.6). Paul used the term in a somewhat wider connotation. He referred to an otherwise unknown couple 'Andronicus and Junias' as being 'outstanding among the apostles' (Rm 16.7). The latter, being feminine, indicates that Paul recognised women as apostles. Paul also links apostles and prophets together as being the foundation of the church whose cornerstone is the Lord Jesus (Eph 2.20). This lack of clear distinction between the ministries was a reflection of the lack of 'church order' during this formative period in the life of the church as new congregations were established right across the Roman world.

False Prophets
The lack of church order and clear definition of ministry roles created problems, especially in regard to true and false prophets. There is plenty of evidence in the New Testament of the activity of false prophets and false religious teachers. Paul's first encounter at the beginning of his first missionary

journey was with 'a Jewish sorcerer and false prophet named Bar-Jesus' (Ac 13.6) who opposed their ministry in Cyprus when they were invited to explain the gospel to the proconsul, Sergius Paulus. There are a number of textual difficulties in this account, notably Luke's statement that Elymas means sorcerer. It was probably a semitic word corresponding to the Greek *magos* (perhaps cognate with the Arabic *alim*, 'sage'). Nobody knows what lies behind the statement (v8) but it would appear from Paul's forthright denunciation of the man that he was not simply dabbling in the occult but claiming some connection with the teaching of Jesus. Paul's indignation boiled over, 'You are a child of the devil and an enemy of everything that is right! You are full of all kinds of deceit and trickery. Will you never stop perverting the right ways of the Lord? Now the hand of the Lord is against you. You are going to be blind...' (Ac 13.10-11). Paul knew how to deal with false prophets!

According to the evidence of the Synoptic Gospels Jesus warned about the problems of dealing with false prophets. 'For false Christs and false prophets will appear and perform signs and miracles to deceive the elect—if that were possible. So be upon your guard' (Mk 13.22,23). Similar warnings are given in the eschatological discourse in Matthew 24 where Jesus emphasises that 'many false prophets will appear and deceive many people' (v11). Jesus warned that prophecy in his name was not necessarily genuine and even words that were accompanied by miraculous signs and wonders were not necessarily from God. 'Many will say to me on that day, "Lord, Lord, did we not prophesy in your name and in your name drive out demons and perform many miracles?" Then I will tell them plainly, "I never knew you. Away from me you evildoers!"' (Mt 7.22,23).

Countering the effects of false prophets was a major problem in the early church. The problems were experienced not only in dealing with unknown men who arrived at a church claiming to be prophets but with the false prophecies that circulated around the churches as a result of their deceptive ministries. Paul refers to this in one of his letters to the churches in Thessalonica.

> Concerning the coming of our Lord Jesus Christ and our being gathered to him, we ask you, brothers, not to become easily unsettled or alarmed by some prophecy, report or letter supposed to have come from us, saying that the day of the Lord has already come. Don't let anyone deceive you in any way ... (2 Th 2.1-3).

Towards the end of the first century the problem was becoming really acute. In the first letter of John he declared that 'Many false prophets have gone out into the world' (1 Jn 4.1). It was the existence of these false prophets that prompted Paul to instruct the churches to 'test everything' (1 Th 5.21). The subject of testing prophecy became one of great importance for the early church and we shall devote the next chapter to examining this. The tension within the early church arose out of the conviction that the Lord Jesus had established the church and that he himself was continually present within the body of believers guiding and directing the mission of the church. They believed that this guidance was given prophetically through the Holy Spirit. Hence Paul's instruction to 'test everything' was preceded by the plea, 'Do not put out the Spirit's fire; do not treat prophecies with contempt.' The tension arose through the desire to hear the authentic voice of the Lord, while at the same time being aware of the presence of deceivers with false prophecies and false teachings that had to be discerned, exposed and rejected. For Paul, however, the alternative to false prophecy was not no prophecy!

Later practices
The later canonical books of the New Testament, such as the Epistles of John and Revelation, give ample evidence of the regular exercise of prophecy in the church of the first

century. Revelation is particularly important as it is the only book in the New Testament which explicitly claims to have been written by a prophet. His understanding of prophecy is summed up in Revelation 19.10: 'The testimony of Jesus is the spirit of prophecy.' Two of the seven churches of Asia Minor were said to be troubled by false prophets and teachers: the church of Pergamum and the church of Thyatira, where a self-styled prophetess by the name of Jezebel was misleading the congregation. It was the presence of so much dubious teaching and practices arising from false prophets that gave rise to the attempt by early church leaders to define orthodox Christian belief and practice. Prophets were highly honoured throughout the first century. This is clear not only from canonical New Testament writings but also from early church documents such as the *Didache* and the *Shepherd of Hermas*. Both these documents are obscure in their origins but nevertheless provide valuable evidence for teaching and practice in the early church.

The *Didache*, whose original title was 'The Teaching of the Twelve Apostles for the Gentile Churches', probably originated from the church at Antioch in Syria around 90 AD. This was the church described in Acts 13.1 as having 'prophets and teachers'. It was the home base for Paul's missionary journeys and it was the church where Agabus prophesied the forthcoming famine throughout the region.

One of the objectives of the *Didache* was to commend to the congregations within its sphere of influence the appointment of local church leaders. The appeal was made that such men should be given recognition and honour in the same way as the itinerant prophets and teachers who served the wider church.

Appoint for yourselves therefore bishops and deacons worthy of the Lord, men who are meek and not lovers of money, true and reliable; for they also perform for you the ministry of prophets and teachers.

Do not despise them therefore; for they are your men of honour together with the prophets and teachers (Did 15.1).

The terms 'apostle' and 'prophet' appear interchangeable in the *Didache* and there seems to be no distinction between their respective functions with the two terms even being used interchangeably in the same sentence.

Concerning the apostles and prophets, act according to the ordinance of the gospel. Let every apostle, when he comes to you, be received as the Lord; but he shall not stay more than a single day, or if need, a second; but if he remains three days, he is a false prophet (Did 11.3).

By the end of the first century AD, all over the Christian world, the subject of prophecy had become a cause of acute difficulty. On the one hand if a visiting preacher was a true prophet, to reject him would be a matter possibly involving the gravest consequences.

Any prophets speaking in the Spirit, you must not test, neither pass judgment on; for every sin will be forgiven, but this sin will not be forgiven (Did 11.7).

On the other hand, bitter experience had shown that dangerous deceivers and false prophets had gone out and were everywhere troubling the congregations. There was an urgent need for clear means of testing prophecy.

Despite all the advice given on testing prophecy in the New Testament, the *Didache* and the *Shepherd of Hermas,* the matter continued to trouble the church throughout the second century and many church leaders took the simple expedient of banning all prophecy. Against such a practice Irenaeus, writing about 185 AD, said:

Others, again, that they might set at nought the gift of the Holy Spirit, which in the latter times has been by the good pleasure of the Father, poured out upon the human race, do not accept that Gospel of John in which the Lord promised that he would send the Paraclete; but set aside at once both the Gospel and the prophetic Spirit. Wretched men indeed, who in order not to allow false prophets set aside the gift of prophecy from the church; ...These men cannot admit the apostle Paul either, for in his Epistle to the Corinthians, he speaks expressly of prophetical gifts, and recognises men and women prophesying in the church. Sinning, therefore, in all particulars, against the Spirit of God, they fall into irremissible sin (Irenaeus, *Adversus Haereses* III, 11.9).

CHAPTER THIRTEEN

TESTING PROPHECY

Anyone who speaks a word against the Son of Man will be forgiven, but anyone who speaks against the Holy Spirit will not be forgiven, either in this age or in the age to come (Mt 12.32).

These words of Jesus warning about the serious consequences of rejecting the Holy Spirit added fear to the dilemma facing the early church that we noted in the previous chapter. To reject prophecy that was genuinely the work of the Holy Spirit could be a mortal sin; but to be deceived by impostors also presented grave dangers. Both Paul and John warned the churches to test everything. John's warning that 'many deceivers have gone out into the world' implied that believers could lose their right relationship with God by allowing themselves to be deceived into believing false teaching. He said, 'Watch out that you do not lose what you have worked for . . . Anyone who runs ahead and does not continue in the teaching of Christ does not have God' (2 Jn 8,9).

Paul's instruction to test everything and only to hold on to that which was good, rejecting the evil, implied a 'sifting process' by which prophecy could be tested (1 Th 5.21).

The problem of false prophecy was not new. It was a

problem that had confronted Israel under the old covenant for centuries. It was one of the problems dealt with in Deuteronomy:

> If anyone does not listen to my words that the prophet speaks in my name, I myself will call him to account. But a prophet who presumes to speak in my name anything I have not commanded him to say, or a prophet who speaks in the name of other gods, must be put to death (Dt 18.19,20).

Here, the penalty for false prophecy fell squarely upon the prophet. He would be held to account for misleading the people. The people themselves were not expected to have that discernment; although there was a collective responsibility, that fell primarily on the shoulders of the leaders. The people were expected to believe what they were told in the name of the Lord. This well illustrates the fundamental difference of the new covenant which was foreseen by Jeremiah (31.31) where each individual believer would be held responsible before God for his beliefs and practices. This, of course, could only be made possible by the gift of the Holy Spirit to all believers and especially through the availability of the gift of discernment. John was referring to this gift when he urged the believers to 'test the spirits to see whether they are from God' (1 Jn 4.1). He knew that believers had been given the ability to detect the presence of evil spirits and to discern that which was of the Spirit of God.

There were tests available for the congregations in the early church, some dealing with the words spoken and others with the character and conduct of the prophet, such as: does he confess that Jesus is the Messiah come in the flesh; does the prophecy glorify Jesus as Lord; does it build up the faith of the church; does it conform with known apostolic teaching?

The tests of prophecy recognised in the early church can

best be summarised under the four headings: *fulfilment; doctrine; edification,* and *the character and conduct of the prophet.*

Fulfilment

The simplest test of the prophet was to examine his teaching and to note if he said anything of a predictive manner. If he did, then the simple test of fulfilment could be applied. Did what the prophet said would happen actually take place; were his words fulfilled? This was the test advocated in Deuteronomy 18.22, 'If what a prophet proclaims in the name of the Lord does not take place or come true, that is a message the Lord has not spoken.' God cannot lie and if the prophet declares God has said something that does not take place, clearly he has not spoken the word of the Lord.

Jeremiah applied this test to the false prophet Hananiah.

From early times the prophets who preceded you and me have prophesied war, disaster and plague against many countries and great kingdoms. But the prophet who prophesies peace will be recognised as one truly sent by the Lord only if his prediction comes true (Jer 28.8,9).

In fact it was because Jeremiah also applied this same test to himself that he went through agonies of mental torture because his predictions of coming disaster at the hands of the Babylonians were so long delayed in their fulfilment. His agonies of self-doubt, 'O Lord, you deceived me, and I was deceived' (20.7), even led him to cry out to God to hasten the fulfilment of his predictions, 'So give their children over to famine; hand them over to the power of the sword' (18.21). All the prophets recognised that the test of fulfilment would be the means by which their predictive prophecies would be judged. Ezekiel spelt this out, 'When all this comes true—and it surely will—then they will know that a prophet has been among them' (Eze 33.33).

The incident concerning the prophet Agabus in the New

Testament indicates that the same test was applied by the early church. He predicted that a severe famine would spread over the entire Roman world and Luke adds in parenthesis 'This happened during the reign of Claudius' (Ac 11.28). It was no doubt important for the readers to know that this man who travelled widely, not only among the churches in Judea but also in Syria and probably farther afield, was a true prophet whose words were fulfilled.

Agabus' prophecy at Caesarea of what would happen to Paul in Jerusalem is an interesting example of how the prophet sometimes receives the main thrust of a message through revelation, but gets the minutiae wrong. Agabus said that the Jews of Jerusalem would bind Paul and hand him over to the Gentiles (Ac 21.11) whereas in fact the Romans rescued him from the Jews and they bound him (Ac 21.33). Agabus was nevertheless recognised as a true prophet whose word was fulfilled.

Doctrine

The fact that a prophet's words of prediction came true did not, however, of itself constitute a test of authenticity. Other tests were also necessary. It was only non-fulfilment that could be regarded as a reliable test, although only in the negative sense. This was made clear in Deuteronomy 13.1 where it is said that if a prophet predicts something that does come true and even if he confirms it with miraculous signs but then says, 'Let us follow other gods and worship them' he should be rejected as a false prophet. The context implies that God has actually allowed the false prophet to have miraculous powers in order to test the love and loyalty of the people. The fase prophet was to be put to death 'because he preached rebellion against the Lord' (Dt 13.5).

The way Jeremiah dealt with the false prophet Hananiah was exactly in line with the teaching of Deuteronomy 18. He said, 'This is what the Lord says; "I am about to remove you from the face of the earth. This very year you are going to die, because you have preached rebellion against the Lord"'

(Jer 28.16). He made a similar pronouncement of punishment coming upon Shemaiah 'because he has preached rebellion' (Jer 29.32). False prophecy and false teaching from the time of Moses through to the post-exilic period was seen as rebellion against God.

The one thing the prophets of ancient Israel stood for above all others was loyalty to God. Over the centuries their teaching formed a body of doctrine that provided the nation with a standard of belief, a plumb-line, to use Amos' term. This became the norm for judging the truth or falsity of any new doctrinal statement or teaching about the nature and purposes of God.

The appeal to established doctrine was a principle that was still adhered to in rabbinical circles in New Testament times. Hence we find Paul stating emphatically in his defence before King Agrippa and Festus, 'I am saying nothing beyond what the prophets and Moses said would happen' (Ac 26.22).

The practice of using Scripture, as established doctrine, to test prophecy or fresh revelation was followed from the early days of the New Testament church. James, presiding over the Council at Jerusalem, used this principle in testing the teaching that Paul and Barnabas brought concerning the gospel among the Gentiles. In his summary statement he declared, 'The words of the prophets are in agreement with this' (Ac 15.15). Paul writing to the church at Corinth, refers to what was evidently a well-known saying, 'Do not go beyond what is written' (1 Cor 4.6).

The principle of regarding Scripture as the norm of truth is clearly stated in 2 Timothy 3.16 which says that all Scripture is divinely inspired and must therefore be regarded as the word of God and the ultimate standard for correct teaching. This was the principle underlying the proclamation of the gospel right from the Day of Pentecost when Peter's speech to the crowds in Jerusalem included quotations from the prophet Joel and the Psalms. His appeal was to Scripture as the norm of truth.

This principle was strictly adhered to wherever the gospel

was proclaimed and in time there is an important addition to the practice of appealing to Scripture—that of appealing to the teaching of the apostles who themselves only taught that which was in conformity with Scripture.

The pastoral epistles contain numerous references to the dangers of false doctrine (*eg* 1 Timothy 6.3; 2 Timothy 2.17) and urge strict adherence to the teaching originally given and approved by the apostles. Hence Timothy was urged, 'What you heard from me, keep as the pattern of sound teaching, with faith and love in Christ Jesus. Guard the good deposit that was entrusted to you' (2 Tim 1.13, 14).

Similarly, Paul warned the Romans:

I urge you, brothers, to watch out for those who cause divisions and put obstacles in your way that are contrary to the teaching you have learned. Keep away from them. For such people are not serving our Lord Christ, but their own appetites. By smooth talking and flattery they deceive the minds of naive people (Rm 16.17,18).

Sound teaching was that given by the apostles (2 Th 3.6) and Paul relates this principle to both the ministry and the gift of prophecy in the instructions he gives the Corinthians.

If anybody thinks he is a prophet or spiritually gifted, let him acknowledge that what I am writing to you is the Lord's command. If he ignores this, he himself will be ignored (1 Cor 14.37).

The *Didache* uses similar words in urging the rejection of false prophets. If the prophet does not proclaim the truth, he is to be ignored (Did 11.1). It is the already established body of truth that serves as the criterion by which any prophetic proclamation must be tested.

The Epistles of John set out clearly both the criterion to be used in evaluating the pronouncements of visiting prophets and teachers and also the steps to be taken in dealing with impostors. John links false prophets with deceivers and deceivers are the antichrist (2 Jn 7). According to John the false prophets had 'gone out into the world'. They had separated themselves from the fellowship of believers. 'They went out from us but they did not really belong to us' (1 Jn 2.19). They proved this by departing from the truth as it had been established and confirmed through the teaching of the apostles.

The true believers would be able to recognise the false prophets by their teaching. 'Every spirit that acknowledges that Jesus Christ has come in the flesh is from God' (1 Jn 4.2). Those who did not acknowledge Jesus as Lord and Messiah, the divine Son of God, born in the flesh, crucified and risen again, were false prophets whose teaching even if given in the form of prophetic pronouncements, was to be rejected.

The true believers have an anointing from the Holy Spirit to enable them to discern the truth (1 Jn 2.20). They were to remain faithful to the teaching they had been given from the beginning and then they could be sure of remaining in Christ.

As for the false prophets who tried to deceive the believers by running ahead and not continuing in the truth, their teaching should not only be rejected but they themselves should be put out of the fellowship.

> If ayone comes to you and does not bring this teaching, do not take him into your house or welcome him. Anyone who welcomes him shares in his wicked work (2 Jn 10,11).

The major emphasis in John's teaching in dealing with false prophecy was the doctrinal test—does it conform with Scripture and with the known body of sound teaching given from the beginning by the apostles and those who have been appointed by the Lord Jesus as leaders in his church whose work and words were confirmed by the Holy Spirit?

Edification

In studying Paul's correspondence with the churches and the record of his life and ministry that we have in Acts there are two outstanding facts in relation to prophecy. The first is that Paul valued prophecy highly and often relied upon prophetic revelation for the direction of the day-to-day affairs of his ministry. The second is that a major test of authentic prophecy for Paul lay in its ability to 'edify' or 'build-up' the church. In order to understand fully these two points they need to be seen in the context of the nature and function of prophecy in its New Testament setting.

The concept of prophecy in the New Testament is identical with that of the major prophets of Israel under the old covenant. It was the revealed word of God that related to the contemporary situation or developments therefrom in the light of the nature and purposes of God. When we come to the function of prophecy, however, there is a major difference between prophecy in ancient Israel and prophecy in New Testament times. Although the basic function is the same, *ie* that of declaring or revealing a word of God, the recipients of prophecy are different. Under the old covenant it is the nation Israel that is addressed, whereas in New Testament times prophecy is addressed to *the church*, to the body of believers in Christ Jesus.

In the New Testament there is no record of a prophecy being addressed to the Roman Empire or to the pagan nations. There is no suggestion of, 'Thus says the Lord to Caesar!' There is not even any evidence in the New Testament, outside the Gospels, of a prophetic word being addressed to the nation Israel. The last prophetic words addressed to the leaders of Israel were by Jesus, 'Woe to you, teachers of the law and Pharisees, you hypocrites! You build tombs for the prophets....' (Mt 23.29).

Paul had an ideal opportunity to prophesy both to Rome and Israel when he addressed the provincial governor Festus

244

and King Agrippa (Ac 25-26). Instead of 'Thus says the Lord' he addressed them politely, respectfully and rationally. To secular men he used secular language to try to persuade them to see the truth that he had received by divine revelation. It failed.

When Paul attempted to describe what had been revealed to him, Festus interrupted and said he was out of his mind. For Paul, this must have been confirmation of the rightness of his teaching that revelation is directed to the church, to believers, not to unbelievers. The only thing that speaks to unbelievers is the basic gospel message of salvation. Hence the Great Commission begins with the command to 'make disciples', rather than teaching them about doctrine or practice. It is the experience of forgiveness of sins and entering a new relationship with God through Christ that speaks to unbelievers. Once they become believers they are open to receive revelation and, through the Holy Spirit, God can communicate with them. Paul knew this from his own experience and from everything that happened on his missionary journeys.

It was because Paul knew that prophecy was addressed to the church to enable it to carry out its primary task of serving the world that Paul made edification or 'building up' his major test of authentic prophecy. If it was a true word from God through the Holy Spirit it would build up the church. A true prophecy would build faith, increase understanding, broaden vision and strengthen the unity of the Christian community. A true prophecy would not be destructive and judgmental even though it might contain rebuke or correction. It would build community, not disintegrate it.

Unbelievers simply scoff at the very notion of divine revelation whereas believers have experienced the presence and power of God through the Holy Spirit, and they expect him to speak because they know his love for them is like that of a father for his children. He wants them to know the truth. And just as children recognise the voice of their own father so believers recognise the voice of their heavenly Father when he speaks to them.

For Paul, it was as simple as that; prophecy was addressed to the community of believers and anything that truly was from God would build community and lead to maturity. Hence his statement in Ephesians 4.12 that the ministry gifts were given to build up the body of Christ for works of service and as they did so believers would no longer be led astray by deceitful men (v14). Instead, they will speak the truth in love and the whole community will be built up in love (v16). In fact, even in private conversation they should only speak that which is helpful for building up the community of believers (v29), otherwise they would grieve the Holy Spirit who had sealed their salvation (v30).

For Paul, the supreme test of genuine prophecy is found in the word 'love'. This is why all three passages dealing with spiritual gifts—and Paul regards prophecy as the highest of the gifts—emphasise the central importance of love. The passages are found in Ephesians 4, 1 Corinthians 12-14 and Romans 12.

Paul teaches that anyone who is genuinely inspired by the Spirit of God to bring his word to the church, whether exercising the ministry of the prophet to the wider church or using the gift of prophecy in the local fellowship, will act in love as the primary and dominant motive. This will be seen in the speaker's humility, not arrogance (Eph 4.2), his sincerity (Rm 12.9) and sensitivity to others (Rm 12.14-16). When speaking a word of rebuke it would be very clearly spoken in love (Eph 4.15) not to crush or condemn. A true prophecy would strengthen faith, encourage the faint-hearted and comfort those in distress (1 Cor 14.3). It would edify the church (v4); it would be a convincing word that would win the sinner (v24).

The true prophet would await his turn to speak (v31); would give way to another who also had a revelation (v30); would gladly submit his words to be weighed by others (v29); would do everything in an orderly peaceful manner (v33);

would speak in simple language intelligible to the whole church (v19); would exercise his mind as well as his spirit (v20), and above all would be concerned for the unity of the body of Christ (12.13).

True prophecy, in Paul's teaching, would edify the fellowship, for prophecy (if rightly responded to) turns division into unity, strife into peace, fear into faith, and binds believers together in love. Paul's overall concern with the exercise of spiritual gifts was that everything should be done in love. Even if a word of judgment had to be spoken in a fellowship it should be done gently and with humility so that the sinner would be brought to repentance and restored to a right relationship rather than driven out (Gal 6.1).

John's teaching was very similar. Throughout his epistles he emphasises the centrality of love. 'This is his command,' he wrote 'to believe in the name of his Son, Jesus Christ, and to love one another as he commanded us' (1 Jn 3.23). For John, the final test of any word purporting to be from God was not simply whether or not the speaker *claimed* to be speaking in love but whether he actually *showed* the love of Christ in his life. 'Dear children,' he wrote 'let us not love with words or tongue but with actions and in truth' (1 Jn 3.18).

Character and Conduct

Towards the end of the New Testament period the major emphasis in testing prophecy moved away from the content of the prophecy to the person of the prophet. Hence we find that neither the *Shepherd of Hermas* nor the *Didache* lay much stress upon doctrine when dealing with the problems of false prophecy. The emphasis is upon the character and conduct of the prophet. The *Didache* gave strict instructions that a prophet who was speaking under divine inspiration was not to be interrupted since to do so was to utter blasphemy against the Holy Spirit. At the same time there was recognition that not everyone who claimed to be speaking in

247

the name of the Lord was sent by him. The false prophets could be detected by their behaviour.

> While a prophet is uttering words in the Spirit, you are on no account to subject him to any tests or verifications; every sin shall be forgiven but this sin shall not be forgiven (Mt 12.31). Nevertheless, not all who speak in the Spirit are prophets, unless they also exhibit the manners and conduct of the Lord. It is by their behaviour that the false prophet and the true are to be distinguished. Thus, if a prophet should happen to call out for something to eat while he is speaking in the Spirit, he will not actually eat of it; if he does, he is a fraud. Also, even supposing a prophet is sound enough in his teaching, yet if his deeds do not correspond with his words he is a false prophet...If any man shall say in the Spirit, 'Give me money' or anything else, you shall not listen to him; but if he tells you to give on behalf of others who are in want, let no man judge him (Did 11.7-12).

This emphasis upon the moral behaviour of the prophet was probably a direct outcome of the teaching of Jesus himself on the subject of testing prophecy. Jesus not only told the Pharisees that he would be sending out prophets (Mt 23.34) but privately he warned his disciples that the situation would become confused by a number of false prophets who would appear actually claiming to speak in his name. 'Many will say to me on that day, "Lord, Lord, did we not prophesy in your name" ...I will tell them plainly, "I never knew you ..."' (Mt 7.23).

In the same passage Jesus warned 'Watch out for false prophets' and the test he gave was 'By their *fruit* you will recognise them.' Jesus used several analogies from nature concerning good fruit and bad fruit. Basically he was saying, you do not get good fruit from a diseased tree, you get only bad fruit. In the same way you can look at a person's life; if it is spiritually diseased and morally corrupt it is not going to produce good deeds. The behaviour and conduct of a person reveals the character of that person. A bad character will produce bad fruit and a good character will produce good fruit. Jesus applied this teaching to testing prophecy. The false prophet will be betrayed by his evil deeds.

This teaching of Jesus is fully in line with that of the Old Testament where the lives of the false prophets were bound up with immorality as well as spiritual apostasy. The true prophets who were sent by God not only stood for loyalty to Yahweh and spiritual purity but also stood against sexual immorality and all kinds of immoral behaviour such as lying, cheating, exploitation and injustice. The eighth-century prophets spoke fearlessly and forthrightly against these sins. But the false prophets actually encouraged the people to sin, 'They strengthen the hands of evil-doers so that no-one turns from his wickedness' (Jer 23.14). In the same chapter Jeremiah speaks of prophets and priests engaging in all kinds of wickedness including prophesying by Baal and committing adultery. They were false prophets who invented visions in the imaginations of their own minds and proclaimed words to the people that God had not spoken.

Similarly, Micah spoke of false prophets as liars and deceivers who would accept bribes from the people and would prophesy any word that the people wanted provided they were paid enough (Mic 3.5); and Isaiah complained that the false prophets got drunk on wine and beer before they had their visions which they used to deceive the people (Is 28.7).

True prophecy led the people into the ways of purity and holiness, for God was holy and he required holiness of his people. They had been warned against allowing their worship of God to become contaminated by the worship of other gods as practised by the other nations. 'They do all kinds of detestable things the Lord hates. They even burn their sons and daughters in the fire as sacrifices to their gods' (Dt 12.31). The false prophets set up Asherah poles as sex symbols and led the people into all kinds of perversions

249

including heterosexual and homosexual shrine prostitution (2 Kg 23.7). Jesus no doubt had these things in mind when he declared, 'By their fruit you will know them.' The false prophets led the people to worship other gods—spiritual apostasy—and they legitimised immoral behaviour. These were precisely the charges that the Spirit of the Lord Jesus brought against two of the churches in Asia Minor recorded in Revelation 2.

In the church at Pergamum the Nicolaitans were giving teaching similar to that of the false prophet Balaam, 'who taught Balak to entice the Israelites to sin by eating food sacrificed to idols and by committing sexual immorality' (Rev 2.14). Similarly, in the church at Thyatira there was a false prophetess referred to as 'Jezebel' who was also leading the people astray into sexual immorality and idolatrous practices.

It was by their deeds that these people were shown to be false prophets. Their words, for which they claimed divine inspiration, were proved to be false because they misled the people and encouraged evil practices. Jesus' teaching here had a clear application—by their fruit you will know them. The true prophet would be leading people into godly ways, that is, into lives of whose behaviour God would approve. Their worship would be pure and holy, acknowledging one God and his only Son Jesus the Messiah who had come in the flesh and who had been crucified and raised from the dead. Every true Spirit would confess the Lordship of Jesus and would glorify Christ.

The true spirit of prophecy would lead people into ways of gentleness and peace, into lives of love and service. They would bear one another's burdens and think more highly of others than themselves. Their lives would be strictly moral. If they were unmarried they would be chaste in their behaviour. If they were married they would be faithful to one partner. In family life they would bring up their children in the love and knowledge of the Lord Jesus. The true believers would shun lustful and immoral behaviour, lying, cheating, stealing and deceitful ways. True prophecy would promote all the things that are good, just and loving.

False prophecy would lead to immorality and lovelessness. The false prophet would be judgmental, self-seeking, greedy and ambitious. The true prophet would be humble, gentle and loving in all his ways, and his words would promote the unity, spiritual health and well-being of the whole body of believers. His character and conduct would be in harmony with the Spirit of the Lord Jesus who had sent him and whose precious word he guarded and proclaimed among the believers so that the whole body of Christ could be built up and come to maturity to carry out its work of service in the world.

The lives of the true prophets and those who exercised the gift of prophecy bore fruit unto righteousness. Through them the Spirit of the Lord Jesus appealed to the believers. 'Let us love one another, for love comes from God. Everyone who loves has been born of God and knows God' (1 Jn 4.7).

CHAPTER FOURTEEN

THE PERIOD OF TRANSITION

Prophecy virtually disappeared from the church by the end of the second century AD although for some churches, notably Thyatira, it remained a powerful influence for several hundred years. In view of the significant role played by prophetic revelation in New Testament times this may seem surprising. Most church historians account for the demise of prophecy as part of the disappearance of all spiritual gifts from the church in the sub-apostolic age. The view generally taken is that spiritual gifts were withdrawn from the church after the deaths of the apostles and first disciples who were eye-witnesses of the Lord Jesus because they were no longer required. The task of the church in the first generation was primarily to be a witness to the historical events of the life, death, resurrection and teaching of the Lord Jesus. After the first generation passed away the task of the second and successive generations was to preserve and pass on the teaching that was handed to them by the generation of eye-witnesses.

Most church historians take the view that the spiritual gifts were given to the church by the Lord at Pentecost for the specific task of taking the word out from Jerusalem and planting churches wherever they were sent. Once the church moved from the initial missionary stage to that of local congregations with settled leadership, the spiritual gifts were obsolescent and were therefore withdrawn. This ignores the fact that the New Testament record clearly shows that the spiritual gifts were not simply given to the apostles and eye-witness disciples who went out preaching and planting churches, neither were they only given to the prophets and teachers who travelled from city to city visiting the congregations established through the ministries of men like Paul and Barnabas. The spiritual gifts were given to the ordinary believers in each congregation, in fact, to all those who received the Holy Spirit. Hence Peter's statement at Pentecost that all who were baptised into Christ would receive the gift of the Holy Spirit which was promised for this first generation *and for their children* (Ac 2.39). Peter also included in this promise 'all who are far off', clearly meaning the Gentiles as well as the Jews. This actually happened according to his own testimony of events in Caesarea when the Gentile believers received the Holy Spirit and immediately began using spiritual gifts. The same happened when Paul prayed for the believers at Ephesus.

Paul's correspondence with the churches makes it clear that it was not only the apostles, prophets and teachers who received spiritual gifts; neither were they confined to leaders in the local congregations. It was ordinary members of local house fellowships who exercised spiritual gifts. When they all came together for their united meetings, as they did in Corinth, they all wanted to use their gifts; hence the chaotic state of affairs with which Paul had to deal firmly in 1 Corinthians 14.

To conclude that the spiritual gifts were withdrawn because they were required only by the first generation of leaders for the apostolic functions of church planting and establishing the faith through the appointment of local leaders, deacons and bishops, and through their writings, thereby leaving a written record of the gospel and authentic apostolic teaching, is contrary to the evidence of the New Testament. Part of the problem facing us in assessing the reasons why prophecy disappeared from the church within two or three generations is the fact that most church historians are clergy whose major interest in that period is with the establishment of church order, the emergence of the ministries and their authentication by what is known as the 'apostolic succession'.

The sociologist, on the other hand, looks at the history of this period from a different perspective. His concern is not to defend a concept of the church and the authority of its ministry that depends upon the laying on of hands by the original apostles. His major concern is to trace the processes of change in the evolving structures of the church. Despite the often quoted statement of Irenaeus that as a boy he listened to the discourses of Polycarp who used to describe how he was taught by John and others who had seen the Lord, there is considerable doubt as to whether John actually did ordain Polycarp bishop of Smyrna, as Irenaeus appears to have believed. But it was nevertheless a powerful weapon in his controversy with the gnostics to be able to say that he received his teaching in a direct line from the apostles.

The major force of change at work in the first two centuries of the Christian era which transformed the early church from a missionary enterprise to an established institution was the process of institutionalisation. At the end of the apostolic generation the church was a loose association of local fellowships, with autonomous local leadership and variable practices, held together by common loyalty to Christ and given cohesion by travelling prophets and teachers. In the following two generations it was transformed into a fixed institution with regulated beliefs and practices dominated by a hierarchical leadership at the heart of which were monarchical bishops. This change came about through a process of social institutionalisation with three major strands: *doctrine, liturgy* and *leadership*. A brief look at each of these three strands will shed light upon the reasons for the disappearance of prophecy from the early church.

Doctrine

The external pressures of persecution and the internal pressures of resisting heretical teaching were forces that continually assailed the early church for the first three centuries. Reports of unsavoury Christian practices circulated widely among pagans, notably that they practised incest and cannibalism. The charge of incest probably came about because the Christians called each other brother and sister, even if they were a married couple. The latter charge was associated with the Eucharist where the eating of the 'flesh and blood' of Christ was thought to be connected with child sacrifice. Pliny, the governor of Bithynia, wrote to the emperor Trajan about 112 AD on this subject, reporting that having examined two deaconesses under torture he had found the charges unfounded. Persecution continued sporadically in different parts of the Roman Empire well into the fourth century and the false charges and misconceptions surrounding the faith were one of the pressures leading to clear statements of doctrine and the regulation of practices within the church.

The major pressure to define orthodox Christian doctrine, however, came from the heretical teaching that continually assailed the church from within. The first three centuries were years of internal strife between those whose teaching was at variance with that of the apostles and first generation eye-witnesses, and those who held steadfastly to the original teaching. These conflicts brought about numerous councils and written statements and were responsible for the credal definition of orthodox belief, particularly concerning the person and work of Jesus Christ. The need to define orthodox Christian faith as a counter to heresy also resulted in the production of the canon of the New Testament and the elimination from Scripture of spurious gospels and sub-apostolic writings.

Later generations of Christians should be grateful for the tenacity and faithfulness with which the fathers of the early church preserved the truth of the gospel. But there was a cost seen in the negative effect of the credal movement. The attempt to define the faith in written statements had the additional effect of leaving little or no room for revelation. Thus the role of the Holy Spirit in the daily life of the early church steadily diminished as the exposition of the faith became the repetition of established doctrinal teaching.

Liturgy

As the apostolic generation of eye-witnesses drew to a close, the unity of the scattered Christian congregations increasingly depended upon two things, that of a common faith and that of a common way of ordering their daily life and worship. From earliest times it had been the custom to break bread together in remembrance of the Lord as well as to sing psalms and have readings and prayers. The rite of baptism became the means by which new believers were admitted to the church. This was a sign of the remembrance of the baptism of the Lord Jesus and the coming of the Holy Spirit upon him as well as an act of the renunciation of sins and their forgiveness as the new believer was incorporated in Christ into membership of his body.

Although practices of daily life and worship in the Christian communities varied from city to city, gradually there developed patterns of regional unity that became the distinctive mark of congregations in each province of the Empire. By the end of the first century there was a recognised form of the Lord's Prayer and an established form of liturgy for the Eucharist that was practised in a number of provinces. This form of liturgy was described in some detail by Justin Martyr at Rome in 150 AD and by this time had evidently become standard practice in a number of other provinces.

As the pattern of worship became formalised there was little room for spontaneity, hence prophecy was increasingly squeezed out. The practice described by Paul in 1 Corinthians 14.26 of the house groups coming together, presumably on the first day of the week, when 'everyone has a hymn, or a word of instruction, a revelation, a tongue or an interpretation' probably did not even survive into the second century. Paul's strictures on disorderly worship at Corinth were no doubt one of the pressures that led to the regularisation of worship and the acceptance by most congregations of an agreed liturgy. This was undoubtedly one of the causes of the disappearance of prophecy from the worship of local congregations.

Spontaneity is always the first casualty of institution-alisation. All new movements are subject to these pressures that begin with the routinisation of charisma. The creativity of the original charismatic leaders is not accorded to the second generation due to a fear of deviant innovation. The second generation of leaders make it their objective to standardise practices according to the pattern they received.

Prophecy, that claimed divine inspiration, would have been seen as a direct threat to the maintenance of first generation purity and thus led to attempts from the second generation onwards, first to control, and then to suppress prophetic revelation.

Leadership

During the apostolic age travelling prophets and teachers, such as those who went out from Antioch (Ac 13), ensured the commonality of faith and practice among the scattered communities of believers across the Empire. With the gradual demise of those who had known the Lord Jesus and heard his teaching, and the increasing number of self-styled, self-appointed prophets and teachers who were troubling the churches, the pressure to establish regular orders of recognised leaders increased. It was apostolic practice to appoint local leaders as, for example, Paul did in Ephesus. Acts 20.28 refers to the *episcopoi*, literally 'overseers' or 'bishops' whom the Holy Spirit had appointed at Ephesus; and Paul similarly refers to the *episopoi* and *diakonoi*—'bishops and deacons' at Philippi (Phil 1.1).

We have already noted that one of the major objectives of the *Didache* was the establishment of local leaders in the congregations scattered across the province of Syria. The tests put forward in the *Didache* for judging prophecy indicate that although the true prophet was highly regarded as one who brought revelation and teaching of great value to the church, the self-authenticated wandering prophets were a doubtful blessing. Nevertheless, although the *Didache* prescribed liturgical prayer to be said at the Eucharist by local elders, if visiting prophets were in the assembly they were to be permitted 'to offer thanksgiving as much as they desire'. This implied that the prophet had a special claim to celebrate the Eucharist. A further indication of the high honour in which prophets were held was the exhortation in the *Didache* to regard them as the Christian equivalent of 'chief priests' and to give them the first-fruits of wine, corn and cattle.

The need for settled leadership to counter deception is apparent in the *Didache* where prophets are urged to settle with a local congregation. Where such a prophet permanently settled, his authority would immediately have been recognised and he would, to all intents and purposes, have become a monarchical bishop. If a prophet settled in an important city his influence would have been even greater. A good example is Polycarp, who was described as 'an apostolic and prophetic teacher in our own time, a bishop of the holy church which is in Smyrna' *(Martyrdom of Polycarp,* 15.2).

Ignatius, also, was regarded as a prophet; or at least, he certainly regarded himself as a prophet! Ignatius was Bishop of Antioch in the transitional period when the church in that city was still controlled by a body of elders of which he was probably the presiding elder. Before leaving Antioch for his martyrdom in the Coliseum at Rome in 115 AD Ignatius used his authority as a prophet to elevate the status and firmly establish the office of bishop. He wrote to the Philadelphians on his way to Rome:

> For even though certain persons desired to deceive me after the flesh, yet the Spirit is not deceived, being from God; for he knows from whence he comes and where he goes, and he searches out the hidden things. I cried out, when I was among you; I spoke with a loud voice, with God's own voice, 'Give heed to the bishop and the presbytery and the deacons' ...I learned it not from the flesh of man; it was the preaching of the Spirit who spoke thus; 'Do nothing without the bishop' (Philadelphians 7.1).

During the apostolic generation the only full-time leaders were probably those engaged in the missionary activities of church-planting and even they sometimes earned their own living as Paul claims to have done while in Corinth (1 Cor 9.5-15). As the local board of elders, subject to the itinerant apostles and prophets, gave way to the settled leadership of monarchical bishops and their deacon assistants, authority became increasingly invested in them and there developed a hierarchical system of church government controlled by full-time professional clergy. The leadership took on a *priestly* rather than a prophetic role; although the office of priest was unknown in the churches of Paul's generation and, in the view of many biblical scholars, it is contrary to the teaching of the New Testament. Their preoccupation was with the *maintenance of established tradition* rather than with openness to new revelation.

Prophecy was increasingly regarded as a threat to the unity of the church. Any deviation from established doctrine or liturgical practice was frowned upon. With the emergence early in the second century of the three greatest cities of the Empire—Rome, Alexandria and Antioch—as the prime centres of authority in the church, anyone who failed to submit to their jurisdiction was regarded as heretical.

The Montanists

It was, in fact, the existence of heresy such as the Gnostic teaching which denied the possibility of God coming in the flesh, that gave the newly emerging episcopal leadership the ideal opportunity for suppressing prophecy. The controversy with the Montanists illustrates this point. Montanus of Phrygia, together with two local women named Priscilla and Maximilla, began prophesying in the churches of Asia Minor around the year 170 AD.

Their teaching was, in fact, in direct opposition to the heretical Gnosticism that was troubling most of the Hellenist churches. It was strongly eschatological and made considerable use of the Revelation of John. They expected the second coming of Jesus to take place very soon, hence there was a heavy emphasis upon personal holiness in their teaching. The reaction of some of the monarchical bishops, including the bishop of Rome, after some hesitation, was to denounce them as diabolically inspired rather than under divine inspiration.

The Montanists reacted by charging their opponents with blasphemy against the Holy Spirit because of their rejection of prophetic revelation. The controversy split the churches in Asia Minor and had a disturbing effect much further afield, even in Alexandria where they were supported by the brilliant preacher and theologian Tertullian, who complained that the control of the church had been usurped from the Holy Spirit by bishops.

It was probably the strict asceticism of the Montanists that also attracted Tertullian. The Montanist movement was in part a reaction to the increasing moral laxity in the church as it expanded in numbers and wealth. There were numerous stories of sexual immorality among the bishops. The Montanists roundly condemned any impurity within the church and both preached and practised a strong puritan ethic. This caused deep resentment among the clergy and was a threat to the authority of the bishops.

The historian Eusebius was scathing in his denunciation of the Montanists. Referring to Montanus he wrote:

> And he also stirred up two women and filled them with the bastard spirit so that they uttered demented, absurd and irresponsible sayings...these people blasphemed the whole Catholic Church under heaven, under the influence of their presumptuous spirit, because the church granted to the spirit of false prophecy neither honour nor admission (Eusebius HEV xvi 9).

Hippolytus, Bishop of Rome, joined in challenging the Montanists, directing his attack chiefly at the women, although conceding that there was nothing biblically wrong with their teaching. He wrote:

> They have been deceived by two females, Priscilla and Maximilla by name, whom they hold to be prophetesses, asserting that into them the Paraclete Spirit entered...These people agree with the Christians in acknowledging the Father of the universe to be God and Creator of all things, and they also acknowledge all that the gospel testifies of Christianity. But they introduce novelties in the form of fasts and feasts, abstinences, meals of parched food and diets of radishes, giving these females as their authority...(Hippolytus, *Refutatio omnium haeresium*, viii 19).

The controversy with the Montanists is significant in assessing the reasons for the disappearance of prophecy from the church. It was not their puritanism, nor their biblical teaching, nor even their expectation of the imminence of the Parousia that aroused the ire of the clergy. It was the challenge of their authority implied in the Montanists' claim to divine inspiration through the Holy Spirit.

In refuting Montanism some early church leaders even went so far as to deny the apostolic authorship of the fourth Gospel on which the Montanists based their teaching on the Holy Spirit. They also refuted the Book of Revelation due to its teaching on the millennium that featured in Montanist teaching.

Hort gives an admirable summary of the beliefs of Montanism. He says:

> Briefly, its characteristics were these: first, a strong faith in the Holy Spirit as the promised Paraclete, present as a heavenly power in the church of the day; secondly, specially a belief that the Holy Spirit was manifesting himself supernaturally at that day through entranced prophets and prophetesses; and thirdly, an inculcation of a specially stern and exacting standard of Christian morality and a discipline on the strength of certain teachings of these prophets. An increase in the numbers and prosperity of the church having brought an increase in laxity, it was not unnatural that attempts should be made to stem it by a rigorous system of prohibitions. To these three characteristics of Montanism may be added two others, fourthly, a tendency to set up prophets against bishops, the new episcopal organisation being probably favourable to that large inclusiveness of Christian communion in which the Montanists saw only spiritual danger, and fifthly, an eager anticipation of the Lord's second coming as near at hand, and a consequent indifference to ordinary human affairs...(FJA Hort, *The Ante-Nicene Fathers*, 1895, pp100ff).

F F Bruce also writes favourably concerning the Montanists. Referring to the two women, Priscilla and Maximilla, he writes:

> Among the new revelations which they communicated were some which imposed a strict discipline on their

followers, in such matters, for example, as fasting and marriage. It appears that at first there was a tendency to renounce marriage altogether, but the later distinctive Montanist teaching on this subject took the form of a ban on second marriages, not only for ministers of the church but for the rank and file as well. One Montanist feature which combined enthusiasm with rigorism was their tendency to court martyrdom. Anything like the judicious withdrawal of Dionysius and Cyprian when the Decian persecution broke out was alien to the Montanist temper. (F F Bruce, *The Spreading Flame*, Paternoster Press, 1966, p 219).

Most church historians have written unfavourably of the Montanists. Accounts of their activities and teaching are usually included under the heading of 'Heresies'. This is no doubt due, to some extent, to a desire on the part of the writers to lend support to established authority in the church. There is, nevertheless, a case for re-examining the history of the Montanist controversy.

Henry Chadwick is typical of many church historians in regarding the Montanists as 'a sect' because of their refusal to accept the authority of the bishops. He said, 'The antithesis between immediate inspiration and mediated authority emerges sharply in the Montanist crisis...The orthodox reply as formulated by Hippolytus of Rome, was unerringly directed against Montanism's weakest point, namely its divisiveness' (Henry Chadwick, *The Early Church*, Penguin, 1969, pp52-53).

There can be little doubt that even if it is conceded that some of the Montanist's beliefs were questionable in regard to the practice and testing of prophecy, the vehemence with which they were opposed by the bishops leads one to the conclusion that the dispute was more about authority than spiritual gifts. Chadwick says that Hippolytus took the view that 'the supernatural is discerned in the normal ministry of word and sacrament, not in irrational ecstacies which lead to pride and sensoriousness' (ibid p53).

The Montanist controversy raised the question; was the Holy Spirit available to all believers or was it only the ordained priests who had any valid claim to divine inspiration? The Montanists' claim to divine revelation directly through the Holy Spirit meant that they were claiming an authority greater than that of the bishops. This was in a period before the formation of the canon of the New Testament and at a time when the church was facing the threat of heretical teaching distorting the gospel. It was therefore understandable that the bishops should attempt to suppress what they saw as a devisive movement. If it were conceded that the Holy Spirit was given to all believers then the exercise of spiritual gifts must also be conceded. The way would then be open for anyone to use the gift of prophecy to challenge the lifestyle or teaching of the clergy.

In the formative period of church order, doctrine and practice, it was important to establish the source of authority or the result would have been spiritual anarchy and the church would have been engulfed in heretical sects and syncretistic cults. The rise of so many false teachers in the early centuries of the Christian era who denied the divinity of Christ or some other fundamental tenet of Christian teaching necessitated firm action to preserve the faith of the apostolic church. The reaction of the clergy was to insist on the absolute authority of the bishops which firmly established the power of the monarchical bishop in each province.

Unity within the church was achieved at the expense of prophetic revelation. The gifts of the Holy Spirit were firmly suppressed and usually those who claimed a special anointing of the Holy Spirit were declared to be under demonic possession, labelled heretics and thus driven out of the church.

The controversy with the Montanists rumbled on for several centuries and caused much bitterness and division.

There were numerous conferences and meetings called to discuss the problems arising. Eusebius records:

> The faithful in Asia met often and in many places throughout Asia upon this matter...and refuted the heresy, and thus these people were expelled from the church and debarred from Communion (*ibid* xvi 10).

Montanism continued in North Africa until the fourth century and was particularly strong in Tertullian's home city of Carthage. It lasted longest in Asia Minor but was finally crushed by the Emperor Justinian (527-565 AD) in Phrygia where it began.

The Suppression of Prophecy

The Montanist controversy is a sad chapter in the history of the church. It caused much bitterness and suffering at a time when Christians desperately needed to be united to face the cruel persecution of a hostile world. The action of the clergy in trying to promote unity by enforcing their own authority is understandable. Nevertheless, the effect was not only to suppress prophecy but to eradicate the spiritual gifts from the mainstream life of the church—an effect that was to last for many centuries, until the birth of the charismatic movement in the twentieth century.

It is arguable that if the bishops had been prepared to deal with the Montanists according to the teaching of the New Testament the split need never have occurred and prophetic revelation could have been not simply contained, but used to continue to pour spiritual life and energy into the church to counter the deadening effects of institutionalisation. Jesus, Paul and John all gave teaching on how to deal with prophets and prophetic revelation in the church. Clearly, it was envisaged that prophecy would be a continuing phenomenon of the presence of the Holy Spirit among believers. Nowhere did Jesus say that the would remove the Holy Spirit from the church after a certain number of years or when all the eye-witnesses had died. In fact, one could argue that after the lifetime of the first generation there would be *even greater* need for the ministry of the Holy Spirit to replace and to continue the witness of the original apostles and teachers. Nowhere does Paul say, 'Be eager to prophesy, but only until my death.' Nowhere does John imply that the time for testing the spirits would soon be past as if the Holy Spirit could be replaced by bishops who would then be the respositories of truth and guarantors of orthodoxy!

It was the establishment of authority through the process of institutionalisation, to which all new movements are subjected, that was a major cause of the disappearance of prophecy from the early church. This is seen not only in the pressures towards the standardisation of beliefs and practices but more especially in the ambitions of leaders to establish their absolute authority. The inability of leaders to control prophetic revelation represented a real threat to this authority. The threat came not simply from those who exercised the ministry of a prophet but from the ordinary believer who exercised the gift of prophecy within local congregations.

Therefore it was not only the ministries noted by Paul in Ephesians 4 that had to be suppressed if the power of the bishops was to be firmly established, but also the whole range of spiritual gifts that according to the teaching of the New Testament were available to all believers. Thus it was not only prophecy but the whole concept of 'whole body of Christ ministry' as taught by Paul that became a casualty of the institutionalisation of Christianity during the second and third centuries.

From the time of the elimination of the Montanists in the sixth century, there was no major movement emphasising prophetic revelation and the exercise of spiritual gifts until the Pentecostal movement of the twentieth century. This does not mean that the Holy Spirit was inactive throughout these centuries. There were many individual Christians who received divine revelation and there were undoubtedly spiritual movements of considerable significance and groups of devout believers among whom there is evidence of the gifts of the Spirit.

Most of the saints were men and women who received divine revelation, including those who became major figures in the leadership of the church. Augustine (354-430) claimed that his conversion was the result of hearing a voice within him telling him to read a passage from Romans, and Jerome (340-420) also testifies to a divine revelation in which Christ appeared to him in a dream that led him to devote his life to the study of Scripture. Karl Rahner, the Catholic theologian, goes so far as to maintain that there is 'no proof that in the early church the wind of the Spirit blew with more vigour than later. In fact, there has always been the charismatic element in the church.' Although, as he admits, you have to look beyond official accounts of church history to discern the work of the Spirit (Karl Rahner, *The Spirit in the Church*, Burns and Oates, 1979, p50).

Numerous examples could be given of the work of the Holy Spirit in the lives of individuals and groups such as George Fox and the early Quakers, John Wesley and the leaders of the eighteenth-century revival, and many others. But it remains true that the gifts of the Holy Spirit were largely suppressed, and divine revelation was not given a place in the mainstream life of the church from the third to the twentieth centuries. Indeed, the attitude of leaders in the institutional church throughout this period is well illustrated by Bishop Butler's vehement opposition to the preaching of John Wesley on the latter's visit to Bristol. The Bishop declared that 'pretending to extraordinary revelations from the Holy Ghost is an altogether horrid thing'.

The place of divine revelation during this period of many centuries that we are attempting to review in a few paragraphs is well summarised in the words of W R Inge: 'The Holy Spirit has never left himself without a witness; and if we will put aside a great deal of what passes for church history... and follow the course of the religion of the Spirit and the church of the Spirit, we shall judge very differently the relative importance of events from those who merely follow the fortunes of institutionalism' (W R Inge, *Things New and Old,* 1935, pp 55ff).

PART 3

PROPHECY TODAY

CHAPTER FIFTEEN

CONTEMPORARY PRACTICE

By the beginning of the third century the church, both in the East and the West, had lost its original character as a company of believers with local leadership whose unity depended upon common loyalty to Christ and the ministry of travelling prophets and teachers. The travelling ministries were eliminated. So too was the exercise of spiritual gifts by ordinary believers and leadership was institutionalised in a professional body of priests with an established hierarchy.

This situation remained unchanged through the centuries until the twentieth with only the most minor roles within the church being assigned to laymen. Today the Roman Catholic and Eastern Orthodox churches still largely use clergy for major administrative roles which ensures that power within the church is kept under the control of the hierarchy. In terms of spiritual activities, the Episcopal churches assign to the laity only relatively minor participatory roles which ensures that the spiritual life of the church is dominated by the priests.

A major objective of the Reformation was to re-establish the doctrine and practices of the church according to the New Testament, which the reformers believed to have been

lost. They said that Peter was referring to the whole church—
the whole company of those who have been redeemed by
Christ—when he declared, 'You are a chosen people, a royal
priesthood, a holy nation, a people belonging to God, that
you may declare the praises of him who called you out of
darkness into his wonderful light' (1 Pt 2.9).

The central concept of Reformation ecclesiology is 'the
priesthood of all believers', but the Protestant denominations
that came out of the Reformation, notably the Presbyterian,Congregational and Baptist, have never found it easy
to establish such an ideal. In practice these churches have
democratised their administration by fully involving laymen
and by investing authority in the local church meeting which
is open to all members, and also by investing authority in
national assemblies of elected representatives. But in spiritual
matters, the Protestants have always relied largely upon a
theologically trained ministry for leadership, especially in
matters of doctrine.

The Reformation emphasised the supreme authority of
the Bible rather than tradition in all matters of belief and
practice. From the earliest days of the Reformation a high
value was placed upon the study of scripture which inevitably
gave advantage to those in full-time ministry. Over the past
four centuries, ministers in the Reformed churches have
become a professional body distinct from the laity. The only
essential difference between such a ministry and that of
Episcopal priests lies in the different concepts of sacramen-
talism. It is arguable that the Protestant denominations have
never succeeded in establishing the priesthood of all believers
in terms of locally autonomous communities of believers
exercising spiritual gifts under the headship of Christ and
directed by the Holy Spirit, because they were unable to
break free from the concept of authority invested in the
institutions of the church and medieval society. Most historians regard this as the reason why Luther backed the
German princes in the peasants' revolt that shook central
Europe at the time of the Reformation.

Changing Social Milieu

The majority of people from the Reformation to the twentieth century had no difficulty in accepting the authority of the Protestant ministry of pastors and preachers. They were used to an elitist form of society in which they readily accepted their subservient roles. It was not until the twentieth century—and the advent of modern democratic, socialist and revolutionary movements that challenged medieval concepts of society and actually changed the old feudalistic social structures—that ordinary believers began to realise that they themselves could exercise spiritual gifts. There are, therefore, sociological as well as spiritual reasons for the resurgence of prophecy in the modern church.

The political challenges of elitism that began among intellectuals in the nineteenth century and developed into powerful socio-political movements in the early twentieth century brought alongside them the possibility of 'people-led', rather than minister or clergy-led, spiritual movements. It is a fact of history that revivals always begin among the poor not among the social elites. For, as Max Weber once penetratingly observed, what do the rich require of religion other than the divine legitimisation of their positions of power and privilege in society?

This is not only true of elites but also of the middle classes. Where any group in society has made friends with 'mammon' there will not only be high levels of personal satisfaction that militate against a hunger after God but also a commitment to the maintenance of the status quo. Hence revivals, that grow out of deep spiritual hunger and a longing for God, begin among the less-privileged rather than the over-privileged. More accurately, all revivals and fresh spiritual movements begin with some form of deprivation. Deprivation is not necessarily social and economic but may be personal, emotional or spiritual. In simple terms, those who are satisfied with life do not hunger and thirst after God. This is the teaching of Jesus (Mt 19.23) and it is borne out in the evidence of revivals throughout the world.

Right up until the twentieth century the Episcopal churches and mainline Protestant denominations were institutions that largely followed the basic social ethos of secular society. They did not challenge it, despite the lone prophetic voices throughout Europe and America that spoke against slavery, colonial and industrial, and the exploitation of the poor. All the churches as institutions were non-revolutionary (conservative) in their structure and teaching, either socially or spiritually, usually both. Leadership was vested in a professional ministry; doctrine was fixed either by church tradition or by biblical interpretation—in either case the theologically educated ministry held unchallengeable authority in this sphere; worship was strictly patterned, even if non-liturgical, which left little or no room for spontaneity. The professional clergy, whether they called themselves priests or ministers, kept a tight control over worship and there was no possibility of ordinary believers exercising spiritual gifts or of prophetic revelation entering the church other than through the established leadership whose training and role-concept closed them to any such possibility.

It was not until twentieth century socio-political movements began changing the mind-set of the masses and attitudes towards authority that conditions were created for a return to the ethos of the New Testament church, the distribution of spiritual gifts among all believers and to the flow of divine revelation into the church that had been missing for so many centuries. Churches dominated by active priests and pastors with passive people are not open to the sudden infusion of spiritual gifts; they are institutions in which spiritual life is strictly regulated and in which divine revelation is institutionalised within the leadership. In such institutions even Protestant ministers perform essentially the same roles as priests.

Priests and prophets have always been in conflict. As Dean Inge dryly remarked, 'A priest is never so happy as when he has a prophet to stone' (W R Inge, *Things New and Old*, p48).

The priest draws his authority from the institution while the prophet receives his from God. The role of the priest is maintenance, preservation of tradition, working within a religious institution; it is essentially conservative. The role of the prophet is creative, challenging tradition, working outside established religious institutions; it is essentially radical.

There are strong links between sociological factors and spiritual movements. This does not in any way diminish the significance of revivals or spiritual awakenings as sovereign works of God. It means that in his own perfect timing God awaits the readiness of man before an outpouring of his Holy Spirit just as he did at Pentecost when he awaited the right moment to fulfil his promise and pour out his Spirit upon the disciples. God uses social movements and secular forces in precisely the same way as he used Cyrus to overthrow the Chaldean empire even though Cyrus had no concept of being 'the Lord anointed' as the prophet hailed him (Is 45.1).

A New Move of the Spirit

In Britain, the first great spiritual revival of the twentieth century began in the Welsh mining valleys among simple Bible-believing industrial peasants. It is no coincidence that the British Labour movement was born in these same Welsh valleys founded by the ministries of prophetic gospel preachers anointed with the power of the Holy Spirit to preach the word of God with the fervour of Amos in calling for justice and the cessation of the exploitation of the poor. Keir Hardie, the first member of the Labour Party to be elected to Parliament, was an open-air preacher in his early days. The fact that the British Labour movement rapidly became secularised and lost its biblical foundations does not detract from the point we are making that God awaits the right timing—the receptivity of the people—for the outpouring of his Spirit.

In Britain the Welsh revival was soon followed by the birth of the Pentecostal churches and in the second half of the century by the charismatic renewal movement that has swept across all denominations.

In America revivals began earlier than in Europe, in the latter half of the nineteenth century among the newly liberated black people in the south and in the growing urban industrial centres in the north. Again there is a clear link with deprivation. It was not until the twentieth century that these sporadic outbursts of spiritual energy became powerful movements sweeping through whole communities. The growth of the Pentecostal churches in the USA since the 1920s has been a major phenomenon of the century. The Pentecostal Movement began in 1906 with the Azusa Street revival in Los Angeles. It has spread throughout the world this century and today numbers, with the charismatic movement, in excess of 405 million believers.

In Third World countries the major movement of the Holy Spirit resulting in phenomenal growth of the church has occurred during the second half of the twentieth century. It did not begin to occur until the movement for political independence, for decolonisation, began to liberate the church in these nations from Western dominance. The European missionary movement of the nineteenth century and its American counterpart of the early twentieth century was closely associated with westernisation. The gospel was taken pre-packaged in Western culture. Church planting meant taking the plant pot as well as the plant. Third World churches were firmly led by missionaries who looked to Europe and America as their bases. This inhibited the development of local leadership and the indigenisation of the gospel. The missionaries created churches where the people were spiritually dependent and knew nothing of spiritual gifts.

It was not until the movement for independence, when Western missionaries were ejected from some regions and the churches began to perceive the urgency of training local leadership, that the process of indigenisation really began. About this same period, in the middle of the century, the

Pentecostal missionary movement began to gain momentum and found a ready response among people whose socio-political aspirations were set on independence. The gospel, together with the teaching that spiritual gifts are open to all believers, was gladly received, became rapidly indigenised and began to spread in many areas like a prairie fire.

In many regions the deadening forces of Western 'churchianity' that suppressed the power of the Holy Spirit, and the exercise of spiritual gifts within the churches, once broken, released a floodtide of spiritual power. Since the mid-1970s the churches throughout central and southern Africa, central and South America, and throughout South-East Asia have been growing at a phenomenal rate. The power of the Holy Spirit has been a major characteristic of this growth seen in divine revelation, the exercise of spiritual gifts, and signs and wonders. Most remarkable has been the spread of the gospel in Communist China where the number of committed Christian believers is reliably estimated to have increased from less than one million in 1949, when Western missionaries were expelled, to between fifty million and a hundred million in the late 1980s. This phenomenal growth has been achieved without a theologically trained leadership or the vast material resources available to Western churches. It has come about through ordinary believers taking the promises of the Lord literally, receiving the power of the Holy Spirit, defying persecution and allowing themselves to be led by the Spirit with the expectation of seeing divine power at work.

The Charismatic Movement

The charismatic renewal movement bears many of the characteristics of the Pentecostal movement which has been gaining momentum throughout the world since the beginning of the twentieth century. But whereas the Pentecostals emphasise the centrality of baptism in the Holy Spirit with its initial evidence in speaking in tongues, the charismatics emphasise all the spiritual gifts and their availability to all Spirit-filled believers. The Pentecostals formed congregations separated from the mainline churches. It was a new movement which produced newly-formed fellowships. The charismatic movement, on the other hand, although it has been responsible for the formation of many independent fellowships, has also entered and had a renewing, transforming effect within many of the mainline churches.

In the Western nations the charismatic renewal movement has taken on some peculiarly Western characteristics. It began in the USA and Britain in the 1960s and spread rapidly throughout North America and Europe through the 1970s and 80s, bringing a new openness to spiritual gifts and prophetic revelation. The renewal movement has crossed denominational lines leaving hardly any of the churches untouched, from Episcopal to evangelical, Roman Catholic to southern Baptist.

There can be no doubt that the charismatic movement has transformed the lives of large numbers of nominal Christians within the traditional churches and has also brought many others into the Kingdom of God. The movement has, however, also had a divisive effect. It has many different expressions which have resulted in the formation of a large number of new denominations, sects, independent congregations and small isolated house groups. It has probably caused more controversy, disunity and schism, than any other movement at any other period in church history. There are a number of reasons for this, one of which is probably to be found in the ethos of the movement itself with its major emphasis upon the 'restoration' of spiritual gifts and ministries to the church.

This highlighting of spiritual gifts is essentially a lay, rather than a priestly, movement which brings it into conflict with church authorities. It is based upon the witness of the New Testament that spiritual gifts were available to all believers in the early church. Paul's teaching in his first letter to the Corinthians encouraged them to exercise spiritual gifts and especially to prophesy (14:1). Such an exhortation finds an immediate response in the social context of Western individualism.

Western society is strongly achievement orientated. The exercise of spiritual gifts opens new spheres of achievement which are particularly attractive to those who lack social status or who are finding it difficult to achieve in a highly competitive secular society. The gift of prophecy is especially attractive because it brings recognition and status to those who are believed to be hearing from God. If God has honoured them by speaking directly to them they should be honoured by other believers within the fellowship. Those thoughts may never be articulated but they undoubtedly represent something of the situation in Corinth with which Paul was attempting to deal in his first letter. In Corinth the Christians were noisy, competitive and unruly, even getting drunk at the Eucharist.

Modern Western society is not only highly competitive and individualistic but it is also essentially lawless. The charismatic movement represents a form of 'do-it-yourself religion'. This, combined with the spirit of lawlessness in secular society, encourages Christians to challenge traditional church order and authority and, in fact, gives them the spiritual justification for setting up alternative authority structures. This is a major sociological factor accounting for the vast proliferation of independent congregations and the formation of new sects and denominations through a process of fission and fusion in the first thirty years of the charismatic movement.

An additional reason for the rapid spread of the movement also has sociological roots in that it is a response to the rapid political, social and economic situation which has engulfed all the nations in the post-World War II era. As the world moves towards the end of the second millenium and the nations are being shaken by the rapid pace of social change, by political upheavals, vast changes in technology and insoluble economic problems there is a general air of uncertainty which gives rise to speculation that the world is moving swiftly into the end times. In such a climate the study of biblical prophecy becomes a fertile field for the purveyors of religious sensationalism. There is much to encourage them with the formation of the State of Israel, Jerusalem back in Jewish hands for the first time since AD 70 and many other indicators suggesting that biblical prophecy is being fulfilled in our lifetime.

All these rapid changes in the secular world generate not only a sense of insecurity, but also a feeling of powerlessness in the ordinary individual. This creates a hunger for power which in unredeemed men often results in crime, terrorism or the rise of the warlords who promote revolutions and lead private armies. Among Christians the hunger for power often results in an emphasis upon power evangelism and 'dominion theology' which are characteristics of some streams in the charismatic movement. This tells ordinary believers that they will possess extraordinary power which will enable them to subdue the nations and achieve greatness in the name of Christ.

It would, however, be an unjustifiable cynicism to imply that the charismatic movement is merely a child of the age. The fact that it does bear some of the social characteristics to be found in secular society in the closing decades of the twentieth century does not mean that it is not a movement of God. On the contrary, there are two important things to note here in assessing any new movement of the Spirit of God.

First, God is a God of perfect timing. He will wait for the right moment to speak into the lives of those men and women who are his servants. He chooses the moment when they are receptive and ready to listen and to receive his word. The twentieth century has been ripe for a major outpouring of the Spirit of God into the lives of millions of men and women from many different cultures throughout the nations of the world.

Secondly, the fact that some of the characteristics of

282

Western secular society are to be found mixed in with the work of the Holy Spirit among Western charismatics should serve as a salutory warning. When God moves among his people in the manner foreseen by the prophet Joel, whereby the Spirit of God is received by all manner of people, young and old, high status and low status, males and females, there are grave dangers that the corruption of the human spirit and the sins of the flesh may interfere with the work of God. This may well account for the incidence of moral failure among charismatic leaders particularly in the spheres of finance and adultery.

Sects and Cults

There has been a proliferation of cults in the twentieth century. Jesus' warnings about deception indicate that he foresaw the rise of cults which certainly fulfil his words that they will 'deceive many'. The danger of the cult is that it usually has links with Christian teaching, often taking selective concepts from the Bible and linking these with the teachings of other religions such as Hinduism or Buddhism to produce a new religion.

Some cults, such as the Mormons or 'Latter Day Saints', and the Jehovah's Witnesses, began with a so-called 'divine revelation' given to the founder of the cult. This revelation is then mixed with biblical teaching or even with their own selective version of the Bible, as in the case of the Jehovah's Witnesses.

Cults need to be carefully distinguished from sects. The cult never becomes a denomination or a church. It only becomes a larger and more highly organised cult. Its teaching and practice never conform to biblical standards, although its leaders usually make claims to divine authority. The leader not only claims to be God's special agent or messiah, possessing supernatural power and wisdom, but he also demands unquestioning loyalty and obedience.

Cults usually thrive when the social order is disintegrating. This is one of the major sociological reasons why there have been so many new cults arising in the second half of the twentieth century. The decline of the family, loosening standards of morality, increasing lawlessness, together with the decline in religious belief, especially the undermining of biblical authority and the declining influence of the church in Western society—these are all factors which have paved the way for the growth of the cults. When society is collapsing due to the decline of traditional beliefs this creates enormous insecurity in millions of people. It generates a search for truth and certainty which provides fertile ground for those who claim divine authority and pose as leaders with special wisdom to point the way to an alternative society, or to usher in a new era of spirituality in the days leading up to the end of the world.

Sects, by contrast, adhere closely to biblical tradition. The Bible is revered as the unchanging word of God. The sect is usually conservative evangelical in its biblical theology and a major objective is to try to reproduce a pattern of church organisation, fellowship life and personal discipleship that is in accordance with the pattern set in the New Testament church. The sect usually begins as a break-away movement from a church or denomination. It arises out of a desire to emphasise some biblical truth which is perceived to have been neglected or under-emphasised in the teaching and practice of the church or denomination from which the group break away. Often the group remains within the parent body for some time attempting to make their witness to what they perceive to be an important truth. Finally they are either driven out or are unable to tolerate the restrictions placed upon them and they soon become a sect.

The sect maintains its Christian characteristics and emphasises the biblical nature of its teaching and practice. The sect is subject to the usual process of social institutionalisation which transforms groups from a loose association of individuals holding a shared belief to a regular organisation. Usually the sect becomes a denomination within two or three generations. This is what happened to the Pentecostal churches which were founded in the early part of the twentieth century. A good example is the Elim Pentecostal church in Britain which has moved from a sect to a denomination in three generations. They began in the 1920s as a small group of individual local fellowships with the shared belief that speaking in tongues is the initial evidence of the baptism of the Holy Spirit.

In organisational terms the Elim church began in a similar way to the house church movement some fifty years later. The need for fellowship with like-minded believers drove them to form an association. As a sect they were known as the Four Square Gospellers. By the time they reached the third generation the pressures generated by the need for organisation, training and support transformed the sect to its present denominational status with a central organisation, national headquarters, ownership of buildings, ministerial training college, ordination of ministers, pension fund and all the trappings of denominationalism.

A similar process of institutionalisation is presently occurring within the new fellowships which have been spawned by the charismatic renewal movement. These are already being referred to as the 'new independent churches'. The need for fellowship and support is bringing many local congregations together into groups or 'streams' in which the leaders recognise each others' ministries. Before long the strongest leader in each group becomes dominant and is recognised as exercising 'apostolic' authority. This is the standard process of social institutionalisation which can be seen throughout church history beginning in the first century AD with the early church.

Prophecy was an important spiritual element in the early days of the Pentecostal sects but gradually, through the effects of institutionalisation which routinised worship and overcame spontaneity, prophecy, together with other spiritual gifts, became suppressed. As ordained ministers gained in status and authority they exercised increasing control over the life and worship of the church, first regulating and gradually taking control of spiritual gifts until the expectation of divine revelation through the body of believers was lowered. Today there are many Pentecostal churches where prophecy is rarely if ever heard and spiritual gifts are only exercised by the leaders. What has happened among the Pentecostal churches in the twentieth century is roughly parallel to what happened in the early church over a comparable period of time.

A similar process can be seen at work in the new sects produced by the charismatic movement. As leaders exert tighter control over congregations they become more suspicious of prophecy being given by ordinary members of the fellowship and usually summarily reject any prophetic messages which challenge their leadership or policy.

As the process of institutionalisation progresses and the independent fellowship becomes a sect and then a denomination and finally a church, so the free exercise of the gifts and the utterance of prophecy gradually disappear. The joy and spontaneity of worship becomes routinised and regulated and the expectation of contemporary divine revelation is lost.

False Prophecy

Whenever there is a fresh move of the Spirit of God it is always accompanied by the counterfeit. The increase of spiritual activity in the twentieth century has also seen a proliferation of false prophets and false prophecy. Jesus warned that this would happen. When his disciples asked him to give them some indication of what would happen at the end of the age and signs of the nearness of his own Second Coming, his first response was a warning about deception. 'Watch out that no-one deceives you' he replied (Mt 24:4). Jesus said, 'Many will come in my name, claiming, "I am the Christ," and will deceive many' (v5).

False prophecy is often not deliberate. There is no intention to deceive. It may simply be the product of wishful

286

thinking, ascribing to God the desires of our own hearts. There are numerous examples of this among charismatics today in the realm of healing. False prophecies often emanate from a desire to please or a genuine love for others. But they always do harm and may even do great harm according to how widely they have been spread and the level of false expectations which have been raised.

There are three levels of false prophecy; namely, (1) the individual, (2) the local congregation and (3) the national or international.

1) Where a false prophecy is received by an individual it may only affect his or her own life, although it will often be known to others and the actions of that individual which are based upon the prophecy may also have an effect upon others. For example, a woman whose husband was suffering from terminal cancer was given a prophecy that he would be healed. The prophecy came from another member of her fellowship whom she trusted. She believed the prophecy was from God, therefore right to the end she continued to pray for and to expect the fulfilment of the 'promise'. Even after her husband died, and right up to the time of the funeral, she expected him to be raised from the dead. Her whole faith in God was shattered when his body was finally buried and no miracle of healing or resurrection had occurred.

This false prophecy, however lovingly motivated, could not have been more devastating in its effect if it had been deliberately designed as a cruel hoax. The damage, although limited, did in fact affect not only the woman and her family, but many others in the fellowship and among her friends and neighbours who had seen her confidence in God broken.

2) An example of a local congregation being misled by a false prophecy occurred at a church in Wales where a prophecy was given that each member should have a prayer partner who would be a close spiritual companion. This, it was said, would aid their growth to spiritual maturity. This prophecy was accepted by the leadership and embraced by

287

the whole congregation. Members paired with one another regardless of sex or marital status. The result was that many people formed close spiritual bonds with someone other than their marriage partner which led to physical and adulterous relationships. This had a shattering effect upon the fellowship and even the pastor was caught up in an unhealthy relationship from which he had to repent.

3) False prophecy may have a much wider effect where it is given publicity by someone in a church leadership position or if the prophecy is given by someone with a recognised national or international ministry. An example of such a false prophecy, which was very widely accepted by charismatics and evangelicals in Britain, occurred in 1990. The prophecy was given by Paul Cain, an American preacher who was associated with a group of men known as the 'Kansas City Prophets'. They were linked with the Kansas City Fellowship which, although only founded some seven years earlier, had attained a lot of attention among charismatics in the USA due to their reported accuracy in prophetic prediction and other charismatic phenomena. Paul Cain prophesied that there would be a great spiritual revival in Europe. This, he predicted, would begin in London in October 1990 and spread throughout the British Isles and across into the continent of Europe. The prophecy was confirmed and repeated by Bob Jones and John Paul Jackson of the Kansas City Fellowship and Brent Rue of the Vineyard Fellowships each of whom were reputed to be 'prophets'.

The prophecy was believed by John Wimber, senior pastor of the Vineyard Fellowship, Anaheim, California, who took a large team from the USA to Britain for meetings climaxing at the Docklands Centre in London in October 1990. Wimber was so convinced that a mighty revival would take place that he even brought his grandchildren over from the States to witness the historic event. No revival occurred and there was great disappointment among those who had believed and worked and prayed for such a time of blessing.

Large numbers of Christians in charismatic churches throughout Britain were seriously misled by this false prophecy. Many were disillusioned and lost their confidence in God. Somewhat incomprehensibly, Paul Cain was not publicly denounced as a false prophet, probably partly because British evangelicals are essentially conservative and therefore too polite to speak their minds in public. But the major reason must also have been that a number of powerful leaders who had publicly backed Cain saw the threat to their own reputation. They took their lead from Wimber who returned to the USA from the London meetings and in various publications attempted to explain away the false prophecy before finally distancing himself from Cain and dropping the subject.

All false prophecy is harmful. It is not possible to construct an ethical system distinguishing between mild and serious false prophecy in the same way as distinctions are sometimes made between 'white lies' and deliberate lies. The only valid distinctions in false prophecy are those given in the New Testament which concern the *source* of the prophecy; *ie*, whether it comes from the human spirit or from an alien spirit (1 Jn 4).

Most false prophecy heard in the charismatic churches today comes from the human spirit and simply reflects the thoughts or desires of the person giving the prophecy. Such prophecies may be given with the best of intentions, such as the desire to encourage or to give good things to others, but they always do harm in building up false expectations.

False prophecy can have a more sinister connotation such as where it is used to manipulate others for the self-gratification of the 'prophet'. Bob Jones, known as the senior prophet of the Kansas City Fellowship, was said to have used his 'prophetic gifting' to elicit sexual favours from women in the fellowship before his removal from ministry in 1991. Although this is an extreme example, any misuse of spiritual gifting to manipulate others is sinful and is an offence against the Holy Spirit. This applies to all false prophecy.

The prophet is claiming to speak as the mouthpiece of God under the inspiration of the Holy Spirit. The speaker is not therefore simply causing offence to other believers, but is actually offending God in whose name the word is being given. Those who glibly give out words purporting to come from God should read the words of Jesus in Matthew 7:15–23.

False prophecy also has dangers for those who accept the false words given to them. The shattering effects upon personal faith have already been noted, but an even more serious effect can result from believing a false prophecy which comes from an alien spirit. It can result in the believer's life taking a wrong direction, thus putting them outside the will of God for their life. Additionally it may result in the one who accepted the false prophecy striving to fulfil something promised that was not from God. An even more serious effect is where the person accepting the false prophecy takes into his own spirit something from the alien spirit and thus pollutes his spiritual life.

In summary, it must be emphasised that all false prophecy is harmful and may be extremely dangerous. It leads believers in wrong directions which may ruin their lives and frustrate the will of God for them. It raises false hopes and false expectations, and may even transmit an evil influence into the life of a believer. It cannot, therefore, be over-emphasised that those who seek to exercise either the ministry of the prophet or the gift of prophecy should exercise the utmost caution and ensure they really are hearing from God before speaking in public. This requires great maturity and considerable experience. Prophecy is something that often excites the spiritually immature and is an area into which new believers often venture enthusiastically but from which they should be firmly and wisely discouraged until they have gained sufficient grounding in the word of God to enable them to exercise spiritual gifts with discernment.

These strong warnings regarding false prophecy and the misuse of prophetic gifting need to be tempered by Paul's encouragement to all believers to seek to prophesy (1 Cor 14:1) which echoed Moses' wish that all the Lord's people were prophets (Num 11:29). The gift of prophecy is one of the manifestations of the Spirit and God can use any believer at any time according to his own choosing to convey a word to other believers. He may choose to use a new believer or even a child who is listening to him with openness and trust. Demos Shakarian records that many Armenian Pentecostals were saved from massacre early in the twentieth century by a prophecy given through an eleven-year-old boy (*The Happiest People on Earth*, Hodder & Stoughton, London 1977, p 21).

When prophecy is given through new, young or immature believers, it is essential that the elders and leaders exercise careful discernment and weigh the words before encouraging other believers to heed them. This weighing is essential if the body of Christ is to be guarded against deception through false prophecy which purports to be 'divine revelation'.

False Messiahs

An outstanding example of the sinister power exerted by the false messiah occurred in 1978. The world was stunned by the mass suicide of more than 900 men, women and children, followers of the Reverend Jim Jones, in the jungles of Guyana, South America. Jim Jones ordered his disciples to drink cyanide. The man they called 'father' saw to it that those who refused to drink the poison were murdered. There were no survivors to report on the gruesome events leading up to the tragedy that engulfed the lives of those who put their trust in a false messiah.

Equally tragic was the holocaust of fire that incinerated the followers of David Koresh, a self-proclaimed messiah who died with ninety of his followers in the spring of 1993. After fifty-one days of siege following a gun battle which left four US agents dead and sixteen wounded, Koresh and his disciples chose death rather than escape when fire swept through their fortified ranch near Waco, Texas. Seventeen of those who died were children under the age of ten, at least seven of them fathered by Koresh who was said to have sixteen wives in his harem.

Koresh believed the end of the world was near. He turned his Waco headquarters into a small fortress armed with machine guns and sophisticated weaponry capable of holding the US FBI agents at bay for more than a month. Koresh, whose real name was Vernon Howell, was thirty-three when he died, convinced that he was the Messiah and that after a final show-down with the authorities he would finally reveal himself to the world as 'Jesus Christ'. He came from a little-known sect of the Seventh Day Adventists and broke away from them to form his own cult.

The twentieth century has seen numerous false messiahs leading many astray with their deceptive teachings. Numerous cults have been formed by these counterfeit messiahs and there have been many accusations that followers have been brain-washed into giving the leaders unquestioning allegiance. One of the best known of these cults is the Moonies led by the Reverend Sun Meung Moon whose disciples travel the world with their false teachings. They are highly active in proselytisation and forming cult communities in many nations.

Many orthodox Jews are expecting Messiah to come in the near future. The ultra-orthodox Lubavitch sect announced early in the 1990s that their leader, ninety-year-old Rabbi Menachem Schneerson, paralysed by a stroke and living in New York, USA, was the long-awaited Messiah of Judaism. They were awaiting the right time for him to return to Israel and to take his place in Jerusalem as the declared Messiah who would be recognised by the whole nation. Since his death they will clearly have to look for another.

The New Age movement also has its false messiahs, one of whom, the Maitreya, was said to be living in the East End of London during the 1980s. He was said to be an Indian guru who, at the right time, would reveal himself to the world. His representative, Benjamin Creme held public meetings giving messages by telepathy from the Maitreya. This followed a full-page newspaper advertisement in 1975 announcing that the Messiah was now on earth and that he would be the fulfilment of the Messianic hopes of people of all religions.

False Prophets and Teachers

Of a different character, but perhaps equally dangerous, have been some teachers who have stayed within the church and whose teachings have been regarded as prophecy. Their method has been to take selective passages of Scripture, piece them together to form a pattern that bears some resemblance to events in the modern world and on this basis predict the imminence of the second coming of Christ, the battle of Armageddon, or the end of the world. Their writings have become best-sellers in an age where fear and credulity grip the masses.

An example of this kind of teaching is *The Late Great Planet Earth* by Hal Lindsey, which was reputed to have sold more than thirty million copies and been translated into more than thirty languages. His book *The 1980s Countdown to Armageddon* is a monument of false interpretation, revealing the author's woeful ignorance of even the first principles of biblical exegesis.

Lindsey's strong anti-Communist line, predictions of a nuclear holocaust, Middle East conflict and catalogue of scare stories showing the inadequacy of American defences in the face of Russian arms technology and weapon superiority were designed to make a strong appeal to the American Right-wing of the 1970s and 80s. His teaching had an enormous political as well as religious influence upon American thinking. Lindsey was even invited to address

Pentagon officials and high ranking military chiefs where, according to his own account:

> As I spoke about the detailed accounts of how the final World War would develop, as recorded in Daniel, chapter 11, verses 40–45, I was impressed by the total attention they were paying to what I said. I continued and discussed the forces that would be involved in the War, the way the troops would move, the battles that would take place and how the War would spread to the rest of the world. I noticed that the men were visibly moved by what I said .... A few days before our meeting, their computer had predicted the same events and outcomes that had been forecast by Daniel. Needless to say, they were more surprised by Daniel's words than I was by theirs (Hal Lindsey, *The 1980s Countdown to Armageddon*, Lakeland, 1980, p6).

It is a chilling thought that American political, military and international strategy could be influenced by false teaching based upon inadequate biblical exegesis of a passage in Daniel that has already been fulfilled in the invasion of Israel and Egypt by Antiochus Epiphanes in 167 BC. It is more than a remote possibility that American politicians and generals who have believed these false biblical teachings may even imagine they are helping to hasten the second coming of Christ by initiating an Armageddon-type nuclear conflict.

The fact that Lindsey was believed by so many Christians is an indication of the lack of sound biblical teaching on the subject of prophecy in the churches. If the churches had only applied the simple range of tests concerning the prophet as insisted upon in the early church and in New Testament teaching they would not have accepted his teaching.

Along similar lines of 'prophetic teaching' have been books about '666' and financial matters. Millions of copies have been in circulation since the 1970s claiming to predict end-time events, cashless societies controlled by 'big brother' dictators who will become the Antichrist referred to in the Book of Revelation and who will place the 'mark of the beast' upon the forehead of all the peoples of the world. These predictions make use of passages from Daniel and Revelation and relate them to contemporary events such as bar-codes on goods in the shops that contain the numerals '666'. Biblical texts and contemporary data are woven together to form a pattern that supports the theory being propounded. Typical of this kind of book is the best-seller *When Your Money Fails* sub-titled *The 666 System is Here* (1981). The writer, Mary Stewart Relfe, states:

> I unreservedly view the international usage of the number '666' by the present world system, to be presided over soon by Mr 666, the false messiah, as the third most significant fulfilment of Bible prophecy in the church age (the past two thousand years) (p59).

She mixes this kind of statement in with a mass of trivial news items and biblical mathematics and then produces bald predictions of the second coming of Christ such as the following:

> Ladies and gentlemen, I have a relentless urgency to share with you that this world is now standing on the threshold of the most critical decade in the history of mankind. I had for years charted the end of this world order as closely corresponding to the close of this century. Today, I am not at all certain that one person reading these lines will see 1990 before they see his Eternal Majesty, King Wonderful, Jesus Christ, Son of the Living God, revealed from heaven in flaming fire taking vengeance on them that know not God and obey not the gospel (p61).

Mary Relfe, actually claims to write under the direction of the Holy Spirit, stating her conviction that she is a prophet. 'I boldly confess that I come to you in the role of a New Testament prophet,' she states on page 202. On the back of the book are several commendations including one in capital letters that says, 'One of the most outstanding books of this generation!' This commendation is said to be

295

by 'Colin Deal, author of best-seller, *Christ Returns by 1988*'. No doubt a commendation from such a source says all that is necessary!

Those who take passages from Daniel and Revelation and apply them uncritically to events in the modern world are doing a grave disservice to the gospel. Their efforts, however spectacular and rewarded by passing popular acclaim, do much harm to the church. Whenever large numbers of Christians are deceived the result is a setback to the mission of Christ to carry the gospel of salvation to all mankind. The gospel is a message of hope, of love, of forgiveness and reconciliation, that God in his great love for mankind has made possible through the Lord Jesus. In total contrast is the lurid scaremongering of the false prophets and teachers who mishandle Scripture, distort the gospel, gain great personal acclaim and make small fortunes out of their wretched ministries of deception.

Interpreting Apocalyptic Literature

It is a fundamental error to try to understand events in the modern world by discovering selective passages of Scripture that appear to resemble them. This is not to deny that Scripture, rightly handled, is a powerful means of seeking divine illumination of the present. But the right starting place is in the understanding of the overall nature and purposes of God that the Bible reveals. Then we may approach the interpretation of contemporary events with confidence and hope rooted in the love of God who is ultimately in control and will not allow his creation to be destroyed by sinful men. The false prophets who revel in bloodshed, destruction and the flames of wrath being poured out upon unbelievers are in total contrast to the true prophets of the Bible where we see men like Jeremiah seeing visions of judgment through eyes filled with tears, and Jesus weeping over an unrepentant Jerusalem.

The right handling of the word of God in Scripture requires an understanding of the circumstances under which the word was given. This is particularly essential in handling the prophetic books and doubly so in attempting to understand and interpret apocalyptic literature. Daniel and the Book of Revelation are apocalyptic, they are not 'straight' prophecy. That is why the Book of Daniel is not included among the prophets in the Hebrew Bible, but is located with the wisdom literature. Apocalyptic literature is written in code; certain words, phrases and numerals have special meanings and these are woven into the picture presented through vision. They are understandable to those who know the code, but they are unintelligible to those who do not.

Apocalyptic literature had special significance during times of persecution when a message of hope and encouragement could be conveyed to believers without endangering their lives if it should fall into enemy hands. Daniel had special significance for the Jews living in the terrible times of suffering and atrocities inflicted upon them by the Syrian tyrant Antiochus Epiphanes. The Book of Revelation was written by John with the particular purpose of encouraging Christians in the churches of Asia Minor whom he perceived to be in great spiritual danger and would soon be experiencing the persecution of Rome.

Like Daniel, John uses a code; for example, *three* stands for heaven and godly things, *four* stands for earth, *six* is the sign of evil, *ten* stands for the fulness of time, while *seven* and *twelve* are combinations of *three* and *four* signifying the completion of the work of God in creation and the accomplishment of his purposes. Finally, 666 is a special sign of evil personified in Revelation 13.18, where it is said to be 'the number of a man'—that is, in the words of F F Bruce (in a private letter to me—quoted with his permission) 'the sum of the numerical value of the letters in somebody's name, no more and no less'.

Through John, the Spirit sent a message to the churches of Asia Minor warning them of the coming persecution, pointing out their specific weaknesses and calling upon them to stand firm and be strengthened by the Spirit of God. This was followed by seven visions containing hidden truth to enable the believers in Asia Minor to glimpse the scene in heaven and to understand the drama that was being played out on earth through the conflict of the gospel with the Roman Empire and through which the power of God overcomes the evil might of man, and the ultimate good purposes of God are worked out. The vision of the great spiritual drama is, of course, in symbolism which would not be understood by the Roman authorities if it fell into their hands, but it would be understood by the believers and would convey a message of hope and encouragement to them to strengthen them as they faced the times of persecution in which so many of them would be martyred.

This does not mean that the messages of Daniel and Revelation have no significance for our age, but rather it is a warning that biblical symbolism cannot be applied literally to random events in the twentieth century without causing vast confusion and misunderstanding. A right handling of the word of God for our times means beginning with those who *first received the word*, standing where they stood, understanding the word as they understood it, deciphering the code, interpreting the symbolism, receiving the message the Spirit of God was conveying through divine revelation, and then taking that essential message and applying it to the contemporary world. Even that should not be done simply as an academic exercise using the tools of intellectual deduction mingled with the fertile imagination of our human minds. It is here that revelation is needed today in order rightly to understand the application of divine truth from Scripture in the context of the contemporary world. We need God's understanding of his word in order to understand God's word for his world in our times.

The false prophets and false teachers care for none of these things. They charge blindly in where angels fear to tread, crushing the truth, distorting the word of God and deceiving the multitudes—even simple believers—as Jesus said, 'even the elect, if that were possible' (Mt 24.24).

Prophets of the New Age

The New Age movement, which has had increasing public profile over the past twenty years, has brought with it its own recognised prophets. Most New Agers are interested in prophecy as part of their fascination with the supernatural. These 'prophets', or gurus, usually operate as clairvoyants using a spiritual master from some bygone age.

Per Johnsen, a Norwegian born-again believer who was once deeply involved in the New Age movement, described in the magazine *Prophecy Today* his own experience of New Age prophecy. Most New Agers believe in reincarnation and Per's 'prophet' was called John Peniel because he believed he had been 'Jacob' and also the 'Apostle John' in former life cycles. Per reported,

> John's prophecies were amazingly accurate in describing people's characters, habits and backgrounds. Virtually everything in the past and the present was correct and to the point. On the future, however, he was not accurate. But he always had excuses; 'The prophecy was right, but the timing was wrong,' or 'The prophecy was right at the time it was given, but it failed because the receiver deviated from God's will for him.'
>
> The first time I met him, during the winter of 1981, I asked him for a prophecy, or a so-called 'life reading'. He did not know me at all but he gave a one-hour prophecy which I recorded on tape. Its accuracy convinced me beyond doubt that it was from God because I thought that no-one else could know such things. This is how the prophecy ended (when speaking through his guiding spirit John always used the first person plural).
>
> 'We say that your life will become more active now, that the changes will come, that you will become more fluid and spontaneous. And we say that joy and peace is coming into your life for the first time ever. You have had much happiness but happiness is on the outside. Joy and peace come from the inside. An incredible joy and peace will come from knowing

exactly why you are here and what you have to do. This will begin near the end of February and by the autumn you will know exactly what you are going to do for the rest of your life.

There will be no problems. No problems at all, because we say very simply this way; God has sent you great help in this lifetime to do mighty works. Because you have worked for God for so many lifetimes in your way quietly, persistently, we are going to see the light in you shine brighter than almost anyone can imagine. Certainly brighter than you can imagine right now. And many people will be quite amazed. You know God's people rise out of the masses. We could not spot them. They are not flashy. They are very quiet, humble people who deeply understand. They even understand more than they understand. And when the moment is right, they rise out of the masses and they do the work that no other man can do, except them. Because the quietly persistent are the people who always succeed, you will succeed—there is no doubt about it.'

The prophecy ended on that note and I wept. Was this really the way God saw me and wanted to use me? Me! I felt such a peace and joy and excitement. I could hardly believe it. My heart leapt with joy. I knew at that moment that I wanted to be around this man who knew such things. I wanted to learn more of his wisdom and to know all the secrets and mysteries of the universe that God had revealed to him.

It took me five years to discover that I was the victim of a great deception. I had to go through a breaking experience; it was like being set free from a spirit of bondage and slavery that had brought my life to the edge of disaster.

It takes considerable discernment to realise that that prophecy comes from a demonic spirit and not from God. Apart from the reference to other lifetimes, much of it sounds very similar to prophecies which are given by charismatic leaders. Per notes these similarities. He says, the key elements are (1) God is concerned with you personally. (2) He proves his concern by revealing personal details of your life to the 'prophet'. (3) You are more virtuous than you think. (4) You are specially chosen by God. (5) God has a mighty work planned for you. (6) Go and fulfil your calling with joy and peace, for God is with you.

Per also notes that he himself became a disciple of this New Age prophet because the man was able to tell him personal details about his own life which he wrongly assumed must have been revealed by God.

The grave danger facing us today in the post-Christian era of secular humanism in the Western nations is that, having ceased to believe in God, millions of men and women not only have no knowledge of biblical teaching, they also are largely ignorant of the spirit world and of the great dangers of deception.

Biblical Teaching

The charismatic renewal movement has brought a new openness to divine revelation but with it has come the inevitable accompaniment of the spurious and the counterfeit in the exercise of spiritual gifts and ministries. The practice of prophecy within the spiritually renewed churches and new fellowships varies enormously but certain common characteristics have emerged.

Among most of the churches and fellowships there is muddle and confusion over the nature and use of prophecy due to a lack of clear biblical teaching on the subject. This can be seen particularly in the following ways;

1) *There is a failure to perceive the distinction between the ministry of the prophet and the gift of prophecy*. This distinction is made clear in both the teaching and practice of the New Testament church.

Paul speaks of the prophet among the ministries that he lists in Ephesians 4. In the New Testament church the prophets were travelling preachers who went from one fellowship to another encouraging and building up the faith of believers by bringing them some direct word of revelation which enabled them to know the direction of the Spirit for the fulfilment of the mission of Christ.

By contrast, Paul refers to the *gift* of prophecy when listing

301

the manifestations of the Spirit in 1 Corinthians 12. This is in the context of his teaching on the exercise of gifts within the local church at Corinth. Hence our conclusion that within the New Testament church the prophet exercised a ministry to the *whole* church, wheras the gift of prophecy was exercised within the *local* church.

Confusion has arisen today because many people are learning to listen to God and there is increasing awareness of the activity of the Holy Spirit. This has resulted in many people thinking of themselves as prophets (even new believers within a few months of conversion) which has caused pain and confusion both to themselves and to others. The ministry of the prophet requires great maturity.

It is not unknown for comparatively new believers genuinely to exercise the gift of prophecy but this also requires a level of spiritual maturity. Wherever gifts are being practised it is essential that those in leadership positions should be able to discern what is coming from the Holy Spirit and what is spurious and also to have the wisdom to know how to handle such situations.

This increased awareness of the work of the Holy Spirit lays a heavy responsibility upon leaders for the exercise of discernment and knowing when to encourage or when to caution or even rebuke. Sound biblical teaching is essential for the right exercise both of ministry and of spiritual gifts.

Discernment is not one of the gifts of the Spirit and should not be confused with the gift of 'distinguishing between spirits' (1 Corinthians 12:10). Discernment comes from the constant study of scripture and right handling of the word of God which enables believers 'to distinguish between good and evil' (Heb 5:14).

If leaders really want to see the right handling of spiritual gifts in the churches they should not only tighten up their own handling of situations in public worship but more especially ensure that every believer is properly taught in the context of small groups. New believers may be

302

encouraged to bring a word from scripture to which they believe God is directing their attention. New believers may also be encouraged to bring words of prophecy in the third person and in ordinary everyday language rather than first person singular King James language.

This makes it much easier to be weighed than if it is prefaced with the awesome imperative, 'Thus says the Lord!' If the prophecy truly is from God and the hearers are men and women of spiritual maturity they will recognise it as a word from God. A low-key presentation beginning 'I believe God is saying to us . . .' also enables the leader to weigh the word carefully and deal with its content objectively without the subjective pressures of having to correct ot refute something which has already been declared to come directly from the mouth of God.

The content of many modern prophecies is a mixture of divine and human origin. Quite often someone will start with a word that has truly been inspired by God, but then drift on into including words of their own. This often happens quite naturally because we do not know how to stop or because we think the 'word' requires additional explanation.

Each of those exercising the gift of prophecy should have the confidence and discipline to say just what they are hearing and no more. It is not uncommon for one person to get one part of the message and someone else to get the second part. If they both speak out what they are hearing, the whole message is received which gives encouragement to the whole body of believers that God is at work among them.

These simple practices make the task of leadership much less onerous and guard the flock against splits and divisions. The leader is able to separate the wheat from the chaff without causing emotional scenes from those who feel affronted that their words were not treated with all the solemnity of Holy Writ. When prophetic words are carefully weighed in the context of scripture the whole congregation grows in spiritual discernment and maturity.

The right handling of prophecy also has two other important effects. It guards the fellowship against deception. It also enables the whole fellowship readily to embrace that which they all perceive to be the word of the Lord to them.

2) *There has been considerable muddle over the use of tongues and interpretation.* Again this is linked to a lack of clear biblical teaching and a failure to realise that through the gift of tongues we are speaking *to* God. Paul says 'anyone who speaks in a tongue does not speak to men but to God.' By contrast he says 'everyone who prophesies speaks to men' (1 Cor 14.2–3). Paul refers to speaking in tongues as 'prayer' and prayer is obviously addressed *to* God and not to men. He says 'If you are praising God with your spirit, how can one who finds himself among those who do not understand say "Amen" to your thanksgiving, since he does not know what you are saying?' (1 Cor 14.16). An interpretation of a tongue is not necessarily a *translation*. The latter would be in the form of a prayer addressed to God. An *interpretation* may enable the speaker or someone else to hear the response of the Father to the heart cry of the believer. This response would be in the form of a message *from* God, but in many churches it is regarded as a translation of the tongue and therefore not tested. Paul says 'He who speaks in a tongue edifies himself, but he who prophesies edifies the church' (1 Cor 14.4). This failure to recognise it as a message from God, which is prophecy, and therefore comes under the strict instructions of the New Testament that all prophecy must be weighed and tested, has resulted in a great deal of false teaching and confusion among churches and fellowships today.

In this connection it is interesting to note that the Assemblies of God in the USA recently acknowledged that they had been making this mistake and accordingly changed their practice, recognising that 'tongues' is *to* God, and prophecy is *from* God, according to the teaching of Paul in 1 Corinthians 14.

3) *There has been widespread failure in the matter of weighing and testing prophecy.* Most leaders simply do not know how to set about this, hence numerous prophecies are simply allowed to pass unchecked in the course of worship. Typical practice is where a prophecy is given during a momentary gap in a time of praise or open prayer. It is listened to in silence by the congregation. Thereupon the worship leader, whose skills are usually more in music than in the handling of spiritual gifts, simply says, 'Thank you, Jesus' and begins the next song.

The word is never weighed by any in the fellowship who have the ministry of prophecy or by those who exercise the gift of prophecy, or indeed by those who have spiritual discernment which may include most of the congregation. The tests insisted upon by Paul and John and regularly practised in the early church are never applied.

4) *Words of divine revelation are often received by fellowships and simply ignored.* If the word is not weighed and tested, which includes sifting out the genuine word of revelation that the Holy Spirit is conveying from the human words of the carrier, the significance of the message is often lost. Many fellowships receive numerous words but fail to perceive the significance of what the Spirit of God is saying to them because they do not know how to handle divine revelation. This again is due to a lack of clear biblical teaching that should be the determining factor underlying current practice in the churches.

This lack of clear biblical teaching on prophecy and the nature and handling of divine revelation lies at the heart of the problem facing multitudes of churches throughout the world today. We are living in a day of great spiritual activity, both counterfeit and genuine.

It is essential that we learn how to handle the word of God rightly which includes learning how to *listen* to what the Spirit is saying to the churches today. Failure to do so results in a situation where either we are prey

305

to the deception of false prophecy or we are shut to divine revelation and thereby cut off from the source of light and power that God has readily made available to his church, including providing the safeguards against deception and the means of discerning the genuine activity of the Holy Spirit.

Prophetic revelation goes hand in hand with the spiritual gifts that God has made available to all believers within the church. The spiritual gifts and ministries are given to encourage, strengthen and build up each fellowship as part of the whole church of Christ. Prophetic revelation is becoming increasingly common as a normal part of the church's worship and spiritual life. This is happening in both small groups and in large assemblies. It is sign of the activity of the Holy Spirit in the church today building up the body of Christ for its mission in the contemporary world.

CHAPTER SIXTEEN

PROPHECY IN THE CHURCHES

Spiritual Activity

The twentieth century has seen a remarkable period of growth in the church both numerical and spiritual. There appear to be three distinct phases of this spiritual activity. The first, at the beginning of this century, was the Pentecostal movement with its emphasis upon the gift of tongues being the primary evidence of the outpouring of the Holy Spirit into the lives of individuals. The first Pentecostal preachers were despised and rejected by other believers but from small beginnings the movement has developed into the fastest growing sector of the church worldwide.

The second phase initiated what we now know as the charismatic movement.

This began in the second half of the century with its emphasis upon all the gifts of the Spirit being available to every Spirit-filled believer. The 1960s and 70s saw the planting of many new independent fellowships, some of which have subsequently linked to form small sects or new denominations.

The third phase began in the 1970s and gained momentum through the 1980s. It is the renewal movement which has run right through the mainline denominations. The Roman Catholic Church, the Church of England, the Episcopal, the Baptist, Methodist, Presbyterian and Reformed churches have all seen many of their local congregations experience new life through the charismatic renewal. The emphasis has been upon a rediscovery of the ministry gifts of Ephesians 4 and the manifestations of the Spirit in 1 Corinthians 12. There has also been a renewed emphasis upon biblical teaching especially in relation to ministry and personal lifestyle.

One of the links between all three waves of spiritual activity during the twentieth century has been the important place given to prophecy. Among the Pentecostal denominations the Apostolic Church gives particular prominence to prophecy and the appointment of prophets to give divine revelation both for the mission of the church and for the lives of individuals. Within the charismatic movement prophecy has been a regular feature in the life of many fellowships, although practices vary considerably. No special role has been assigned to prophecy and the messages are usually concerned with bringing comfort and encouragement to the fellowship or personal prophecy for individuals. A major use of prophecy, both in the new independent sects and in the renewed mainline churches, has been through words of knowledge especially related to the exercise of gifts of healing.

It is, however, notable that so far throughout the twentieth century, with its major emphasis upon spiritual gifts within the contemporary church, there has been very little recognition of the wider biblical role of prophecy. Prophecy has largely been seen in terms of meeting individual needs or bringing comfort and consolation to the local fellowship. We have not seen prophecy used to bring creative drive to the message or mission of the church in the declaration of the gospel or its application to the injustices and evils of society. Neither has prophecy been used as in the early church for the direction of the mission of the church and its leadership. Perhaps it will be another generation before prophecy is fully restored to its biblical role within the community of believers and their outreach into the secular world.

Popular Prophecy

The post-World War II period was a time of reconstruction and optimism which saw the birth of the charismatic movement. In the USA the movement had many extremes and gave rise to a number of different groups, some of which expanded into independent denominations whilst others developed a variety of bizarre practices and teachings. Most of the latter had some biblical derivation such as the 'Faith Movement' or 'prosperity gospel', 'dominionism' and 'manifest sons'.

All these teachings and a number of others arose out of what is now known as the 'Latter Rain' movement which had its beginnings in 1948. Latter Rain grew out of the classical Pentecostal churches and it is this movement which has given birth to a variety of 'charismatic' streams, most of which have the common theme of 'restoration', *ie* that we are living in the 'last days' during which God is restoring to his church the five-fold ministries of Ephesians 4 and the spiritual manifestations of 1 Corinthians 12.

The Latter Rain movement has had a continuing influence upon the church for the past fifty years. It has spawned a number of related teachings such as 'manifest sons'. The term 'manifest sons' comes from Paul's reference in Romans 8:18 and 19 where he says that the whole creation 'waits in eager expectation for the sons of God to be revealed'. The AV, which is more usually read by some evangelicals, says, 'For I reckon that the sufferings of this present time are not worthy to be compared with the glory which shall be revealed in us. For the earnest expectation of the creature waiteth for the manifestation of the sons of God.'

Most of the 'Latter Rain' groups, and those derived from them, believe that in the last days the final generation leading up to the end of the age or to Armageddon will receive an incredible outpouring of the power of the Holy

Spirit, *ie* the 'latter' or spring rain of Joel 2:23, which will enable them to do mighty exploits. They will see amazing miracles and be given the power to do mightier works than Jesus himself, in fulfilment of his promise 'anyone who has faith in me will do what I have been doing. He will do even greater things than these . . .' (John 14:12). The 'manifest sons' are expected to be the final generation of believers who have been selected by God for immortality.

Those who teach 'dominionism' believe that the restored church will overcome the enemies of the gospel, subdue the nations and prepare the way for the Second Coming of Christ. Dominionism is based upon the belief that the true believers will actually rule the nations through the divine authority and power that will be given them. They will exercise dominion over the whole created order and will take over all the instruments of government in the nations throughout the world.

One of the major figures in the early days of the 'Latter Rain' movement was William Branham, a self-proclaimed prophet, whose followers believed him to be the prophet Elijah. Branham himself believed this and when he met an untimely death in a road accident his disciples fully expected him to rise from the dead.

A one-time associate of Branham was Paul Cain who became disillusioned with the prophetic/healing ministry and retired from public life for a number of years. When he reappeared towards the end of the 1980s he claimed that God had told him to attach himself to an established ministry. Having failed in a number of approaches he wrote to John Wimber, leader of the Vineyard Ministries, predicting (accurately as it transpired) that there would be an earth tremor in California on the day they met. This convinced Wimber and he took him into partnership and proclaimed publicly that he and Paul Cain would never be parted. Wimber used his considerable influence in charismatic circles, both in the USA and internationally, to promote Paul Cain as a prophet using him at large gatherings to perform a mixture of clairvoyancy and popular personal prophecy. Before each meeting Cain would write down various messages for people he believed would be present.

During the meeting he would produce a number of cards with these messages which he would read out. This caused great excitement among the crowds. Cain would call out a name and give various personal details such as things that had happened in the past which gave credibility to the 'prophecy' which followed. These were usually predictions of how God was going to use that person in the future.

Those who practise clairvoyancy or divination are usually accurate in their knowledge of the past but are unreliable in regard to the future. Paul Cain's prophecy that there would be a great spiritual revival in England has already been mentioned. His much publicised prediction that this revival would commence in October 1990 was not fulfilled and caused great disappointment which led to the decline of popular prophecy.

This kind of prophecy which caused a lot of excitement and brought together large crowds of charismatics in the late 1980s and early 1990s soon subsided both in the USA and in Britain. There was much controversy surrounding the Kansas City Fellowship and in 1991 Bob Jones, their 'senior prophet' was exposed for what John Wimber described as 'gross sexual sins'. John Paul Jackson had already been taken out of public ministry for a period for what Wimber referred to as a time of 'theological training'. The following year Wimber distanced himself from the Kansas City Fellowship and severed his partnership with Paul Cain. Then, in May 1993, Brent Rue, Wimber's deputy, died of cancer and John Wimber himself had to cancel his engagements for a period in order to undergo treatment for cancer in the throat. He subsequently suffered a stroke which severely limited his active ministry.

Paul Cain lost support in America following the election of President Clinton whom he prophesied would be the greatest president since Lincoln. He had accurately foretold the headlines in American newspapers on the day following the presidential election. But his prophecy that Clinton would restore greatness to America and re-establish America's declining moral foundations proved to be far from accurate. He further lost face in 1994 when he visited Iraq and had a personal interview with Saddam Hussein. He was widely reported as declaring that Saddam Hussein was a good man, much maligned and misunderstood who had been unjustly treated by the Western powers.

The great wave of popular prophecy which had taken the charismatic churches by storm appeared to be over, but the legacy of bitterness and disillusionment rumbled on. Inevitably, when a ministry is given high profile promotion, it evokes controversy. In the two or three-year period of the link-up between Vineyard and KCF considerable harm was done to the fragile unity which was developing across the Pentecostal/charismatic/renewed sector of the church. A number of fellowships in the United States and in Britain split as a direct result of this ministry.

David Pytches, a Church of England clergyman, and strong supporter of John Wimber, went out to Kansas City in 1989 to investigate reports of the new 'prophetic' phenomena there. On returning he wrote a sensational book, *Some Said it Thundered*, describing the exploits of the men known as 'the Kansas City prophets' which caused considerable excitement among the less discerning charismatics in Britain. Some of the more bizarre anecdotes recounted in the book were said by Wimber and Cain to be either exaggerations or untrue.

Wimber later said that he had strongly advised Pytches not to publish the book, which was timed to promote the visit of the so-called 'Kansas City prophets' to London in July 1990 which Pytches organised. At these meetings Mike Bickle, senior pastor of the Kansas City Fellowship, confessed to numerous 'serious errors' in their teaching and practice. Perversely, this 'confession', plus the hype surrounding the ministry and the teaching given by Wimber served to enhance the ministry. The confession was seen as commendable humility by British evangelicals not used to such public displays as they are in the USA.

Following these meetings a number of leading British charismatics signed a statement saying they had examined the teaching of these men from Kansas and were happy to commend their ministry to the churches in Britain. This statement, published in the religious press, paved the way for the meetings in October that year where the great revival was supposed to begin.

Opinion will no doubt be divided on this ministry for a long time to come but there can be no doubt that the mixture of excitement, exaggeration and controversy surrounding it did untold harm to the serious study of prophetic revelation and to an understanding of the activity of God in the contemporary world. It was a setback to the cause of promoting a biblical understanding of prophecy in the churches.

The Toronto Blessing

The Toronto Blessing sprang to prominence in 1994 and by the middle of 1995 it had reached most countries in the Western world. Britain was said to be the most affected and it was variously estimated that some three to five thousand churches had embraced the phenomena. Its characteristics were uncontrollable laughter, falling down, a variety of uncontrollable physical movements and many strange sounds including screaming and animal noises.

The fruit of the Toronto Blessing was said to be seen in healings, usually of an emotional nature such as healing hurts from past experiences and the healing of broken relationships. But most of the testimonies were about having a greater love for Jesus. The fruit was therefore largely subjective and difficult to assess. In the first eighteen months of the phenomena there were very few claims of conversions and none of the usual signs of revival.

The Toronto Blessing was usually passed on at what were

known as 'receiving meetings'. These were characterised by a lengthy period of worship with the repetition of songs and choruses which have become a familiar mark of charismatic meetings. A new departure for evangelicals was that there was very little emphasis upon preaching the word and many meetings had little or no scripture reading at all. When the scripture was read it was often accompanied by outbreaks of laughter which made hearing the word difficult. The emphasis at these receiving meetings was always on 'ministry'. Worshippers were often prepared for this by leaders telling them what to expect and advising them not to use their minds but simply to receive whatever the Spirit wanted to give to them. The ministry time usually began with testimonies from those who had already received the Blessing. When invited to give testimony the recipients would often lose the power of speech and eventually fall to the ground again to do more 'carpet time', as it became known. Many people went back time after time to these meetings to repeat the experience.

The Toronto Blessing brought great division among evangelicals wherever it reached. Many leaders embraced it uncritically. This was usually because, according to their own testimonies, they were spiritually dry, discouraged and hungry for the power of God to come upon them and transform their ministries. The Toronto Blessing came at a time of world economic recession, political instability and revolutionary social change. Standards of morality had been falling dramatically in all Western nations since the 1960s, marriage and family life was disintegrating and there was a general air of hoplessness and despair which was weighing heavily on most people especially those who mourned the loss of traditional social values and biblical standards of morality.

In addition to these sociological factors, which were influential in the rapid spread of the Toronto Blessing, there were theological roots which make it relevant for this present study. These theological concepts were rooted in prophecy—prophecy which emanated from the Latter Rain movement to which reference has already been made. Rodney Howard-Browne, a South African evangelist who was said to have originated the Toronto Blessing, was a one-time associate of the Johannesburg Rhema church and closely associated with the Word Faith movement linked with Kenneth Hagin and Benny Hinn. It was through these two men that the Blessing got into the Vineyard churches and was picked up first by Randy Clark, a St Louis pastor, and then by John Arnott, pastor of the Toronto Airport Vineyard church. Arnott invited Clark to do a four-night series of meetings in January 1994, a series which stretched to three weeks. This engendered great excitement and attracted visitors which rapidly swelled into a flood so that by September 1994 it was estimated that 35,000 people had visited the Toronto Airport church, most of them being overseas visitors.

Howard-Browne openly prophesied that his meetings were a fulfilment of the Latter Rain prophecies of a great outpouring of the Holy Spirit in power upon believers. He prophesied that this was a 'second Pentecost', continually reading Acts 2 at his meetings where he would emphasise that the drunken behaviour being witnessed was similar to that on the Day of Pentecost. He prophesied that those who experienced the Blessing would never be the same again, they would receive mighty power to do amazing miracles. He said that people would fall down at their feet in the streets and shopping malls and say, 'I see Jesus in you'.

At the time of writing there is no evidence of these prophesies being fulfilled. Even more importantly, there is no evidence of the great revival foretold in the Latter Rain prophesies. There are, however, reports of scenes of genuine revival in a number of Baptist churches and colleges in the USA which are said to be quite independent of any influence from the Toronto Blessing. These are characterised by confession of sin, repentance, reconciliation with God and with others, plus many young people offering

315

their lives for full-time ministry. These authentic marks of revival are in strong contrast to the emotional scenes, animal noises, hysterical laughter and drunken behaviour that characterise the Toronto Blessing meetings.

Personal Prophecy

The combined effect of the growth of Pentecostal churches and the development of the charismatic and renewal movements has resulted in the recognition of spiritual gifts in churches and fellowships throughout the world. This in turn has created growing interest in the whole subject of biblical prophecy and contemporary prophetic revelation. Undoubtedly the most popular form of the latter is personal prophecy.

Most people are curious about the future. In secular society the first page in the daily newspaper read by millions of people is the horoscope with the astrological prediction for the day. In an age of 'secular spiritism' more and more people are turning to astrologers, diviners and fortune-tellers to obtain guidance in the complex issues facing them in their business and personal lives.

Christians are by no means immune from curiosity concerning the future and most have a deep desire to receive divine guidance for their lives. There can be few Christians who would not wish to receive a direct word from God or to speak with him face to face if that were possible.

There are times when all believers seek guidance through prayer or through reading the Bible, or through some other means, before making important decisions which may perhaps have far-reaching implications for their lives. The Victorians had a promise box full of texts which they would pick at random when seeking a word from the Lord. Many people today still use the pin in the Bible method of pointing to a verse which they hope will give them guidance. Others pray for the Holy Spirit to bring into their minds some verse of Scripture which will have significance for them.

316

PROPHECY IN THE CHURCHES

It is in the context of this longing in the human heart for divine guidance that the popularity of personal prophecy has to be seen. Since the earliest days of the Pentecostal movement at the beginning of the twentieth century there have been some Pentecostal churches which have placed a particular emphasis upon the importance of personal prophecy. The Apostolic Church, for example, is amongst those who appoint ministers to the office of prophet. Ministry appointments and the movement of pastors or evangelists from one place to another are all undertaken only on the basis of prophetic revelation. They see this as a practice which was a regular feature of life in the early church. For example, it is recorded in Acts 13,

> In the church at Antioch there were prophets and teachers
> . . . While they were worshipping the Lord and fasting, the
> Holy Spirit said, 'Set apart for me Barnabas and Saul for the
> work to which I have called them.' So after they had fasted
> and prayed, they placed their hands on them and sent them
> off. (vv1–3)

In many charismatic churches personal prophecy has taken a place of considerable prominence. It is not simply used for major decisions in the ministry of individuals and the mission of the church but for meeting every kind of personal need. The self-centred individualism of secular Western society has had its effect upon the charismatic movement. This can be seen in the exercise of spiritual gifts where there has been considerable emphasis upon meeting personal needs. The gifts have often been seen as being given for the healing, the health and the wealth of individuals rather than for building up the body of Christ in order to fulfil the mission of the church in world evangelisation and growth in spiritual maturity.

This emphasis upon 'self' has created a spiritual atmosphere within many charismatic fellowships in which there is a hunger for personal prophecy. It is small wonder, therefore, that meetings are very popular where there is

317

known to be an emphasis upon personal prophecy or where individuals who exercise such ministry are known to be present. The danger is that such meetings, often advertised as 'celebrations' become more like charismatic cabarets.

Nevertheless, while it is wrong to make a public spectacle of spiritual gifts, it would be a grave error to despise all personal prophecy. The New Testament has many examples of prophecies being given to individuals. Paul reminds Timothy of prophecies he had been given earlier in his life, 'Timothy, my son, I give you this instruction in keeping with the prophecies once made about you, so that by following them you may fight the good fight, holding on to faith and a good conscience' (1 Tim 1:18–19). Paul himself received a powerful prophecy through the prophet Agabus when he was on his way to Jerusalem for the last time, 'Coming over to us, he took Paul's belt, tied his own hands and feet with it and said, "The Holy Spirit says, 'In this way the Jews of Jerusalem will bind the owner of this belt and will hand him over to the Gentiles'"' (Acts 21:11).

Paul received that prophecy but did not heed the pleas not to go up to Jerusalem. Instead, he took it as confirmation of the warnings he had already received from God (Acts 20.23) and no doubt went on his way strengthened in the spirit.

If Paul was right in going up to Jerusalem he could easily have been deterred from doing so by the prophecy of Agabus. Also, if he had been a weaker character he could have been manipulated by the pleas of others who heard it. This underlines the danger of personal prophecy being used consciously, or unconsciously, to manipulate.

On the other hand there are great spiritual benefits from receiving a true word from God for giving guidance not only in our personal lives, when we are facing important decisions, but also for ministry in whatever sphere of service we are being used within the body of Christ.

Bill Hamon, a Restoration minister in the USA, who claims

to have given many thousands of prophecies to individuals over more than forty years of ministry, wrote in 1987,

> I believe that the decade of the 1980s has been designated in the counsels of God as the time for the calling forth of the prophetic ministry. Before the 1980s are over, God will have raised up and called forth thousands of prophets. . . . They will no longer be denied and ignored but rather accepted and activated into their full anointed authority within the office of prophet.

Hamon believes that we are presently witnessing a great prophetic movement in which there are those called to be prophets and others exercising the gift of prophecy who together fulfil the biblical expectation of the return of Elijah in the last days. He says,

> The emerging company of prophets with the prophetic mantle of Elijah will prepare the way for Christ's Second Coming in full manifestation of his ministry as King of kings and Lord of lords. The cry of the Holy Spirit is for prophets to come forth. The church is crying out for holy and truly God-anointed prophets. And the prophets are coming, for the Spirit and the Bride are now saying, 'Come!' (*Prophets and Personal Prophecy*, Bill Hamon, Destiny Image, Shippenburg, PA 1988 pp. 55, 56).

Whether or not this proves to be a true prophecy or merely wishful thinking only the passage of time will tell.

There are twelve elements in the testing of prophecy which are basic to biblical teaching. From the evidence of the New Testament, the Didache and other early church documents, we may say that they were standard practice in the early church. The following is a brief summary of these tests which may provide a code of practice for the handling of prophecy in the church today.

Tests of Prophecy
1 Prayer
Prophecy should always be received in prayer. This provides the right foundation for weighing anything that purports to be divine revelation. Prayer opens the believer

to the channel of the Holy Spirit and enables discernment to take place, particularly the primary discernment of 'spirits' referred to in 1 John 4.1 (*cf* 1 Th 5.17–22).

2 *Witness of the Spirit*
There is an immediate witness of the Spirit that bears testimony either to the falsity or the truth of what is being heard. If someone is speaking something that has been inspired by another spirit there will be an immediate sense of revulsion and rejection like a strong warning bell ringing within the mind of the believer. By contrast, if the word is from God, there will be a leap of response from the Spirit of God within the believer. This is not a rational or an intellectual process that can be taught or acquired. It is the gift of God. It is rather like when Mary the mother of Jesus, and Elizabeth the mother of John the Baptist, met during their pregnancies. When Mary came into the room Elizabeth testified that the babe leapt within her womb at the presence of the Lord Jesus within Mary. That is how the Spirit of God leaps within the believer in answering response to a true word from God (*cf* Jn 10.14–16).

These first two elements in weighing prophecy are purely concerned with the gifting of God—*what the Holy Spirit does for us*. The next ten tests are what we have to do in response to the Spirit to weigh, check and confirm the rightness of what we are hearing and how it should be interpreted. These tests all require the exercise of what may be described as 'sanctified intellect', 'adult thinking' to use Paul's term in 1 Corinthians 14.20.

3 *Scripture*
The content of prophecy should always be checked and compared with Scripture in the same way as the early church used the known teaching of the prophets and apostles to check the teaching of visiting preachers. The instruction given to the church through Titus (1.9) was that a leader 'must hold firmly to the trustworthy message *as it*

320

has been taught so that he can encourage sound doctrine and refute those who oppose it'. The word of God is unchanging. He does not contradict himself (*cf* 1 Cor 4.6; 2 Tim 3.16).

4 Meditation

Sometimes it is necessary to take time to ponder over a particular word—to spread it before the Lord and wait upon God in order to understand its significance, particularly if the Spirit has borne witness that this is a word from God, but there is no clear understanding of how it should be handled. We cannot hurry God and sometimes it is we ourselves who are not ready to receive the word with understanding. We must await his perfect timing (*cf* 2 Tim 2.15).

5 Confirmation

An important word will always need to be confirmed. God never objects to our asking for confirmation. This is not a lack of trust. It is the right exercise of caution in handling revelation. God does not want us to be deceived. He was extremely patient with Gideon in the tests he requested when seeking confirmation of the word he was hearing. God will often confirm his word through the mouths of others who had nothing to do with the original word, or through a sign; *ie* an event that has a spiritual interpretation. There is no 'blue-print' for confirmation. God uses many ways to communicate with us according to the measure of our faith (*cf* 1 Cor 14.20).

6 Unity

If a word is given for a particular fellowship there should be agreement within the body that this is truly a word from the Lord. The word of God is not divisive. It may not always be to our liking but if we are truly listening to God and we have the right attitude of love, humility and obedience, we will all hear the same thing and even through tears and penitence we will embrace the word and one another in love and unity (*cf* Titus 3.9–11). Division occurs where there is a lack of love, and unresponsiveness to the word of God.

7 Build up

If revelation is truly from God it will build up the faith of the church. It will strengthen, encourage and comfort believers. This is what Paul called 'edifying' the church. A major objective of the Holy Spirit in speaking to the churches is to build up the body of Christ, to give clear vision and power to meet the demands of mission in the contemporary world (*cf* 1 Cor 14.3).

8 Love

Is the word spoken in love? Any word that comes from God will be permeated through and through with his love. Love, of course, is never weak, or indecisive, or compromising with evil. Love, even if it rebukes, does so with tears and an unbreakable desire for the good of the loved one, and for the restoration of close fellowship. 'Love is patient, love is kind, . . . it is not rude, it is not self-seeking . . . love does not delight in evil but rejoices with the truth' (1 Cor 13.4–7).

9 Glorify Christ

A true word from God will always glorify Christ. It will never be boastful or bring honour and glory to the speaker, who is but a humble channel of the Spirit (*cf* 1 Pet 4.11). John made this a major test. If the spirit of the speaker is truly the Holy Spirit speaking to the church the word will glorify Jesus (1 Jn 4).

10 Conditions

If the word is one that promises blessings or brings rebuke there will be conditions. God's blessings are usually conditional upon *obedience* while even his words of judgment carry the call to repentance—'If my people will humble themselves and pray . . .' (*cf* 2 Chr 7.14; Jer 18.7–10).

11 *Fulfilment*

If the word is predicting future events the simplest test is to wait and see if the things predicted come to pass. If God has truly spoken through the prophet the events will happen. If the event prophesied does not happen at the predicted time, God has not spoken (or the conditions in the prophecy were not fulfilled). But this alone is not to be regarded as a test of prophecy, or of the prophet, in isolation from all the other tests (*cf* Dt 18.21,22).

12 *Character*

The moral character of the prophet was a major test applied by the early church and should still be regarded as of paramount importance in the exercise of ministry or gift within the church of Christ. Scripture teaches us that none of us is truly holy in the sight of God and all have fallen short of the glory of God. But those whose lives are being lived contrary to the word of God cannot be used as a channel for the Holy Spirit. Jesus taught that a major test of prophecy is to be seen in the *fruit* of the prophet's life (*cf* Mt 7.15–20).

The Prophetic Task

If the church is to be the prophet to the world to carry out the task God has given to his people that will enable him to fulfil his purposes in each generation, there must be obedience to basic biblical teaching in the supremely important task of handling the truth that God reveals to his people. It is only as the people of God become a 'listening people' that they will also become an obedient people empowered by the Spirit of God and radiating his glory among the nations. It is God's intention that the church of his precious Son should be the prophet to the world in this crucial period of history so that through the church his good purposes to bring forth the Kingdom may be fulfilled and thus glorify the name of the Lord Jesus unto whom all knees will one day bow.

PROPHECY PAST AND PRESENT

The prophetic task for which God has given the Holy Spirit to his church is:

—to reveal to the world the nature and purposes of God
—to discern the signs of the times
—to interpret what the Spirit is saying to the churches
—to guide and direct the mission of Christ
—to encourage and build up the body of Christ
—to correct error and discern the truth
—to warn and give forewarning of danger
—to declare the 'now' word of God
—to bring all men to a knowledge of God
—to intercede for the saints and for the nations
—to bring glory to Christ
—to prepare the way of the Lord

CHAPTER SEVENTEEN

PROPHETIC REVELATION—
GOD'S GIFT TO HIS CHURCH

Shaking and Harvest

In April 1986 there was a small but significant gathering at Carmel in Israel of international leaders with prophetic ministries. The objective was to share with one another what was happening in different regions of the world particularly relating to the activity of God; to seek for an understanding of the contemporary world situation in the context of the purposes of God as revealed in Scripture and to seek the word of God for our times.

There was a clear leading of the Spirit to an obscure prophecy in one of the minor prophets, Haggai 2:6 and 7.

> This is what the Lord Almighty says: "In a little while I will once more shake the heavens and the earth, the sea and the dry land. I will shake all nations, and the desired of all nations will come, and I will fill this house with glory," says the Lord Almighty.

It was noted that this prophecy is repeated in Hebrews 12 from verse 26 which indicates that it was still unfulfilled towards the end of the period of the writing of the New Testament.

There was a strong witness of the Spirit at the Carmel

325

gathering that what is being seen in the contemporary world is in line with this prophecy. God is shaking the whole created order plus the political, economic and social systems of the nations. He is also giving a period of unprecedented growth of the church throughout the world. Hebrews 12:28 implies that the purpose of the great shaking is to prepare the way for the Kingdom.

The Shaking of the Nations

The twentieth century has been a century of phenomenal change. It would be impossible even to attempt to summarise the sweeping changes in science and technology, in industrial production and communications, in political, environmental and social structure, as well as moral values, to mention just a few headings. The speed of change has increased throughout the centuries so that in the final decade the changes on the international scene have been occurring at a bewildering rate. The demise of the Communist Empire in Eastern Europe and the dismemberment of the Soviet Union took place in an incredibly short space of time once the shaking of the Warsaw Pact nations began.

The continuing ferment in the Middle East is a constant source of international uncertainty. The 1991 Gulf War really settled nothing and the rivalries for leadership of the Arab world continue between Syria, Iraq and Iran. Islamic fundamentalists have for many years been attempting to destabilise countries in the Middle East and Mediterranean areas such as Algeria, Egypt, Jordan and Lebanon. Additionally, despite peace agreements, the old hostilities between Muslims and Jews continue to complicate the Palestinian/Israeli situation.

The great famines in the Horn of Africa, together with political unrest and civil war plus the population explosion, grinding poverty and the legacy of white colonialism have made Africa a highly unstable continent through most of the twentieth century. The century has also been a black period in the history of Europe with world wars, constant conflict and upheaval climaxing in the final decade with the rise of a new phase of 'tribalism' which has resulted in the horrific slaughter of the civil war in former Yugoslavia. All these situations have added to the complexities of the international scene and are vivid evidence of the shaking of the nations in the contemporary world.

The rich Western nations have not escaped the shaking. The effects of the severest economic recession for sixty years hit the whole Western world at the beginning of the 1990s, dragging on far longer than any economist could predict. In ten years the economy of the United States was transformed from being the world's banker to becoming the world's largest debtor nation. Lloyd's of London, backbone of the world's insurance market, began struggling for survival from the beginning of the 1990s as the shock waves of huge insurance claims hit the City of London following a spate of international disasters, both manmade and natural, arising from storms, hurricanes and earthquakes as the natural order of creation was shaken together with the social, economic and political systems of the nations.

By the final decade of the century it was clear from reports coming in from all over the world that something extraordinary was taking place in every region and in every area of life—God was shaking the nations.

The Great Harvest
Since the middle of the twentieth century the church worldwide has been growing at a faster rate than at any time since the Apostolic age. Christianity is now the largest religion in the world with more than one-third of the world's total population claiming to be adherents of the faith. This, of course, is a global figure which includes people of every denominational background and theological persuasion, some of whom would undoubtedly be 'nominal' rather than active believers. Nevertheless, the significance

of what has been happening throughout the second half of the twentieth century lies in the growth rate of new believers rather than in the diversity of belief and practice.

Church historians such as Kenneth Latourette (*A History of the Expansion of Christianity*, volumes I–VII, Eyre and Spottiswoode, London, 1948) have amply demonstrated that the growth of the church throughout nearly two thousand years has proceeded in 'waves' rather than in a linear growth pattern. Each advance has been followed by a recession, but the wave of each advance has reached a new high-water mark and the trough of each dip has been correspondingly less. The present great advance is bringing millions of new believers each year to acknowledge Jesus as Lord.

Significantly the vast majority of this growth is taking place among the economically poor nations of the world whereas the rich industrialised nations have been seeing a decline in church attendance for half a century. Europe, which during the nineteenth century was the greatest missionary-sending continent, has seen the greatest decline. This, no doubt, is linked to its political history and the disillusionment of two devastating twentieth-century wars. By contrast, many of the poorest nations have been experiencing what can be justly described as a great 'spiritual awakening', especially during the last two or three decades of this century.

South East Asia is a region that has seen phenomenal growth. By 1990 the church in China was said to be growing at the rate of ten million new believers each year. Similar phenomenal growth has been seen in Indonesia which until recently was the largest Muslim nation in the world. Some estimates show that Christians now outnumber the Muslims whereas in 1965 they were less than ten per cent. A similar growth pattern has been seen in Korea which boasts some of the largest congregations in the world.

Central and Southern Africa, as well as South America, are also regions which have seen phenomenal growth in the numbers of new Christians. Christians in Third World nations now greatly outnumber those in Europe and America, the traditional Christian nations. The common factor is the indigenisation of the gospel that has taken place during the last half-century. Missionary strategy has been to plant the gospel and to allow it to grow within the local culture, developing local leadership, styles of worship and different practices appropriate to local needs and customs.

Another significant phenomenon of the second half of the twentieth century has been the considerable increase in persecution of Christians. The twentieth century has been a century of colossal bloodshed through war, political purges, terrorism and inter-racial and religious strife. It is estimated that in the Soviet Union, during the seventy years of Communist power, some 66 million people were murdered in political purges. (See *The Day Comes*, Clifford Hill, Collins, London, 1982, p 184.) It will never be known how many of these were believing Christians who suffered for their faith.

It is, however, an established fact that the number of Christian martyrs has increased sharply in recent years. Research carried out by David Barrett and published in the *World Christian Encyclopaedia* shows that by 1990 the annual figure for the number of Christian martyrs had risen to 300,000 and since then it has shown a steady increase of an additional 10,000 per year. The fanatical opposition of Islamic fundamentalists is one of the major factors in the rise of violent opposition to the gospel. Nigeria, for example, has have seen large-scale massacres of Christians by militant Muslims who have burned churches and murdered whole communities of Christians. In China the opposition of the Communist authorities steadily increased through the 1980s and became even more violent following the student revolution of 1989 which culminated in the Tiananmen Square massacre.

One of the most significant things we are seeing today is the link between the shaking of the nations and the spread of the gospel. It is nations such as China, Korea and Indonesia, each of which has been shaken by bloody revolutions and enormous political upheavals, which are seeing the most phenomenal growth in the number of believers. Despite opposition from the authorities the growth in the spread of the gospel is unstoppable. It may be that it is part of God's strategy to link the shaking of the nations and the growth of the church worldwide. If we are right in such a conclusion then we may expect the rich Western nations also to be shaken in order to open them up to the word of God.

Moses' Wish

Moses once expressed the wish that all God's people should be prophets. In response to two of the elders of Israel prophesying in the camp, instead of in the 'tent of meeting' where religious ritual took place, he said, 'I wish that all the Lord's people were prophets and that the Lord would put his Spirit on them!' (Num 11:29). If we take the word 'prophesy' to mean 'declaring the word of the Lord', rather than its narrower popular meaning of predicting the future, then we can say that Moses' wish is undoubtedly being fulfilled today in many parts of the world.

The great harvest we have just been noting which is taking place in some of the poorest nations and in places where there is violent opposition to the gospel is a 'people-led' movement of evangelism. It is not a movement in which famous Western missionaries or well-known evangelists are conducting great crusades. Such activities are forbidden in these nations. It is the ordinary people who are the evangelists. Despite fierce opposition, beatings, imprisonment and martyrdom, the believers cannot keep quiet. Even the newest converts are impelled to share their faith with others. The words of Tertullian in the third century still hold true, 'The blood of the martyrs is the seed of the church'.

It is in the context of the shaking of the nations that

there has been a great outpouring of the Holy Spirit upon believers throughout the twentieth century. This is the significance of the Pentecostal/charismatic/renewal movement of this century. It has to be seen as part of God's strategy for these times. It may be that Mary was foreseeing something of this in her song of thanksgiving before the birth of Jesus, when she spoke of God performing 'mighty deeds' and 'scattering the proud', bringing down rulers and lifting up the humble poor (Luke 1:46–53).

Joel also foresaw a mighty outpouring of the Spirit of God upon all people, those of high status and low status, young and old, male and female, and Peter saw the significance of the Day of Pentecost as inaugurating the age in which this prophecy would be fulfilled.

The gospel undoubtedly turns the values of the world upside down and it would be fully in harmony with the teaching of Jesus and the whole witness of the Bible that God would want to use the humble poor to establish his Kingdom. But the nature of God has not changed, neither have his ways. Just as Jesus instructed the disciples after the Resurrection to wait in Jerusalem until power came upon them to enable them to fulfil the Great Commission, so today he is giving the same power of the Holy Spirit to all believers. It is for this reason that we are seeing a reappearance of the spiritual gifts after many centuries when they were not in evidence among ordinary believers. It cannot be denied that there has been a phenomenal increase in spiritual activity in our lifetime. This is one of the signs advanced by those who believe we are living in the last days of the present age.

End of Millennium

Not all the spiritual activity today can be ascribed to the Holy Spirit. In the Western world there has been a remarkable revival of witchcraft and occult practices at a level not seen since the Middle Ages. Undoubtedly some of this activity is linked to the widespread loss of faith

331

in the former Christian nations of Europe. The reasons for this secularism are complex and here we can do no more than note it as a fact. This loss of faith has left a spiritual vacuum which has been filled by all kinds of spurious spiritual activities which have coincided with the rise of the New Age movement which New Agers believe is in preparation for a 'new age of the Spirit' in the third millennium.

In the final years of the second millennium it was to be expected that there would be a considerable increase in prophetic activity. A similar thing happened at the end of the first millennium which many people at that time expected would see the end of the world. Eschatological prophecies for this period have been multiplying throughout the second half of the twentieth century. The New Testament, however, including the teaching of Jesus, abounds with warnings about false prophecy, false messiahs, false prophets and teachers. The believers are warned not to be disturbed by these things but to expect them to multiply as the time for the Second Coming of Christ draws closer.

End of the Age
The Bible declares that the world did not simply evolve over a period of millions of years, but it began with an act of creation which was the activity of God himself. A belief in the 'big bang' theory of creation is now respectable among physical scientists. But the Bible also declares that the world will come to a sudden end. God has set a time when he will draw all things to a conclusion and that he himself will judge the nations. This time of judgment will be both a day of light and of darkness, of joy and of sorrow. It will be a time of great rejoicing among believers and of fear among unbelievers, especially those who have deliberately rejected the word of God.

The New Testament declares that the nations will be judged by the Lord Jesus and that he will return to the earth in a way that will be seen by all people. His coming will be in power and glory to establish his sovereign rule upon the earth. His parousia will mark the end of the present age and he will return suddenly 'like a thief in the night' when most people are not expecting him (Mt 24:36 and 2 Pet 3:10).

The New Testament also declares that no one knows when the end of the age will occur. Jesus in fact specifically told his disciples not to speculate, 'It is not for you to know the times or dates the Father has set by his own authority' he said (Acts 1:7). His instruction was that his followers should be a watching and praying people who were ready for his coming at all times. His followers are required to be a people who are watching events in the world with understanding so that they can interpret the signs of the times. Jesus spoke scathingly to people in his own generation who were blind to the spiritual significance of events in their day (Luke 12:54–56) and he pleaded for them to be ready at all times (Luke 12:35–40).

It is obvious to all those who are watchful and follow the news in the rapidly changing events of the contemporary world that we are living in a period very similar to that which is described in many of the prophetic passages in Scripture, both Old and New Testament. This should therefore make us highly alert and watchful. At the same time believers need to heed the warnings against deception and false teachings and be on their guard against spurious spiritual activity.

In one of the parables of the Kingdom, Jesus praised the servant who was found doing what his master had commanded him at the master's return. This should be the major objective of every believer today. The command Jesus left with his disciples was to evangelise the whole world. This Great Commission has never been rescinded. The primary objective of all prophecy today in the con-temporary church is to enable the body of Christ to fulfil the Great Commission and thus glorify the name of Christ. It is therefore with these words of Jesus that we conclude this study of prophecy past and present. 'Therefore go and make disciples of all nations, baptising them in the name of the Father and of the Son and of the Holy Spirit, and teaching them to obey everything I have commanded you. And surely I am with you always, to the very end of the age' (Mt 28:19–20).

SELECTED BIBLIOGRAPHY

Anderson, George   Wishart The History and Religion of Israel (London, England: Oxford University Press, 1966).

Baron, David   Commentary on Zechariah (Grand Rapids, Michigan: Kregel, 1988).

Bruce, F.F.   The Spreading Flame: The Rise and Progress of Christianity from Its Beginnings to the Conversion of Zechariah (Grand Rapids, Michigan: Eerdmans, 1980).

Buber, Martin   The Prophetic Faith (New York, New York: Macmillan, 1949).

Carley, K.W.   Ezekiel Among the Prophets: A Study of Ezekiel's Place in Prophetic Tradition (Geneva, Alabama: Allenson, 1975).

Chadwick, Henry   Early Church, Pelican History of the Church, Vol. 1 (New York, New York: Penguin, 1968).

Clements, R.E.   Isaiah and the Deliverance of Jerusalem (Winona Lake, Indiana: Eisenbrauns, 1980).
New Century Bible Commentary on Isaiah 1-39 (Grand Rapids, Michigan: Eerdmans, 1980).

Cunliffe-Jones, H.   Book of Jeremiah (New York, New York: Macmillan, 1961).

Davidson, A.B.   The Theology of the Old Testament (Minneapolis, Minnesota: Fortress, 1904).

Davies, Eryl W.   Prophecy and Ethics: Isaiah and the Ethical Traditions of Israel (Winona Lake, Indiana: Eisenbrauns, 1981).

Driver, S.R.   An Introduction to the Literature of the Old Testament (Minneapolis, Minnesota, 1913).

Ellison, H.L.   Men Spake From God (Exeter, England: Paternoster Press, 1972).
Ezekiel: The Man and His Message (Exeter, England: Paternoster Press, 1967).

Elmslie, W.A.L.   **How Came Our Faith?** (New York, New York: Scribner and Sons, 1949).

Freeman, H.E.   **An Introduction to the Old Testament Prophets** (Chicago, Illinois: Moody Press, 1968).

Hanson, P.D.   **The Dawn of Apocalyptic: The Historical and Sociological Roots of Jewish Apocalyptic Eschatology** (Minneapolis, Minnesota: Fortress, 1979).

Harrison, R.K.   **Introduction to the Old Testament** (Grand Rapids, Michigan: Eerdmans, 1969).
Old Testament Times (Grand Rapids, Michigan: Eerdmans, 1970).
Jeremiah and Lamentations (Downers Grove, Illinois: InterVarsity, 1973).

Herschel, A.J.   **The Prophets** (New York, New York: Harper and Row, 1962).

Hill, Clifford   **The Sociology of the New Testament Church to 62 AD** (Unpublished thesis, University of Nottingham, 1972).
The Day Comes (London, England: Collins, 1982).
A Prophetic People (London, England: Collins, 1986).

Johnson, A.R.   **The Cultic Prophet in Ancient Israel** (Cardiff, Wales: University of Wales, 1962).

Koch, Klaus   **The Prophets,** Volume One (Minneapolis, Minnesota: Fortress, 1982).

Lang, Bernhard   **Monotheism and the Prophetic Minority: An Essay in Biblical History and Sociology** (Winona Lake, Indiana: Eisenbrauns, 1983).

Lindblom, J.   **Prophecy in Ancient Israel** (Minneapolis, Minnesota, 1963).

Mowvley, Harry   **Guide to Old Testament Prophecy** (London, England: Lutterworth Press, 1979).

Noth, Martin   **History of Israel: Biblical History** (New York, New York: Harper and Row, 1960).

Osterley, W.O.E.
and Robinson, T.H.   **Hebrew Religion: Its origin and development** (New York, New York: Macmillan, 1949).

Pederson, J.   **Israel: Its life and culture** (London, England: Oxford University Press, 1953).

Peterson, David L.   **The Roles of Israel's Prophets** (Sheffield, England: JSOT Press, 1981).

SELECTED BIBLIOGRAPHY

Prior, David — **The Message of 1 Corinthians** (Downers Grove, Illinois: InterVarsity, 1985).

Pusey, E.B. — **The Minor Prophets** (Grand Rapids, Michigan: Baker, 1956).

Robinson, Theodore H. — **A History of Israel, Volumes 1 and 2** (Oxford, England: Clarendon Press, 1934).

Rowley, H.H. — **The Servant of the Lord** (Oxford, England: Blackwell, 1965).

Streeter, B.H. — **The Primitive Church: Studies in the Origin of the Christian Ministry** (New York, New York: Gordon Press, 1977).

Tertullian — **The Ecclesiastical History of the Second and Third Centuries** (London, England: Griffith Farran, 1825).

Theissen, Gerd — **Sociology of Early Palestinian Christianity** (Philadelphia, Pennsylvania: Fortress Press, 1975).

Welch, A.C. — **Prophet and Priest in Old Israel** (New York, New York: Macmillan, 1953).

Wevers, John W. — **Ezekiel** (Grand Rapids, Michigan: Eerdmans, 1982).

Whybray, R.N. — **Isaiah 40-66** (Greenwood, South Carolina: Attic Press, 1975).

Williamson, H.G.M. — **1 and 2 Chronicles New Century Bible Commentary** (London, England: Marshall Morgan and Scott, 1982).

Wilson, Robert R. — **Prophecy and Society in Ancient Israel** (Philadelphia, Pennsylvania: Fortress Press, 1980).

Wiseman, D.J. — **People of Old Testament Times** (Oxford, England: Clarendon Press, 1973).

Wood, Leon J. — **The Holy Spirit in the Old Testament** (Grand Rapids, Michigan: Zondervan, 1976).
The Prophets of Israel (Grand Rapids, Michigan: Baker, 1979).

Young, Edward J. — **My Servants the Prophets** (Grand Rapids, Michigan: Eerdmans, 1974).

BLESSING THE CHURCH?
Clifford Hill
and
Peter Fenwick, David Forbes, David Noakes

The Charismatic Movement is an established feature of late-twentieth century Church life. Whilst opinions have always been divided concerning spiritual gifts and their application, nothing has recently polarised Christians more than the Toronto Blessing. *Blessing the Church?* reflects that concern.

Dr Clifford Hill, editor of the magazine *Prophecy Today*, looks at the social setting of the Charismatic Movement and at the current hunger for 'belonging' which provides fertile ground for those offering 'power', 'healing' and a 'me-centred' faith. He also examines the evolving role and importance of prophecy in the direction of the Charismatic Movement.

Peter Fenwick, a businessman who leads a House Church in Sheffield, offers an overview of twenty-five personally experienced years of change in charismatic beliefs and practice.

David Forbes, Deputy Director of the Prophetic Word Ministries Trust, looks at the so-called Latter Rain movement, its origins and evolution into the Toronto Blessing.

David Noakes, a solicitor now exercising a full-time itinerant teaching ministry, examines both the shift of biblical emphasis and the changing public practices (worship, celebrations, manifestations) within the Charismatic Movement.

Finally, Dr Clifford Hill concludes by asserting that the Charismatic Movement has turned from Christ-centredness to spirit-centredness; from Bible-centredness to experience-centredness; from Cross-centredness to me-centredness and is further drifting into New Age theology.

Blessing the Church concludes with a timely prophetic call for evangelicals to a Bible-centred witness without abandoning their witness to the presence, power and gifts of the Holy Spirit.

0 86347 186 2

Eagle